BILLY HILL
GODFATHER OF LONDON

WENSLEY CLARKSON

BILLY HILL
GODFATHER OF LONDON

THE UNPARALLELED SAGA OF BRITAIN'S
MOST POWERFUL POST-WAR CRIME BOSS

Pennant Books

This paperback edition published 2009.

First published in hardback 2008
by Pennant Books.

Text copyright © 2008 by Wensley Clarkson.

The moral right of the author has been asserted.

British Library Cataloguing-in-Publication Data:
A catalogue record for this book is available on request from
The British Library

ISBN 978-1-906015-43-5

Pennant Books' True Crime series is edited by Paul Woods

Design & Typeset by Envy Design Ltd

Printed and bound in Great Britain by Clays Ltd, St Ives plc

Pictures reproduced with kind permission of Getty Images and the author.

Photographs on page 3 of the picture section © Getty Images.

Pennant Books
PO Box 5675
London W1A 3FB

www.pennantbooks.com

"There will never be another Billy Hill."

– Reggie Kray

"Bill had a great brain. There's no two ways about it."

– Frankie Fraser

"I made Billy Hill. Then he got over the top of me. I should have shot Billy Hill. I really should. I'd have got ten years for it but it would have made me happy and I'd be out now – laughing."

– Jack Spot

"I have no doubt that during his career Hill had some very senior officers in his pocket."

– Leonard 'Nipper' Read, legendary Scotland Yard detective

ACKNOWLEDGEMENTS

I cannot begin to express the depth of my feelings for the many individuals who've made this book possible. I owe them my deepest and most heartfelt gratitude.

To my publisher, Cass Pennant, I say many, many thanks. Without him and the superb editing skills of Paul Woods, this book would never have been possible. Their support and guidance has been very much appreciated. Then there are Bob Duffield, John Irvin, Oein McCann, Jimmy Smithers, Frank Page, Dave Barry, Jordan Reynolds, Jason Moody, Freddie Foreman, Dave Barry, and many other friends and associates of Billy Hill who would rather that their names did not appear here in print. Also, a final tribute to the memory of so many great Fleet Street reporters, including the gentlemanly Victor Sims and the legendary Duncan Webb – plus Jack Spot's ghost-writer, Steve Francis (aka Hank Janson), whose whitewashed villa in Rosas, on the Costa Blanca, marked the beginning of my love affair with Spain.

AUTHOR'S NOTE

Some of the dialogue represented in this book was sourced from available documents, some was drawn from tape-recorded testimony and some was reconstructed from the memory of participants. References to the cost of items such as clothes and food are as they were at the time. I've adapted the Billy Hill story to read as closely to a novel as possible, and have had to make some informed deductions for dramatic purposes. But the actual facts are as they occurred.

In Billy Hill's era, robbery was the equivalent of the drugs trade in today's underworld. Fortunes were made and lost with alarming regularity. Some villains paid for their mistakes with their lives. Back during my childhood, I encountered a few of them (and many of the reporters mentioned in this book) through my father, a Fleet Street tabloid journalist . . .

PROLOGUE

The People, 3 October 1954

'BULLION SECRETS – DUNCAN WEBB scores another crime scoop!'

At the end of the most dramatic week in the history of British crime, Scotland Yard was last night having to face the grim truth that the £45,000 worth of gold stolen in the Great Bullion Robbery is now unlikely to be traced. They will now be lucky indeed to get even a clue as to how it has disappeared.

This sorry result is not due to lack of trying on the part of Scotland Yard. On the contrary, its top detectives turned on last week the biggest search London's underworld has ever known.

The stripping-down of houses, flats, offices and even motor cars of known criminals reached a scale that has hardly been equalled in Hollywood crime films.

The Yard were convinced that if raids and inspections were carried out on a big enough scale, they would be bound to find some clue that would lead them towards the recovery of the gold or the arrest of the thieves.

My information is that they were left last night with nothing of material value except a more detailed account of how the bullion robbery was done.

This was supplied to them by the notorious Billy Hill, the self confessed gangster boss of London, who declares that he has retired from crime – he has spent seventeen years in prison – and is now "in legitimate business".

TEDDY BEARS

Hill claims to know what goes on in the underworld: the police take the view that he knows far too much. So last week they submitted a toy business with which he used to be associated to a search more fantastic than anything in fiction.

The Yard decided that Hill had organised the bullion robbery and had stolen the idea of the comedy film *The Lavender Hill Mob*, by actually concealing the gold inside the 50,000 dolls and teddy bears inside the toy warehouse.

So squads of policemen were set to work taking every doll and teddy bear out of its box and examining it.

The search of the warehouse building took nine hours, and, by the end of it, Billy Hill – urbane as ever – said he was sorry they had found nothing but he could pass onto the police the account he had heard of how the bullion robbery was done.

HIS STORY

Hill, who has been telling in *The People* his reasons for giving up crime . . . "the police are bound to win in the end," he says – then agreed to tell me for publication the story of the robbery.

As a crime reporter of twenty years experience, I had heard nothing to equal his account of life in the underworld as told on the word of a super-gangster.

Ace crime reporter Duncan Webb's breathless report was perfectly in keeping with the mood of London in the mid-1950s. His close association with London 'godfather' Billy Hill had reaped many scoops, but Webb had to sacrifice a certain level of editorial independence in order to keep the crime boss on his side.

BILLY HILL: GODFATHER OF LONDON

The bullion robbery had rocked Scotland Yard to the core. It had been a brilliantly executed crime, carried out after some masterful planning by . . . . . . Billy Hill.

But Hill's metamorphosis into the leader of Britain's underworld is no overnight story. It represents a history of crime in the first half of the last century, as Hill moved from abject poverty all the way to the top of London society, through a criminal hinterland that seems a million miles away from today's high-tech gangsters and drug barons . . .

ONE

Seven Dials, sandwiched between Leicester Square and Covent Garden in the heart of London's West End, was said by the police to have more pickpockets per square yard than anywhere else on the globe. To outsiders, the West End in the first half of the twentieth century was considered a seedy city centre teeming with petty crooks. Visitors to the area turned their eyes away as women paraded their bodies on street corners, while their pimps lurked in the shadows nearby.

Over in nearby Oxford Street and Tottenham Court Road, gangs of petty criminals ruled the pavements and illegal bookies took bets from passers-by. After nightfall, lowlifes roamed the narrow streets and illegal dives, rat-holes of dirty divans and sackcloth curtains, frequented mainly by criminals and bargirls. In Piccadilly, street hustlers – some as young as six or seven – tried their hardest to hawk dodgy goods.

In those days Seven Dials was a violent pocket of the West End, filled with destitute, often drunken families living in tenement blocks. As local beat copper Ted Greeno later recalled: "Suicides were commonplace in the West End back before World War One. And the nearby Thames was the favourite location for a dramatic exit. To some it was a happier prospect than a life of poverty and violence."

It was into such a world that William Charles Hill was born, on 13 December 1911. Little Billy, as he was always known, didn't get out of the Hill family's cramped flat in Seven Dials much during the first couple of years of his life. But then his mother, Amelia, didn't have much time on her hands thanks to her many other children. Billy's mum was an Irish emigrant, and for her, family took preference over everything else. She bore a total of twenty-one babies, though several were stillborn or died in infancy. She was renowned as a tough but fair mother, always looking out for her many kids. But despite this, Billy later recalled that he was lucky to get his older brothers' and sisters' leftovers at meal times.

When the First World War broke out in 1914, the Hills moved to Number 23 Netley Street, just off the Hampstead Road, between Tottenham Court Road and Camden Town. The tall Victorian house, with a basement, was a vast improvement on their previous home. But then, as Billy said many years later, "With twenty-one kids in the family we needed a bit of space."

As the First World War raged in the trenches of France and Belgium, duckers and divers like Billy's Irish father avoided the call-up by claiming to be conscientious objectors. There was a feeling amongst such people that the war wasn't theirs to worry about.

Billy attended the local Netley Street council school until he was fourteen years old. His later overview of his education was typical: "I was not a good scholar, as perhaps you can imagine. The only thing I reckoned on learning was figures. I knew unconsciously that I would need this knowledge later on in life." Life inside the Hill household was a hub for local villains, who used to pop round at all times of the day and night offering stolen goods in exchange for cash. Alice Diamond, one of Britain's most notorious hoisters (or shoplifters), was a regular at the Hills' house. Another visitor was the infamous Eddie Guerin, already an underworld legend after being arrested for a bank robbery in France. He'd been sent to the notorious Devil's Island prison but escaped with six other inmates. However, Guerin was the only one to survive after they tried to make it across the sea in a flimsy wooden rowing boat. (Guerin never said much about what happened to the other prisoners, but there was a rumour in the West End that he survived the journey by eating them after they perished.)

Guerin was a great friend to the Hill family, and to the young, impressionable Billy he was larger than life. As Hill later recalled, "I looked up to him like other kids looked up to Jack Dempsey, who was then world boxing champ. You know how it is when you're kids. Gangsters are about the most exciting heroes of all. It was like cowboys and Indians to an older generation."

His conclusions as to what made a hero and what made a villain provide a fascinating insight into the way his mind worked, even back then. "After all, they told us all about Drake and Raleigh and Clive and Cook at school. And weren't they all gangsters? Weren't they nicking something that didn't belong to them? Only because it was on behalf of their Government that made it legal. I guess it's all right if the Government says you can nick something. But if it says you can't, then I suppose it's all wrong."

In Billy's mind, there was little moral difference between what his family and their friends got up to and the deeds of the great British adventurers. In some ways he had a point, although it would be many decades before wider society would start to understand his moral relativism. As he later explained, "The real crime in life, as I see it, is in being found out." But then, that's the way that Billy Hill had seen it for the whole of his life.

His logic makes more sense to us today. In his so-called autobiography *Boss of Britain's Underworld* (more of a hagiography designed to improve his public image – though it provides some fascinating insights), Hill observed, "Look at the way world public opinion made us give back India to the Indians and part of West Africa to the Africans. Well, if we gave it back to them, it must have belonged to them in the first place."

Young Billy's street in Camden Town was virtually an Irish immigrants' ghetto, dominated by hardworking womenfolk like Billy's mum, constantly feeding and looking after her vast family. There were no playgrounds back in those days, so kids like Billy and his mates made do with strips of wasteland. Local rubbish tips often provided the raw material to make everything from box carts to wooden swords and guns.

Though they often stayed out on the streets until late at night, their parents didn't worry because they were just glad to get the kids out of the house. Occasionally, there would be a visit to Arsenal Football Club on a Saturday afternoon or a trip to the picture house to watch a silent film. But that often ended in scuffles and punch-ups between kids who talked non-stop to the screen.

Children were not allowed inside pubs back in those days, so many of them would be expected to loiter outside while their mums and dads sat inside supping a few drinks. If they were lucky, the kids would be offered a bottle of pop while they stayed out on the street.

Life was undoubtedly hard for those who lived in London slum areas. Billy's dad frequently struggled to find work as a painter and decorator and there was no unemployment benefit, but he always managed to make a few bob through his ducking and diving. Unlike most families in the street, the Hills didn't use coupons from the doctor for a bowl of soup, which was usually collected from a basin in the local school.

Families like Billy Hill's were constantly on the breadline. Food and clothes were always in short supply. Many pawned family heirlooms, including wedding rings and a lot else besides.

At school, the really poor kids were provided with boots, complete with holes punched in the side as a mark, so that they couldn't be pawned.

It was hardly surprising, therefore, that many of London's slum dwellers were virtually obliged to commit crimes. It was all a matter of survival, but there was no organised crime network back then so it was very much a case of each man for himself. And the golden rule was that you didn't steal from your own. The rich and the well insured were legitimate targets. Kids like young Billy Hill grew up knowing that the only way to make 'good money' was to steal. They knew only too well how hard life had been for many of their parents.

* * *

Vicious prejudice against the Irish existed on the poverty-stricken streets around Camden. Before Billy Hill reached the age of ten he found himself in constant scraps with other youngsters, many of whom had been brought up by their parents to hate the 'bogtrotters'. Many of them had only moved across the water during the previous thirty years, and were considered stupid or 'thick' because they didn't speak with the same accents as the locals. Billy rapidly worked out that, even at his young age, he needed to be in a gang in order to survive on the mean streets of London. So, still under ten years old, he formed his own street gang and recruited bigger, older kids. Strong as an ox despite his small size, Billy stood up to them all and they soon showed him the utmost respect.

When young Billy listened avidly to characters like Eddie Guerin and another local criminal legend, Brummy Sparkes (who later married his sister Maggie), talking about what they'd been up to, it all seemed completely normal and acceptable. Survival on the rough and dangerous streets of Camden took a special kind of cleverness, which the young Hill possessed in bucketloads. So it was that, when Billy and his mates stole fruit from the stalls in Seaton Street, near his family home, his undoubted powers of leadership emerged for the first time.

Pinching apples was all well and good, but it didn't exactly bring in a fortune and often ended in a thick ear from an angry stall holder. Young Billy had bigger plans. He'd built himself a soap-box on four wheels, and took it to the end of Seaton Street which ascended up a slope. On the way, Billy told his mates to station themselves at various stalls in the market. Minutes later he was going full pelt through the market, knocking customers flying and even pulling a few stalls down on the way. In the chaos which ensued, Billy's pals threw all their stolen produce into his makeshift cart as it whizzed by. By the time the soap-box came to a halt more than a hundred yards further down the street, it was crammed full with nicked greengrocery.

All the produce was quickly resold at cheap rates to local barrow boys. Billy and his gang also specialised in stealing second-hand books from one shop which were quickly resold to another.

And he had soon learned that violence had to be countered by more violence. Whenever he arrived home in tears after taking a belting from other kids, Amelia Hill would shriek, "Well, get the bleeding chopper and go out and murder them!" As Billy himself admitted many years later, "And if we didn't do that we'd get another belting from our mother, who was more than well built. That's how we learned to keep our end up. You had to in Camden Town in those days."

*　　*　　*

When Billy was fourteen he showed a violent side to his nature, which would evolve into his trademark in later years. Out on the mean streets of Camden he got into an argument with a young serviceman. As he himself later explained in cold, stark terms: "Suddenly he took a liberty with me. Without the slightest qualm I got hold of a pair of scissors and drove them into his back. It was as easy as that. And it came quite natural to me."

For Billy Hill's reputation preceded him in Camden Town, even though he was still just a kid. He always seemed to have a smile on his face, and he had a self-deprecating sense of humour, but beneath that friendly exterior was a razor-sharp mind. Billy's eyes and ears were constantly on the lookout for opportunities, which he'd then bounce off his pals before deciding on a plan.

Billy got all his cigarettes and pocket money by thieving, so it was inevitable that the long arm of the law would catch up with him sooner rather than later. A 'screwing' (theft) with some other kids from a tobacconist's kiosk in Regent's Park ended in his arrest as he was fleeing the scene.

To teach him a lesson, the teenaged Hill was sentenced to a ridiculously long five years in a reformatory school. Billy's family, friends and neighbours in Camden Town were outraged by the severity of the sentence. Even the traders of Seaton Street market, from whom he had nicked so much 'gear', joined in the protests, and a petition was signed by five thousand people. As a result, when young Billy appealed his sentence it was reduced to two years probation, on the condition that he resided with a family member on his release.

Billy went to live with one of his older sisters, Dolly, and even managed to get a job with an electrical firm, until he ran off with £50 given to him by his boss to buy equipment. Soon after starting another straight job, for a greengrocer, he was asked to make a delivery when the owner of a house was not in.

It was like a red rag to a bull for the young career criminal. As he later recalled, "Almost without thinking I went round to that house and screwed it. It came to me as natural as a child weaning from its mother." For the next few weeks, Hill kept himself busy screwing the empty homes of the greengrocer's customers. His employers had no idea what he was up to. Eventually, he was swamped with so many potential victims that he did a deal with his sister and her husband, Bert, who'd just moved to a flat in Adelaide Road, Swiss Cottage. Billy would telephone Dolly and Bert, and they'd pay the empty house a visit themselves.

Billy soon gave up his job at the greengrocer's shop. Before he'd turned sixteen, he'd chosen a career path as a fully fledged burglar. Even at such a young age, he was a brilliant planner. Every morning he'd get out his bicycle and ride around all the nearby expensive residential areas. Often he'd carry some greengrocery with him, which meant he could knock on people's doors to see if anyone was in without raising much suspicion. If anyone answered the door he had the perfect cover story by claiming he had the wrong address.

Hill was soon an expert at slipping a stick between a patent lock and the wood of the door. It usually took no more than a second for the door to pop open. Billy would then immediately bolt the front door and check out the best means of escape before casing the joint, usually a garden door or a back window.

*   *   *

Less than a mile to the south of Billy Hill's Camden home were the sleazy neon lights of Soho, London's so-called 'Square Mile of Vice'. Hill was attracted to the area, almost like a moth to a light-bulb. He'd heard all the stories about how the streets of Soho were lined with young prostitutes, overshadowed by sinister looking pimps prepared to slice up any punters who didn't pay their dues. Then there were the countless illegal drinking clubs, many of which featured special back exits for a quick getaway from the law. In some of them the dreaded marijuana leaf was openly smoked, and Hill soon heard rumours about some of the strange things narcotics did to people.

But drugs didn't interest young hoods like Billy back then; he and his gang much preferred Soho's illegal gambling premises, where cardsharps ruled. These were known as 'spielers', where all sorts of cons and tricks occurred, such as the 'hold-out' which could whisk a chosen card up a sleeve so fast that no one would notice. Spielers were ripe for the sort of con artists who'd often buy marked cards at a conjurer's shop. Other, bigger money cheats would mark the cards during a game, using a smear of 'daub', a crayon-like paste. One renowned cardsharp hid the daub on his waxed moustache, which he'd stroke throughout a game. Hill was also partial to the odd game of billiards in one of half a dozen halls, where he had the added bonus of seeing a punch-up any night of the week.

By the end of the 1920s, there were two hundred and ninety-five registered clubs within that sleazy square mile called Soho. And just behind Leicester Square were at least fifteen more unregistered premises, all known to the police. It was a veritable melting pot of sleaze. Perfect territory for someone like Billy Hill.

*   *   *

Billy Hill's attitude to life was that, even though he knew the difference between right and wrong, he didn't really give a toss about it.

Besides the spielers, horseracing was the other major gambling attraction for young nascent villains like Billy. Legal betting was only allowed with official bookmakers at each track and the competition for bookies' pitches was fierce. Gangs of criminals charged those same bookies for so-called 'protection' at most tracks.

Just after World War One, a gang of five Italian brothers called Joe, Darby, Charlie, Young Harry and Fred Sabini – from London's Little Italy, off of the Clerkenwell Road – started a gang war that would be waged relentlessly for almost twenty years. During that time many men were horribly mutilated, and the Sabinis earned a fortune by demanding protection money from intimidated bookmakers.

This period saw the emergence of so-called 'slashers', gangsters who knew precisely how to mark their victims with a razor without killing them. These men had their weapons strapped to their palm, in a piece of cork held in place by string so it didn't show in a clenched fist. With just one eighth of an inch of blade exposed, it would not penetrate deep enough to cause serious injury but could leave a horrible scar for life with one deft movement. In the confusion that followed, the slasher would soon disappear into the crowd; naturally, nobody ever saw what happened.

The slashers also used a second technique which was just as effective, but a tad clumsier. The slasher would wear an ordinary cloth cap, which contained a blade. Once again, the cutting edge would protrude slightly, and when the assailant snatched off his cap and struck his victim with its peak, it would lay the victim's face open.

There was even a ruckus at London Bridge Station, before the Sabini mob got on the trains for Plumpton racecourse one day, and a number of men were taken to Guy's Hospital for treatment. At Plumpton itself, there were also flare-ups, and by the end of the day the Sabinis proclaimed themselves the outright victors. The truce which followed lasted just a few hours, before the ringleader of the Loonies, a rival race gang, was found shot outside a club. The Sabinis and their soldiers pulled in vast sums of cash, which bought luxury flats, flashy 'clobber', diamond rings and fancy women. They were known in London as the 'Easy Come, Easy Go' boys. For the first time in British history, criminals were living better lives than most ordinary citizens. But then the Sabinis' henchmen began demanding better pay and conditions. Rival factions sprung up. Four brothers named Cortesi – later known as the 'Frenchies' – acted as unofficial shop stewards for some of the gang's discontents.

These new gangs moved from their shabby hideouts, often in the suburbs, into Soho, where they began taking over the smaller clubs and spielers, making their presence felt throughout the manor. Territorial rights were fought over as savagely as they were across the Atlantic, in prohibition Chicago (although with blades, rather than the deadlier machineguns), but the Sabinis would reign supreme until the mid-thirties.

*　　*　　*

Still in his teens, Billy Hill was already making a healthy living out of crime and learning from every job. In many ways, Hill considered thieving to be virtually an art form. He soon learned to look further afield, to even richer areas, for "better quality swag". The predominantly Jewish suburb of Golders Green was a classic example; in Hill's terms, it was "where people emigrate to when they've made money."

One day, the teenaged Billy took an accomplice called Albert Smart with him to a flat which had been unoccupied for a week, while the owners were away. Hill later said that he and his pal took their time on the job, even making themselves a meal from food in the fridge. Then Albert used the toilet and foolishly pulled the chain. Billy was furious, because he knew only too well how much noise it would make throughout the block of flats. As he later explained, "I could have brained Smart, who was anything but, for pulling that chain." Billy grabbed his partner in crime and they hotfooted it out of the flat, loaded with swag. But, unbeknownst to them, a neighbour had already called the police. Hill and Smart were picked up a few streets away, armed with the tools they'd used for the raid. They were charged and eventually sentenced to three years in a borstal next to Wandsworth Prison, in south London. As Hill later explained, "I could not wish for a better academy than that borstal institution. Whatever kind of boy or youth you put into one of those places you can be certain that he'll be a far better criminal when he comes out than when he went in."

As he also quickly learned, in borstal one had to be able to fight in order to eat. If you didn't fight you wouldn't survive. After three months at Wandsworth, he was transferred to Portland Prison in Dorset, and set to work in a quarry. It was back-breaking to carry loads of stones in baskets up the quarry face, which was nearly ninety degrees steep. Inmates like Hill were often harnessed to trucks like horses, and ordered to pull them along the sandy surface of the quarry. Each night, Billy and the other inmates had their backs washed down with iodine to prevent infection from the cuts, abrasions, sores and scabs. As he later explained, "I don't know what society expected from me. I don't know what they hoped to make out of me by sending me there. I might have been a horse. Had I been a mule owned by an Arab I would have been treated better."

So here was Billy Hill, just turned seventeen years of age and already a hardened criminal. And as ever, he had a plan up his sleeve.

One day he dared ask a screw for some water, as he was humping bucketloads of stones up the quarry face. Naturally, Hill's request was turned down. But it fuelled his determination to execute his masterplan. Later on that very same night, 18 September 1929, Billy and a prisoner called Lawrence Edward Harding escaped by climbing over the main wall and jumping to freedom. Both were dressed in borstal clothes, grey short trousers and grey shirts.

Needing to ditch those uniforms, they broke into a nearby house belonging to a naval officer called Commander Bowen. After getting in on the ground floor, Hill and his fellow escapee heard noises from upstairs. Billy hid behind a door until someone came in, then pounced and gave the figure a crack with his home-made cosh. It wasn't until the body fell to the floor, unconscious, that he saw it was a housemaid called Valetta Mary Matthews.

Billy typically summed up his attitude to this attack in his autobiography: "Lesson Number One to all housemaids. Never stalk a burglar. Always break a window and scream like hell. The burglar will always scarper."

Hill and Harding felt so bad about the maid that they carried her to the kitchen tap and brought her round. Then they waited for the police to turn up, and gave themselves up. They were both charged with breaking and entering, and robbery with violence. As Harding was over twenty-one, he got twelve months hard labour on top of his other sentence, plus twelve strokes of the cat after the housemaid accused him of attacking her (whereas it had, in fact, been young Billy). Hill got only nine months' hard labour. Afterwards, he showed great loyalty towards Harding by making a confession to the police, and Harding's sentence was reduced.

As a result, Billy was going to face the birch, a bunch of tightly wrapped twigs about three and a half feet long. Into them was inserted a handle of a similar length, making the whole contraption about seven feet overall. A special one was sent down to Portland from the Home Office in London. It had been soaked in brine to make it more pliable.

The young, wiry prisoner Billy Hill was escorted into the prison yard, his wrists handcuffed and crossed. His ankles were then outstretched at the base and handcuffed at each corner separately. Hill wasn't permitted to see the face of the actual prison officer but he already knew from other inmates who it would be. Hill later recalled, "They gave me the strokes on my bare backside and afterwards dressed the bleeding wounds with a medicated pad, and then sent me straight back to hard labour. No, I didn't holler when they belted me. If you live by the sword you've got to expect to die by it. So I took all they could give me and lived for the day when I could get out of that nick and get back to work."

Hill's next punishment was to be made to live around the clock in a rectangular cubicle, just high enough for him to stand in if he stooped. It wasn't even wide enough for him to bend down properly. As he recalled, "If I stood crouched at the shoulders, my body did not touch the roof or sides. If I moved it did. They gave me either some stones or bones. These I had to pound with a pounder into powder. I had to fill a bucket with the powder in the forenoon and another bucket in the afternoon."

Billy later said that, when he was first given a bone to pound, he felt sick to his stomach because of the disgusting stench it gave off, "but I had nothing in my stomach to be sick on." Later he did spew up his guts on occasions, including one time when he was sick all over himself and collapsed against the wall of the tiny cubicle. After that, Hill claimed, he taught himself to control his nausea through strength of mind.

It was a barbaric punishment by today's standards, and undoubtedly contributed to Billy's cold criminal character by installing in him a determination not to be beaten – by anyone.

Billy Hill turned into a virtual machine inside that tiny cubicle cell. His day became a cycle of pounding, shovelling what was virtually dog food into his mouth from a tin plate at mealtimes, then stumbling onto the wooden plank which was his bed. He later recalled, "If I did go to sleep I don't remember. I think I fell unconscious a few times. But in the nick you've always got to wake up and see another day through. Death is the only thing that lets you out of it."

Billy's hard labour finally came to an end when he was sent to Rochester Borstal, in Kent. Still just seventeen years old, he had suffered more pain and anguish than someone twice his age. He didn't care about losing remission through bad behaviour, and would remain incarcerated for another two years as a result. He perfectly summed up his attitude in his autobiography: "What the hell did it matter! Learn crime? I knew more than most of them after coming from Wandsworth and then Portland."

Hill's recollections of these gruelling punishments reveal the intelligent, analytical mind he would put to use in pursuit of his criminal aspirations. Yet, as one psychiatrist later insisted, he could so easily have been encouraged to channel that intelligence into something much more worthwhile. As Hill himself once conceded, "If only I'd had the opportunity at a young age to take a different path."

He remained convinced for his entire life that, if it hadn't been for those three gruelling years in borstal, he might not have remained a career criminal. "I learned nothing which would have been of any use to me even had I intended trying to go straight. I just spent three years being pushed around like an animal. So did thousands of other youngsters."

So by the time Billy Hill was finally released from borstal, aged nineteen, he was hardened in every sense of the word. He had a criminal record. He'd been brutally punished and was known to the police as a professional thief, a bad character with no calling in the straight world. "Society did not want me. They only found me useful when they wanted to exact a sycophantic and hypocritical revenge on me and my likes. We were useful only to keep the law busy while we were out of gaol. Who the hell do you think would have employed a boy of nineteen with the record I had? To do what – run errands? Sweep the floor? Would that buy me clothes, feed my starved guts, shove vitamins and nourishment into my body, pay my rent, give me a hope of living?"

On his release Billy's saviour was his older sister, Maggie, who, despite making a return visit to Holloway Prison, had managed to leave some money for her kid brother. It came from the proceeds of stolen property which she'd handled.

Billy was out on parole, which meant he'd be sent back inside if he was caught breaking the law. It didn't bother him. He purchased two new complete outfits of clothing plus a first-class set of workman's tools – including a brace and bit, some drills, a set of master keys, a screwdriver and, most important of all, a jemmy made from the half-shaft of a car. Hill called it his 'Peter cane'. 'Peter' had been the name for a trunk back in the 1600s, which was then converted into British criminal slang meaning a safe or jail cell. Hill also had another stick made from steel, which was shorter. Now he was ready to break the law with a vengeance.

TWO

London in the late 1920s and early 1930s was going through quite a boom period. The West End thrived on the rich and famous, and the city was attracting more visitors than ever before. Britain seemed to have fully recovered from the slump which occurred straight after the end of the First World War. It meant lots of pockets to pick, and houses to steal from, for a young tearaway like Billy Hill.

However, Hill knew only too well that he needed to be 'in the know' about all the other mobs of criminals in or near his manor of Camden Town. Back then, the Elephant mob controlled the Elephant and Castle area across the river. In Hoxton there was the Titanic team, who were mainly highly organised burglars and pickpockets. (The Titanic team even had a fund into which all gang members made regular contributions. This meant that, when any were sent to prison, their families were given financial support.) Then there was the Angel gang in Islington, and an East End mob so adept at stealing cars that they could virtually nick one while it was being driven along the road.

Within just under a week of leaving borstal, Billy Hill, still just nineteen years of age, had formed a gang and carried out two screwing jobs. Then, on his seventh day of freedom, he got arrested in Maida Vale for what was known back then as 'loitering with intent' – in other words, being a suspicious person. He had his parole revoked on 19 September 1931, and was sent back to the borstal section at Wandsworth where he quickly established himself as an up-and-coming leader of men. Coming from one of London's toughest families, he'd already spent so much time in prison that he had the respect of most inmates. By the time he finally came out, he was twenty years old and even better prepared for a life of crime. And this time he was determined to get away with it.

It was 1931. London was buzzing. Britain had just gone off the 'gold standard', which defined a national currency in terms of a fixed weight of gold and allowed a free trade in the precious metal. For the government of the day believed Britain's economy had been dragged down by other countries and could afford to go it alone. Politicians and the rich seemed to be having the time of their lives. Billy Hill wanted a piece of the action and he was now running his own mob, a team of criminals he intended to become the best screwing gang in the country.

And he continued to prove he was never afraid of violence. He was frequently set upon by other Camden Town toughies, who considered him a "lippy Irish git". With the Irish so looked down upon, Hill relished becoming known as a protector to many of them. Not surprisingly, his tough guy reputation was also attracting the attention of other local criminals.

*   *   *

'Race gangs' like the Sabinis looked on Soho as their manor. They even encouraged other gangsters to set up 'joints' – small underground drinking dens which were out of bounds to any unknown faces and mainly patronised by the so-called 'get-rich-quick' boys – self-acclaimed graduates of Soho's own academy of crime. Protection rackets sprang up, some of which still exist to this day, to provide extra cash for running these dens. Young colts like Billy Hill noticed all this action and wanted a piece of it.

In Soho's spielers, games of faro and chemin-de-fer saw vast sums of money change hands every evening. Soho's criminals began opening illegal casinos with roulette tables and croupiers, although these shady establishments were run from behind locked and heavily guarded doors. Inside, alcohol was encouraged while uniformed 'commissionaires' stood to attention, ready to raise the alarm if the boys in blue appeared. Illegal gambling between the wars in Britain was later estimated to have an annual turnover of £450 million, more than any other industry besides the building trade.

* * *

Despite his youth, Billy Hill was deeply respected by his boys. He was no fairground bully, drunkenly forcing them to commit crimes. He was a thinker, and that made him very different from most of the street criminals in London. Hill took an almost scientific approach to burglaries. He liked to time jobs to the second, sometimes spending hours calculating every possible detail with a specially devised schedule. As a result, many burglars on his manor began relying on him to put up jobs which were safe and profitable, and many were soon desperate to join Hill's Camden Town mob.

He was also scrupulously fair in how he shared out the proceeds following a job. If it was a five-hander, he split it fair-and-square five ways, while others might have been tempted to take two shares and then split the rest. Hill also began to get to know the best fences on his manor, who were vital in disposing of the swag as quickly as possible.

He also handled his mob differently from most others in the underworld, becoming a master at settling arguments without resorting to violence. He rarely raised his voice, even when he got worked up, priding himself on staying low-key and not drawing too much attention to himself and his gang. As he later explained, "It doesn't pay to be noticeable. I always dressed well, but conservatively. I might have worn my hat on the back of my head when I was younger, but I did not go in for flash suits and loud ties. I could be with four people and you wouldn't know I was there. But let anyone take a liberty and my chiv was on his cheek before he knew I was about."

The key to Hill's power always remained the low-key threat of violence. Always being armed with a chiv was the perfect way to ensure most of his enemies (and his friends) watched their step. When Hill did resort to actually using it, he was partial to carving a 'V for Victory' sign, or a cross on the cheek. "They remember that, and whenever you saw anyone wearing one you knew that it was Billy Hill who had done it."

But he always insisted he never chivved anyone "unless I had to . . . I was always careful to draw my knife down on the face, never across or upwards. Always down. So that if the knife slips you don't cut an artery. After all, chivving is chivving, but cutting an artery is usually murder. Only mugs do murder."

Even when talking about violence, Billy Hill was always able to make it sound like a reasonable response to a problem. It was controlled, and all decisions were taken with the utmost care and consideration.

The Camden Town gang included Square Georgie (real name Georgie Ball), Button, Birdie Short and Teddy Hughes (aka Odd Legs), most of whom went on to work for Hill for more than thirty years. They were young, hungry thieves, happy to be led by the well organised Hill. Then there was Georgie Sparkes, his sister's brother-in-law, who brought with him a girl known as Coloured Queenie whom Hill later claimed was an actress in a leading West End musical at the time. "No one in the world would have suspected this olive-complexioned coloured girl, a smashing looker she was too, of drumming for a burglars' gang."

Hill had no problem with women in his gang. He also adored their company outside working hours. He believed his obsessive love of women probably came from having been deprived of female company throughout so much of his youth, while incarcerated in various borstals. In Hill's mind, he was simply making up for lost time.

On his home manor of Camden, Hill quickly became a local celebrity thanks to the success of his criminal enterprises. Women were falling at his feet, but Hill knew only too well that most of them were after his money. He picked and chose his girlfriends with great care. "When you're skint or in trouble they're not so friendly any more. Dozens of them came my way, and dozens of them I passed by."

Hill eventually got himself a flat in Camden Town, which he used as his headquarters. Typically, he chose a relatively modest apartment. Nothing too flash, so as to keep at bay the cozzers or any rival criminals who might be tempted to go after his loot. It was in a house owned by a local man who Hill knew could be trusted.

Despite spending a lot of his money on women, spielers and drink, he also prided himself on never neglecting his work. He didn't rest on his laurels, seeing screwing as a trade which provided a regular living. He was always planning the next job, and he expected all of his mob to graft for their living.

Every week, Hill and his team were out scanning the streets for any potential targets. One gang member might be in a hotel when he spotted a woman with expensive jewellery. He'd then tail her for as long as a week, until he got the perfect chance to steal it. Pubs and clubs were watched for potential wage snatches. Hill later compared his vocation to being a policeman, or even a newspaper reporter.

A lot of jobs brought in modest amounts of money, but now and again they'd have what he called "a real tickle". Big money in those days meant takings in excess of £1,000. But within days of even the big hits, Hill and his mob were back on the streets looking for more opportunities.

Billy Hill was already earning in excess of £50 a week – a huge amount back then, the equivalent of probably £2,000 a week today – at only twenty-one years of age. He chose his team carefully, knowing only too well that one careless whisper could land them all in jail.

But on the mean streets of Camden Town, being a member of Billy Hill's gang was already a badge of honour, although he warned his men against boasting. In some ways, Hill would have preferred it if no one even knew who he was – although his local fame did bring him some excellent inside information. People would come to him from all over London with tips about possible burglary targets, and he prided himself on giving those informants a fair share of the proceeds of any resulting jobs.

But it was the buyers of 'bent gear' – the fences – who were the most important sources: "Fences are always trying to get burglars to do jobs so that they can buy the stolen gear at a profit." But Hill was wary of some, as he knew a large number of fences had been planted amongst the criminal fraternity by the police. Hill had learned all about such grasses when he was banged up in prison. He also knew from his 'training' that it was always a good idea to carry plenty of cash around, so that if he was nicked he'd be able to bribe his way out of trouble.

By this time, his mob was carrying out at least a dozen burglaries a week. But Hill cleverly continued to change his *modus operandi*. He knew the police were no fools, and in any case had the utmost respect for them. "They're smart. In any case, you've got to admit it, they're the finest police in the world, that Metropolitan Police Force. And if you don't have both eyes open they'll be feeling your collar all the time."

So Hill decided to stop committing burglaries after calculating there were too many other local villains 'at it'. The police would also try to get whoever they arrested to plead guilty to other jobs, even if they were nothing to do with his gang. They liked to clear their books, irrelevant of who had actually committed the crimes. So Hill decided to turn his hand to robbery – or 'blagging', as it was known on the streets of London. He knew it would pay handsomely. The key to it was inside information, knowing exactly when a payroll was being brought from a bank, or the time when a particular person was delivering a large sum of cash. Hill knew that some people would get hurt, but it didn't bother him when it was part of the job. As he later recalled, "The only way to succeed in this venture is to use sufficient violence on the person carrying the dough in order to relieve him of it." Although he did add, "Not too much, mind you, but enough to get the dough and escape with it."

Blags had a lot of advantages over burglaries. For starters, most of them involved hard cash so there was no need for a fence. Currency notes were rarely identifiable back in those days, and even if they were marked, Hill knew that a quick trip to the local dog track would soon get rid of them. It all made it much harder for the police to prove anything.

Naturally, Hill was soon being given tips about potential blagging targets. In pubs and clubs on his manor, so-called respectable bank clerks would seek him out in the hope of a lucrative tip-off fee. Other informants included embittered employees of wealthy businessmen.

He had one particularly important inside man called Peter the

Pole, who kept him informed re all the big banks. This Polish immigrant was known in the trade as a master 'switchman', which meant that he watched banks for days at a time and then focused on a particular employee who regularly went to a bank to drop off or pick up money. The Pole would then obtain an identical bag to his target, waiting for the perfect opportunity to switch his bag full of newspapers for the bag full of money. As a result, Peter the Pole knew all about the movement of money in and out of banks and his information was invaluable to Hill.

Billy and his mob would also often tail a man for days on end. They'd study all his habits – from stopping at a certain café, to popping into his favourite pub, to the people he spoke to when he was out and about. The key was the exact timing of each of the target's movements, and any changes in his daily habits. However, there was always the risk that something unpredictable might happen. A target might spend three weeks arriving at a bank at precisely the same time, and then the following day he'd be there an hour later, just as a policeman was passing. Ultimately, it was all in the lap of the gods.

A classic example of this was a blag carried out by Hill and his team in the East End. He was standing by the door of a bank, waiting for their target to walk out with his money. Hill described what happened next in vivid detail in his autobiography:

"Our client, who was a prominent West End businessman, got out of his car. It was parked behind ours. Then, as he walked across the pavement, a smaller man got out of his car with the bag containing the gelt. It was as though some instinct made the businessman look straight at me. There I was, leaning on the corner of the bank doorway. I was dressed in my well-weathered raincoat with a soft hat pulled down over my eyes. My hands were in my pocket, the right hand firmly holding the cosh, which I had bought from a store the day previously. I guess I looked like a gangster. They say Humphrey Bogart could go for my twin brother, and he looks like what a gangster's supposed to look like."

Hill kept his eyes locked on the businessman, who was speeding up his pace. Then he suddenly broke into a run. "There was no time to think. I ran after him to try and cut him off from entering the bank doors." Hill pulled his cosh out of his pocket and smashed the man over the head with it. Then he grappled the businessman to the ground as they began an almighty struggle for the bag containing the money.

Luckily, Hill had Odd Legs covering him, and his accomplice whacked the man over the head some more. The full force of it made him release his grip on the money bag. Hill and Odd Legs scarpered out of the front door of the bank, diving straight into the car where getaway driver Harry Ryan was waiting. Within seconds they were out of sight. The entire raid had taken just three minutes from start to finish, leaving Hill and his gang £1,700 (all in £1 notes) better off.

Odd Legs was the most experienced member of Hill's team back then, and had got his nickname following a car accident which left him walking with one leg trailing the other. Fellow gang member Tosh Saunders was renowned as being, in Hill's words, "as cool as a cucumber". He was known throughout London as a superb driver, his nickname dating back from when he and Hill were in prison together. Tosh – slang for 'rubbish' – was renowned for collecting lenses from other prisoner's glasses and making a homemade telescope, which was then used to watch the warders' married quarters opposite. Tosh rented it out to other inmates, who enjoyed only partially obscured views of the screws' wives bathing. Eventually, Saunders was caught red-handed and given a long spell inside solitary confinement. But his name became legendary inside prison because of his ability to turn "any old tosh" into a money-making concern.

Hill felt a great deal of loyalty towards Tosh, after the first job they did together almost ended in disaster. The gang were about to hit a bank in the City. They had been tailing a messenger and his minder for more than a week. The messenger took the cash takings from a travel agency to the bank every Wednesday at precisely noon. The plan had been for Hill to go after the big minder and stun him, while Tosh and Odd Legs looked after the smaller man who had the money. As Hill explained, "I knocked the big man on the head and he dropped like a log. I only gave him a tap. But he swallowed it and didn't want to know any more. The other two tackled the smaller man, but he fought back like a tiger." In the end Hill and his men grabbed a bag carried by the bigger man and didn't bother with the smaller target. They were lucky to find it contained about £1,200 in notes and silver.

The blags themselves were extremely risky undertakings. Often the gang's car might break down, or another vehicle might block its getaway route. Back in those days any robbery with violence was punishable with 'the cat' (flogging), as well as a hefty jail sentence.

Hill and his mob chanced upon one very lucrative East End job when they ran into a villain called 'Runner Beans George', who offered them a blag his team didn't fancy. Hill grabbed at the chance, after having to abandon a job earlier that same day. They were told by George that two men were exiting a specific East End bank with three bags of money between them.

Hill checked out the bank door, the street outside and the nearest junction for their getaway, where there was a set of traffic lights. He didn't like traffic lights as they could hold up the gang's escape, but he knew he had to make a decision on the spot. "It was ten minutes to wait. I decided to give it a go."

There was an extra gang member called Long Stan in tow that day. He tended to be a bit of a nuisance, so Hill tried to dissuade him from joining the actual job. But he was determined to get involved, and Long Stan, all six feet five of him, headed to the nearest telephone box to black up his face as if he was going on a commando raid. Hill was appalled. The way he later described it made it sound like something out of an Ealing comedy:

"He looked a right pretty picture standing before the mirror of a public telephone box piling black greasepaint on his face to try and disguise himself. And to add to his nonsense, there was a bunch of navvies digging the road up a few yards away looking at him."

Hill had long been convinced that disguises simply were not worth the bother. "It's amazing how few people recognise you on a blag job. All they know is the knock they get on their head or arm." So he pulled open that telephone box door and grabbed Long Stan's arm, yelling at him to get the black face paint off. "The navvies laughed like hell. If only they had known what they were about to laugh at next."

Just then the two targets came out of the bank. One of them was carrying two bags of money on his shoulders. The other man, his minder, carried a third bag of swag. But as Hill, Odd Legs and Runner Beans George converged on them, one of the men dropped his bag and ran. Hill went after him to make sure he kept quiet, and eventually gave him a severe knock on the head. His other two accomplices dealt with the bloke with two bags. Within two and half minutes all three were in the getaway car with the three bags of money.

With Harry Ryan at the wheel, the gang ran straight into a red light at the end of the street, which was choked with traffic. Hill knew they'd be nabbed if they hung around, so he ordered Ryan to drive on the wrong side of the road against the oncoming traffic. Ryan slammed his foot down on the throttle and swung the car right around. Buses skidded out of the way. Taxi drivers shouted and swore, and a couple of lorries mounted the pavements, but Ryan managed to steer the car safely past them all. Slouched in the back seat, Long Stan yelled for him to be careful but he took no notice. Moments later, the car skidded right into the path of an oncoming lorry. Ryan wrenched the steering wheel over and tried to pull them out of the way, but it caught one of the door catches and sent the car spinning out of control.

Hill's getaway vehicle shot clean across the road, directly in front of the oncoming traffic, before Ryan managed to bring it in line with the traffic heading towards the City. Ryan then slammed his foot down again and headed around a corner leading towards Old Street, hitting speeds approaching seventy miles an hour. The remains of the car door lay twisted on the side of the road almost one mile back.

Minutes later, Ryan expertly pulled the car to a halt. Hill and his gang of four grabbed their cash and scattered down the deserted streets. They'd all earlier agreed to rendezvous at Hill's flat by four o'clock that afternoon. He eventually counted out more than £4,000 in five and one pound notes. "Not a bad day's work."

* * *

Billy Hill may have initially prided himself on keeping a low profile, but by the early 1930s he undoubtedly began revelling in the notoriety of his crimes. The newspapers splashed stories about his gang's exploits across their front pages. He and his gang were never arrested for their series of blags. Hill insisted that no one got badly hurt during the raids, and even later claimed he had designed a cosh specifically not to cause any lasting damage. But it was a risky strategy, which wouldn't have got him much sympathy in a court of law.

By the end of 1933, his average weekly takings were close to

£100 a week, a very tidy sum back in those days. Typically though, his criminal brain continued to work overtime on various schemes. Hill knew it was time to go back to screwing houses and businesses, to keep the Old Bill off the scent.

He decided that all jobs would from now on be carried out in daylight. Most people were away from their homes then, and if the law did apprehend you, they couldn't nick you for being 'in possession of housebreaking implements by night'. Even if they did arrest you on the 'sus' law – being a suspected person, 'loitering with intent' – then you'd only end up with a fine in most circumstances.

But not all of Hill's jobs went perfectly. He was turning over a doctor's house in Bromley, Kent, when he heard the owner moving around upstairs. Hill bolted through the garden door, over the fence and down a railway track. As he was running across the track, he tripped and fell onto an electric line. He was badly burned, and two policemen soon caught up with him.

On 11 January 1934, Billy Hill would be handed down a three-year sentence and a trip back to his old *alma mater*, Wandsworth Prison . . .

THREE

Billy appealed against his three-year sentence and was given twelve months hard labour instead. He slept on bare boards for the first fourteen days at a borstal in the Wiltshire countryside. On the floor of his windowless cell was a tin for drinking, another one for washing and a china bowl which doubled as a toilet. For the first three months he wasn't allowed to read one single book. No wonder he sat in solitude, planning dozens of crimes for when he got out.

The only book he was offered was a bible. Although brought up as a Catholic, Hill hadn't been to church since he was a child, although he did later concede that he thought religion "was alright". Along with many other inmates, he found it difficult to equate religion and forgiveness with the brutal regime inside prison. "Prison screws were sadistic bastards. Hardly a day went by without some prisoner being beaten up until he was unconscious. It was routine for a bunch of screws to lock the door of a bloke's peter [cell] and kick him to death nearly."

During the day, Hill and his fellow prisoners sewed mail bags before being locked up at 4pm in their cells, not allowed out again until the following morning. Those who did not perform their prison duties properly were put on bread and water. Smoking was prohibited in prisons throughout the land back then, though inmates were permitted to chew tobacco, which made for a thriving black market in 'snout'. Some of the prison officers were crooked enough to bring more in for the richer inmates, like Hill. He'd tell his tame screw to call in at a certain address for a specific appointment, where he'd be given, say, £5 in cash. The screw would keep half the money for himself and then invest the remainder in snout, which he'd bring into prison. It was the only release for many inmates, and Hill was soon organising a healthy trade in chewing tobacco.

Even at that young age, Hill displayed a remarkable degree of self-awareness. He was determined the system would never beat him, seeing prison as the ultimate challenge. As he later explained, "I had long ago acquired the facility of being able to mentally transport myself out of that nick and to some place where life was pleasant and rosy. I can still do that, so I don't suffer from neurosis. Why, many a long night from 8pm to 6am I've had the time of my life living in a wild fantasy of dreams."

Hill knew that the system would never beat him so long as he had the ability to switch off. He managed to divorce himself from the grim reality of prison, in effect living a life apart. In many ways, Billy Hill had the intense mind of a writer or an artist. There was a vast area of his imagination where he could lose himself and create a world that kept him sane.

Hill spent many hours every day in pursuit of criminal perfection, going over his previous blags, screwings and mistakes all over again. While in prison, he also started thinking seriously about getting married. He'd met a 'young lady' called Aggie a few months before being nicked for his latest offence. Aggie was rosy-cheeked with brown hair, brown eyes, full lips and a smile that reduced tough guy Hill to jelly. She was a shy creature, which made her even more attractive to him as he didn't feel comfortable with loudmouthed women. Neither did she wear showy outfits like the prostitutes that Hill usually socialised with. As he said, "There was something different about her." Hill kissed Aggie the first night he took her home, but didn't dare take things any further out of respect. It was the first time in his life he had felt like this about a woman.

Hill later claimed he was so smitten by Aggie that if she'd asked him to give up his life of crime, and work an honest living, he would have agreed. (Although he did later admit it might have been a bit of a stretch.) But it was only after he got sentenced to prison that he realised how special she was. She wasn't after his money or his lifestyle. She just wanted him.

Hill had always been quite shy unless he was with familiar people, such as his gang or his family. He had great difficulty making ordinary conversation, and when he met Aggie for the first time he was similarly tongue-tied. It didn't help that she had a strange northern accent. Their courtship was littered with confusion; he would ask her to repeat what she'd just said, and she'd hit back with accusations that he must be deaf. But Hill had fallen head over heels in love, and didn't know what to do next. The couple had taken it 'nice and easy' for the following few months, until he got arrested. Then she immediately wrote to him in prison. It convinced Hill that she was going to become someone really special in his life. He had never read a letter like it before. It wasn't full of gushing 'I love you's' or "I'll stand by you forever," but instead was crammed with news about the world outside, asking Hill how he was feeling and telling of how she hoped to see him really soon.

Hill read that first letter from Aggie over and over again, until he could recite it off by heart. He later recalled, "It just made me feel good. And I didn't mind doing me bird after that." He only had a year to serve.

The offshoot of being in love was that Billy Hill kept a low profile for the remainder of his sentence. Naturally, by the time he walked out of the prison gate, he had many new criminal enterprises lined up. But there, standing at the end of the approach to the vast gates of Wandsworth Prison, was his sweetheart Aggie.

Hill takes up the story: "It seemed funny after all this time to see her standing there. I think she was blushing. And I felt a bit of a berk too. Fancy a dame waiting outside the nick when you came out from doing your bird!"

As she walked towards him, he suddenly panicked. "I wanted to turn and run back into that nick again. But I knew this was something I had to face," he later explained.

"How are you?" said Hill, trying to be as cool as he could.

"All right. How are you?" Aggie asked back.

"All right," said Hill, awkwardly.

Within seconds they were walking arm in arm up the road leading away from Wandsworth Prison. Hill later recalled that they barely exchanged another word. "I felt I had known her all my life." But he was secretly very bothered by the fact that none of his gang had been at the prison gates to greet him, although he didn't dare say anything about his gangster life to Aggie.

When he turned and asked if she had any money on her, she replied, "The boys asked me to give you this." It was £20 in cash. Hill now realised she had set it all up with his boys. He was genuinely touched. The couple hailed a taxi and, within an hour, Hill was sitting around a table talking to his old mates Button, Chilly Dicky, Taffy and the rest of the team.

*   *   *

Another criminal operator had been causing quite a stir in the London underworld at that time. His name was Charlie 'Ruby' Sparkes. He'd become the self-acclaimed king of the capital's smash 'n' grab raids, but earned the nickname after stealing rubies in a burglary in Mayfair and then throwing them away because he thought they were worthless. It was 1934, and the Flying Squad (although formed not long after the First World War) was still in its infancy. The squad didn't even have many vehicles, and it was only the occasional skilful lone detective who would put it on the map in the long term.

Back then, there were no two-way radios and messages were tapped out in Morse code between police cars, only sent on one wavelength at a time. Only a handful of Flying Squad vehicles were ever out at the same time in London. Other police used so-called 'area cars' and 'Q cars', and 999 calls to police head-quarters didn't even exist. To contact the police, you lifted a telephone receiver and asked for either the local police or Scotland Yard. At night, the phones were often not answered for up to ten minutes after the original call. It was little wonder that smash 'n' grabs were popular with London's underworld.

It wasn't until Hill began looking more closely at Ruby Sparkes' jobs that he realised Sparkes' reputation might not be all it was cracked up to be. At the time of Hill's release, Ruby was on the run from the notorious Dartmoor Prison in the West of England. His daring escape seemed to have backed up his reputation more than the actual crimes he'd committed on the outside.

So Hill decided to get together a team who'd become the most formidable smash 'n' grab gang in London. He assembled his favourite boys, Georgie Square, Chilly Dicky, Taffy, Birdie Short and a few others 'faces'. Hill would later explain, "The proper way to do a smash 'n' grab is to time every move to the split second. There's no room for improvisation, nor is there any point in deciding on one plan and trying to put another into operation. Every man must work like a machine, with the precision of a handmade watch."

Hill had no difficulty picking targets for his newly formed gang.

He knew just about every jeweller's shop in London and most of the furrier's stores as well. For his first job since getting out of prison, he picked on a crowded jeweller's shop near Baker Street, with plenty of escape roads to Camden. Hill went over the route with a fine toothcomb in the week before the raid, examining everything from the timing of the traffic lights to the places where most people crossed the street.

His team also spent days getting to know the habits of all the shop assistants. The gang consisted of Taffy, a superb driver, Georgie Square, who had been working with Hill for years and was considered 'a natural', and Chilly Dickie, who was as reliable as Big Ben. Armed with a driving licence in a false name, they hired themselves a getaway vehicle for the princely sum of £1 a day.

The gang drove up to Baker Street early one evening. Dicky and Georgie Square held the two front doors tight, while Hill calmly strolled up to the store window, threw the head of a sledgehammer into it and took out two large diamond solitaire rings, worth almost £1,000 each. (The rings could be traded for straight cash.)

Not one member of the public batted an eyelid. No one yelled out. Once Hill had the stolen gear in his hands, he headed across the pavement, back towards the getaway car, where Taffy had the engine running. The entire operation had taken no more than thirty seconds, and within ten minutes they were all safely back in Camden Town. The robbery hit the headlines and was hailed as the first of a big wave of such raids to hit London in 1934.

Hill genuinely believed that the sheer audacity of many of his jobs made them relatively safe. It was as if the authorities simply couldn't comprehend how anyone could carry them out. Virtually every day, he would drive around London looking for new targets. He'd get out of his car to take a closer look at the window displays, assessing the street value of virtually any piece he saw within seconds. If he didn't know, then he'd get a fence to take a stroll with him to look at the jewellery, before deciding on whether to pull off the job.

Hill quickly concluded it was always best to dump the getaway car before the gang reached their home turf. The police had soon worked out that they were hiring cars for their robberies, and garages were warned against dealing with suspicious characters. They got over that little problem by stealing their getaway vehicles, replacing the plates with new ones made for them by a specialist who lived in Camden. The car would then be kept in a lock-up until the day of the job.

Hill thought of everything. He'd get the gang to drive around and around in the hope that someone would note down their number. Then they'd pull up in a quiet mews and replace the plates with another set, just to confuse the police.

Scotland Yard were soon put under immense pressure by Fleet Street, who were calling the robberies an "epidemic of smash 'n' grab raids". The Yard's commissioner, Lord Trenchard, made it clear he wanted some fast results. In the *Daily Mirror* of 8 February 1935, the headline 'LORD TRENCHARD ORDERS GREAT VIGILANCE' said it all. On the same day, the *Daily Express*'s headline ran, 'RAIDERS STRIKE AGAIN. ONE POLICEMAN TO EVERY TEN MILE BEAT.' On 10 February 1935, the *Sunday Express* breathlessly reported, 'THIEVES – £13,000 IN ONE WEEK'. The following day, the *Daily Herald*'s headline screamed, '£2,800 JEWELS STOLEN IN THREE RAIDS'.

Insurance rates on jewellers' shops soared. Outraged citizens formed home protection groups and demanded more action from the authorities. The newspapers became more and more hysterical, with the old, bible-thumping *Daily Express* screaming, 'CRIME WAVE RISES IN THE SUBURBS'.

The Home Secretary felt obliged to make statements in the House of Commons about the smash 'n' grab epidemic, and the *Daily Herald* perfectly summed up one fortnight in the criminal career of Billy Hill: "More than £50,000 worth of jewels have been stolen in a series of lightning raids which have swept London and the Home Counties in the last two weeks."

But Hill was nothing if not a realist. He knew the odds would eventually turn against him and his gang. The Flying Squad was being increased in strength. He had to change tactics again, and switched to night-time raids instead.

*   *   *

Billy Hill was still in his twenties, and already a rich man by the standards of that era. He'd later reflect that he might have become even richer if he hadn't been so generous, but he didn't regret a thing. He always looked after his mother and father, and many of his relatives. "After all they had fed and clothed me well as a kid," as he later explained. Hill's parents were still living in Camden Town; he kept in close touch and constantly "bunged them a few quid". Then there was his sister, Maggie, who'd looked after him after he first came out of borstal. Hill made sure she never went short, and many of his numerous other brothers and sisters also got a helping hand. Then there were all his friends and cronies on the manor, who hadn't enjoyed his kind of luck.

Hill came from a traditional Irish family, which meant that he was expected to help out similar clans in Camden Town. They all had dozens of kids and many of them were straight, law-abiding citizens who struggled to pay the rent. Families with names like Murphy, Reilly, Flanagan and Flaherty were all living on the breadline. Hill "worked a few quid their way", and in the process got himself something of a reputation as the Robin Hood of Camden Town. But the master thief actually had a social conscience. As he later explained, "It didn't seem right that I should have all that dough when they had so little."

Then there was Aggie, the love of his life. He bought her jewels and rings, and would insist that none of it was nicked. It was as if he didn't want to directly expose her to his life of crime.

Hill later said this was one of the happiest periods of his life. He had a comfortable flat in Camden Town, and a good lifestyle, which allowed him to eat in decent restaurants and drink fine wines. He didn't even mind that so many on his manor constantly tried to put the touch on him for money. That was the price you paid for local fame. People were constantly onto him in pubs and clubs for a few quid and he usually obliged, looking on it as yet more evidence of his standing in the community. Hill also knew that if he turned down any of these 'touches' he could make an enemy for life, which could lead to all sorts of problems.

So despite earning a small fortune on the streets of London, Billy Hill needed to maintain his income. As he later pointed out, "Being crooked is like any other job, when you come to think of it. The more successful you are the more successful you've got to be."

It got him thinking about his next move, and he decided that fur coats were to be his next big criminal campaign. He took a trip around the West End and spotted dozens of furriers, with tens of thousands of pounds worth of fur in their front windows. But Hill could foresee problems. "It was not going to be like putting your hand into a hole in a window and picking hold of a tray of rings. To get furs you have to smash the window wide open so that you can walk to the window itself and lift the furs off the models. And once you've made the smash, you can't walk into the window a second time. One grab and you've got to get out and into the car." He also worked out that he couldn't get away with many furs in daylight robberies, because of their bulk. Eventually he decided to take a buyer along with him, who could tell Hill exactly which furs to grab and what they were worth. Hill planned to carry out all raids at night, and reckoned on as many as two or three in an evening. With a plan imprinted on his mind, he then returned to Camden Town to brief his boys.

Once again, it was imperative that their getaway car was the right model for the job, and that they had what was called a 'run-in' – a place where they could doctor a vehicle so it couldn't be traced back to them. Hill demanded that every car was carefully checked out mechanically, and also decided to start using a so-called 'block car' – a vehicle that would cover the main team and enable them to make a safe getaway. If necessary, the block car would be deliberately stalled at a nearby junction to give the main vehicle a clear escape route. Sometimes the block car was a vehicle genuinely owned by a gang member who, if caught by the police, could claim he was innocent of any involvement.

Hill and his gang would often dump their getaway car near a cab rank, get out of the vehicle with suitcases containing the furs, and hail a ride to a decoy destination. All these little planning touches were typical of Billy Hill. He left no stone unturned when it came to trying to ensure a job would be both safe and lucrative.

His first fur job was a shop in Regent Street, which he knew from his own sources was a long way from the nearest Flying Squad patrol car. (Hill had ears and eyes inside the police, as well as amongst the criminal fraternity.) As usual Taffy was at the wheel of their getaway vehicle, alongside Hill, as they pulled up near the store. In the back were the redoubtable Ruby Sparkes and Georgie Square.

Hill hunched his mac up to his shoulders. His mouth was bone dry from nerves, although he'd never have conceded that at the time. There were loads of pedestrians around, including a couple walking arm-in-arm towards Hill. He waited for them to draw parallel with their car.

"Give us the spare wheel," he ordered Georgie. "You keep that door held on the catch, Ruby."

Hill, wearing gloves, grabbed the spare in both hands, held it firmly in front of him and headed towards the store window. His trilby hat was pulled well down on his head, his mac buttoned and belted tightly so that it would not flow in the wind when he ran away.

A woman walked past and almost collided with him. He immediately apologised. Then he lifted the spare wheel and tyre above his head and smashed it into the shop window. Glass splintered in all directions and a great hush enveloped the area. An old-fashioned taxi horn sounded in the distance. Hill took hold of the wheel again and bashed the bottom part of the glass out of the window, so that he could walk clean into the shop.

Then he grabbed every fur within reach, all of which had been marked for theft by the buyer he'd bought to the store. He lifted some off their mannequins and put them over his left arm, not once looking behind himself as he knew the others were covering him. Then he clambered out from amongst the broken glass and ran across the pavement to the waiting car.

The ever-dependable Taffy had the engine running. But as Hill headed for the getaway car he noticed a man running towards him. He chucked the furs in and jumped aboard, with Ruby slamming the door behind him. Taffy was about to screech off up the road when Hill ordered them to wait a moment. He watched as that same man suddenly stopped running and stared intently at the car. Hill hoped he was memorising the registration number. Just to make sure he got a good look, Hill made Taffy wait for the best part of a minute before they drove off.

The block car, driven by a gang member called 'Horrible Harry', was on their tail in case of any unforeseen problems. No one seemed to be trying to chase them, but Hill ordered Taffy to slow down. The rest of the team sat in silence, knowing full well that Hill had a golden rule about not speaking during a job unless absolutely necessary. In fact he had earlier calculated when all the traffic lights would turn green, and knew that if Taffy slowed down a tad they'd pass through the next set.

As they headed towards Broadcasting House in Portland Place (where BBC Radio is based to this day), Hill and his boys spotted the block car stalled in the middle of the road. Then it started forwards and backwards, just as Horrible Harry had been instructed to do. It meant no other vehicle would get across the lights for at least two or three minutes.

Meanwhile, in the back of the car, Ruby and Georgie were packing the furs into suitcases. Taffy pointed the car towards a cab rank in Tottenham Court Road. Moments later they dumped the 'drag', Georgie and Taffy taking the suitcases to one taxi while Ruby and Hill hailed another. They went as far as Russell Square and then grabbed another cab for Euston tube station. Then they jumped on an underground train to Chalk Farm, where they walked down the road towards nearby Camden Town before hailing another cab, which dropped them three streets from their base. The other two had already arrived ahead of them with the booty from the raid.

A few minutes later, Hill's fence arrived. Within another minute of that, all the furs were in his car and on their way off of Hill's manor. The fence had just passed over £1,000 in readies, with another £500 due to be paid to Hill the following day.

FOUR

Nineteen thirty-nine turned into a busy year for Billy Hill, now one of London's most successful young criminals. He had a touch of class about him, which made people sit up and take notice of him despite his age. Four or five smash 'n' grab raids in a week were nothing unusual for Hill's mob.

On his home turf of Camden, at pubs such as the Victoria, the Bedford and the Brighton Arms, everyone knew Billy. They didn't know exactly where he got his cash from, but he was a good spender and that was all that mattered. Even the hangers-on knew there would usually be a drink in it for them if he was feeling flush. Hill saw himself as a bit of a soft touch. "Like the money I was getting, I was easy. I never had the guts to resist a touch, especially if the story was good."

*   *   *

Meanwhile, Hill's young girlfriend, Aggie, was beginning to get a tad irritated with the way he was always out 'working'. She told him she was fed up of him coming home so late "there's nothing else to do but go to bed." And she chipped in with the ultimate insult for good measure: "Why, even policemen see something of their homes at some time or other."

Hill was irritated by his Aggie's attitude, feeling that, as long as

43

he saw her alright for money and possessions, she shouldn't really give him a hard time. After all, the best he could expect in the straight world would be a job as a lorry driver, if he was lucky. And once they found out he was a jailbird, he'd probably get fired and end up on the streets.

Billy Hill, master criminal of Camden Town, refused to be thrown on the scrapheap. He'd chosen his career path and there was no turning back. But Aggie was never far from her favourite subject: "Billy," she said. "Why take the chance of getting knocked-off at all? We could buy a café or something like that. A small business and you could get out of the game altogether."

As Hill recalled, many years later, "Of course, she didn't know that once you're in my business you can never get out. Imagine me opening a café. Who d'you think my customers would be? Why, crooked people of course."

Aggie wasn't going to give up that easily. "But Billy. Just try it out. I'll work hard. We can both work together. And if we fail, then we both go down together." She was worried sick about her husband going to prison again, telling him, "I love you. I want you to be with me. I don't want money and not you. I don't want only money from you. Don't you understand these things? Don't you understand how a woman thinks?"

Something in her words touched the so-called hard man. As he later explained, "I had known little kindness in my life. Less still real love from a woman." Profoundly moved, Billy asked her to marry him. He even promised that he'd only do a few more jobs before switching to a straighter occupation, like a bookmaker.

The following day, Hill got hold of a couple of his lads and asked them to act as witnesses at his wedding. (But not before swearing them to silence.) Then Billy Hill and his pretty young wife went straight from the registry office to the Brighton Arms to celebrate. It seemed that everyone on the manor wanted to congratulate them.

"By the time I got round to buying everyone a drink I was half-boozed and so were all the others. So we kept it up all day and right through the night. Jewellers' and furriers' shops were safe that night. If the law had only known, they all could have gone home to bed. For the first time in my life I felt happy."

But to support his married life he'd have to work even harder. As he looked at it, "I couldn't stop working. The more I worked the luckier I seemed to be."

Hill's reputation had, by the middle of 1935, spread so far and wide that professional thieves were virtually queuing up to work for him. He had actually become cocky enough to feel sorry for his long suffering enemies, the cozzers. As he would explain, "Many of them aren't bad blokes. You hear a lot of nonsense about policemen. I, at least, can speak with some authority. And I can say that many police officers are genuine characters worth knowing."

He may have sounded like his tongue was firmly in his cheek when he spouted off about the "lovely cozzers" he knew, but he needed certain policemen to feed him the right sort of information. Without them, his criminal career might have been over much sooner. And the police knew all about Billy Hill, as was their job.

Hill often retold the story of how one police contact was convinced that another north London villain, Massy Johnson, was responsible for the spate of smash 'n' grabs carried out by Hill and his gang. He naturally found it hilarious, especially when the same copper claimed he'd spotted Johnson's getaway car on his manor. "If only that policeman had known why I was laughing so heartily! It was I who had left that stolen car in his area," he testified in his autobiography.

Coppers on the beat were shown little respect by the poor during the 1930s. And they were paid such paltry wages that it wasn't surprising the long arm of the law was prone to bribery, as well as using excessive violence if payments were not forthcoming. Scotland Yard had only fourteen hundred detectives out of a force of twenty thousand men to cope with ever-rising crime in the capital. Even the so-called elite units, Special Branch and the Flying Squad, only totalled four hundred detectives. And all those plainclothes officers relied on networks of 'snouts' or 'grasses' – if they had any.

* * *

Often, Hill would have so many jobs on the go at the same time that he'd farm out less important work to old boyhood mates and characters he'd first come across in borstal. A classic example was Button, from Camden Town. Hill soon realised he wasn't bright enough to go out on a proper job, but gave him a few quid to mind his flat when he was out smashing and grabbing in the West End.

One night the team arrived back with more than fifty fur coats, and Button helped carry them into the flat. But as Hill and two other gang members were sorting out the swag, Button started making strange hand signals. Eventually Hill pulled him into another room to find out what was on his mind.

"Look Bill," he said, pulling some furs out from under a bed. "Here you are, five for you and five for me."

For a brief moment, Hill wondered how in hell Button had got hold of these furs. Then he realised they were part of the loot he'd just helped bring in from the car. Button coolly explained he had stolen the coats as he was unloading them, and now he wanted to make a secret deal to share the spoils.

Hill was furious at such blatant disloyalty, and clipped Button around the ear. He knew that, once his team thought he was cutting them out, there would be an internal war. For Hill knew how to manage people and how to keep his team happy. He and the other gang members laughed about it later, but Button was lucky he didn't pay a more severe price.

Behind the bravado, Billy Hill was bright enough to know it was only a matter of time before he was tumbled. So he decided it was time to change his tactics yet again, devising a crime which no one had ever tried before. He heard from his brother-in-law, Brummy Sparkes, that many jewellers in the West End allowed potential customers to examine goods in the light of day before purchasing them.

So Hill 'trained up' a young screwsman called Connolly to pretend he was a customer. He dressed him for the part in a clerical grey suit, bowtie and bowler hat, adding a pair of neat spats together with brolly, horn-rimmed specs, yellow gloves, a copy of *The Times* and a briefcase. The young villain was then taught some stock phrases. "Say it posh like we've taught you," instructed Hill.

They chose a jeweller's in Mayfair. Connolly entered the store at eleven o'clock one bright and sunny morning. Nearby, Hill and two more gang members waited in their getaway car, just close enough to see what was happening through the jeweller's shop window. They watched as a staff member took a tray of rings out of the window, which looked to be worth at least £3,000. Hill told Tosh Saunders to start the vehicle and keep the engine running, as he knew Connolly would be out soon.

Then, just as Connolly was tearing out of the store with the rings, a milk float pulled up right in front of the getaway car. Tosh slammed the car into reverse then shot forward, only to smash so hard into the float that it ended inside a shop doorway. Connolly, feverishly clutching a tray of rings, hopped in the back of the car as they belted up the street. Within half an hour they were all back at Hill's Camden Town headquarters.

Next day, Hill and a couple of his gang went to their local cinema where a newsreel of the smashed-up milk float made headline news. But when young Connolly started mouthing off about it around the manor, he ended up being arrested and sent to prison. Hill was furious, but relieved that at least Connolly hadn't grassed on them.

Yet again Hill managed to later have a laugh about it all, even joking about Connolly's obsession with having his hair curled (after the event) as part of his disguise for the Mayfair job. Hill loved recalling how, when Connolly was banged up, he was spotted by prison officers putting his hair in paper crackers so that it would stay curly. (Hair curlers were in rather short supply in men's jails at the time.)

A typical day in the life of Hill and his gang at this time consisted of cruising around London in a stolen motor, looking for likely robbery targets. He knew it was best to use young males with no criminal records on a job, in case they were stopped and checked out by police near the scene. He claimed these 'employees' included public school boys from Eton and Dulwich College. Others came from as far afield as the army and Cambridge University.

He was turning into the stuff of criminal legend, even though his actual name had not yet been publicly linked with any of the audacious crimes. Hill seemed to have no fear of anyone – even a reporter from one of the big Fleet Street dailies, who'd become a regular at one of his favourite pubs in Camden Town. The journalist made it clear he was fascinated by the gang and their criminal lifestyle.

For his part, Hill believed this reporter could be trusted – especially when he tipped them off about a potential target, the house of the mother of a rich friend in the country, filled with jewellery. So Hill's gang broke in one night and stole the lot. But the reporter's friend was so suspicious that he went to Hill and told him where the journalist's family jewels were hidden, as a reprisal. They nicked all of that as well. It had turned into a classic vicious circle, and the only winner was Billy Hill.

Then the same reporter hit on hard times, and asked Hill if he could go on a job with him. Hill reckoned he was ideal because he looked like such a middle-class citizen. It was perfect cover for an outrageous plan. The reporter was introduced to a pretty West End chorus girl called Gerda, who was a part-time prostitute. Hill then made sure she thought the journalist was "worth a stack". In fact, it was the reporter who was taking her for a ride. After one boozy lunch date he persuaded her to go into a West End jeweller's store. She thought he was about to buy her a ring, when instead he grabbed a tray of rings and rushed straight out the door, towards the getaway car waiting nearby.

Gerda was then arrested by police and taken to the local nick. Eventually she was acquitted of involvement in the robbery, but started boasting around the West End that the reporter was a gentleman thief. As she told one friend of Hill's, "They took me down to Scotland Yard and showed me the photographs of crooks in the Rogue's Gallery. I saw a picture of that Billy Hill there, but my friend's picture wasn't there. No, he's not just a common thief like Billy Hill. He's a real life Raffles."

Hill eventually paid the reporter his £600 share of the takings, by putting it into an envelope and dropping it through the letterbox of his family home. The journalist's father found the envelope with the cash and a 'thank you' note from Billy Hill.

The reporter warned Hill that his father was planning to pay him a visit. Eventually, the angry father turned up at Hill's flat and gave him a complete rollicking for being a bad influence on his son. As Hill later explained, "It was as good a verbal broadside as ever any judge had given me. At any moment I expected him to hand out a ten stretch for luck. Instead, he threw my six centuries on the floor and stalked out." Hill never used him again, and the journalist went back to his job on a national daily newspaper.

He then began coaching old school cockney villains to "act posh", but this never guaranteed success. One character called Canary Joe insisted on dressing himself up more like a racecourse tipster than a city slicker. Hill knew he didn't look right, but, when he got away with his first job, decided to stick with him. But on the next, Canary Joe was hit very hard by an angry jeweller and Hill had to drag him into his getaway car. Days later Joe was arrested for another robbery, breaking the underworld's cardinal rule by boasting about his jobs with Hill. Hill never got pulled but saw it as a warning sign to be on his guard.

When a fence called Sammy Grant popped round to buy some stolen fur coats, Hill smelled a rat after Grant declined to purchase any and kept trying to leave the premises in a hurry. Eventually, Hill made Grant sit down and have a drink with him, just in case the fence had tipped off the police.

A few days later, Hill asked Grant if he'd be interested in purchasing some more stolen furs from a team in Paddington he knew well. By this time he was so suspicious of Grant that he refused to give him the address, insisting on them meeting up an hour later to discuss the deal. After their rendezvous, Hill took Grant to the address in Sussex Gardens where the fur coats were being kept. After ringing the doorbell, the door flew open and Hill was smashed in the chest so hard he fell back into the hallway.

When he staggered to his feet he found himself facing Detective Inspector Robert Higgins, one of his oldest Scotland Yard foes. Hill knew the moment he saw Higgens and another detective that he'd been caught bang to rights. They grabbed the two brothers who'd stolen the furs, charging them and Hill with robbery. Grant sloped out of the flat without a word.

Hill managed to grease the right palms to get bail, but knew he was in deep trouble. So he set out to make as much cash as possible for Aggie while he was banged up. He worked a smash 'n' grab job in Enfield, Middlesex, and only took Taffy as a driver to keep costs and share-outs down.

Using a three-foot cobbler's iron bar, Hill smashed the window of a jeweller's shop and then grabbed two trays of rings. As he stuffed them into his pocket and turned to make a run for the waiting getaway car, an assistant in the shop came after him and tried to swing a punch, but completely missed. Hill jumped in the car, Taffy keeping to a slow speed so as not to create any attention. After a mile, Hill ordered Taffy to dump the car and they both got a Green Line bus after Hill had torn off his gloves and thrown them in a dustbin.

En route back to central London, Hill began worrying about the gloves he'd borrowed from the wife of a close mate, then on the run from prison. He wondered if the woman could be trusted, and whether they could be traced back to her. Worse still, one of the gloves was saturated in Hill's blood because he'd cut himself on the jewellery store window. He knew that if the cops found it they would be able to match it to his blood group.

But then Hill's devious mind went into overtime. He stage-managed a fight in a cab with another gang member in which a window was broken. The cabbie was furious, but agreed to drive them to a local hospital because of Hill's supposedly cut hand. The cab driver also insisted on calling the police.

Hill carefully took a note of the number of the PC who interviewed him at the hospital, as it could provide perfect cover if the Enfield job blew up in his face. A few days later, Hill was arrested for that robbery after being picked out in an identity parade by the girlfriend of the store assistant.

While awaiting trial on those charges, Hill came up in court for the Paddington fur coat raid. He knew he stood no chance, and so, by pleading guilty on 23 October 1936, ensured he only got a twenty-one-month sentence. At his trial for the Enfield job on 9 December that same year, the chairman of the Middlesex Quarter Sessions complimented Hill on his artfulness in organising an alibi, but added, "Unfortunately for you it did not quite come off." He got four years to run concurrently with the twenty-one months he was already serving. This time he got sent to Chelmsford Prison, in Essex, which mostly housed young convicts.

*   *   *

Billy Hill's time in Chelmsford Prison didn't prove such a great hardship. Now aged twenty-five, he was one of the oldest inmates in the nick, which rather suited him as it bestowed a certain status. He also had a few cronies behind bars with him, including childhood pal Franny 'the Spaniel' Daniels, Square Georgie, and four or five others. Being Londoners they all naturally stuck together, a formidable mob compared with the youngsters from the provinces.

Even the screws inside Chelmsford nick weren't as bad as in many other prisons. Hill soon discovered that, as long as he was prepared to splash out a few bob, then he could pretty well have just about anything he wanted. But he was careful with his cash, as he needed to support Aggie – especially since his sister, Maggie, had just been sent down to Holloway yet again, which meant Aggie had to run her sister-in-law's home as well on a meagre income. So Hill started running a book in prison, and earning snout money on the side to maintain a half-decent lifestyle for himself.

Then Hill learned from sources back in Camden Town that Maggie's husband, Brummy Sparkes, had been knocking her around before she'd been banged up. He also heard Sparkes was mouthing off around town about his wife and her family. Yet he remained in the home which Hill had helped him to buy, which was a further source of outrage. Sparkes had so upset Hill's family that his younger brother, Archie, decided he should be taught a lesson.

One afternoon, Archie Hill caught Brummy Sparkes walking up Shaftesbury Avenue with four other villains. Archie steamed into Sparkes and gave him an almighty belting, before slicing him with a chiv. The attack almost killed Sparkes, but it was intended as a message from the entire Hill clan for him to keep away from their manor. He would never again take any liberties with the Hills. Indeed, he was never seen on their patch ever again.

Back in Chelmsford Prison, Hill and his boys were virtually running the place, while Aggie wrote to him regularly to keep him abreast of all the news from the outside world. Hill later admitted he found actual visits by his wife very difficult to handle, because she reminded him of what he was missing. But he treasured her letters.

Running a book inside prison provided him with enough income to start paying a tame screw to bring him in messages from his mob. The officer's 'duties' were to phone a specific number in London every day, as well as passing on any instructions from Hill. As Hill would recall, "It was an invaluable service, because from it I could prepare for a few more jobs to be done as soon as I got out."

Just three months before completing his sentence, Hill's father was suddenly taken ill and died. He was deeply upset because he'd been close to his old man throughout his life. As he later reflected, "He wasn't as smart as me, but he was a good 'un, and always looked after my mother."

Hill's family applied to the Home Office for him to be

temporarily released on parole, so that he could attend the funeral. He even offered to serve any extra time the authorities stipulated, if they'd let him out to attend the burial service. But his request was turned down flat. He was pragmatic about it, but later conceded that it further hardened his attitude towards authority. He felt he was being told he wasn't a good enough citizen to attend his own father's funeral. That night in his cell, Billy Hill said prayers for his father and promised himself he'd never allow the 'other side' to rule his life.

A few days later the Second World War broke out. Ironically, Hill and all his fellow inmates were slung out of prison – whether or not they'd finished their sentences.

Aggie was at the gates of Chelmsford nick when he came out. Hill immediately noticed how she looked exhausted, compared with when she'd last made one of her rare visits. She could only pull a half-smile when he cracked a joke. He desperately wanted to thank her for running their home and his sister Maggie's place, not to mention his mum's following the death of his father. But he later admitted he was so shy about discussing such personal subjects that he never actually got around to saying anything.

Instead he took her hand and squeezed it tight. But then the two of them gave each other a strange glance. "It's all right," she said reassuringly. "I know what I'm doing. I didn't marry you for what you've got or what you haven't got. If I don't stick by you, no one will. I know you'll go away again, but you'll always find me waiting. Let's go home and go to bed."

Hill later summed up Aggie thus: "She'd go through hell-fire and water for me, and always be at the right spot at the right time when I wanted her. A cracker in every way, but what a woman if I upset her! I'd rather upset the worst villain in the world than upset her."

On the outside, Billy Hill soon got his feet back under the table.

He assembled all his old team including Tosh Saunders, Teddy Odd Legs, Franny the Spaniel, Horrible Harry, Bear's Breath, Soapy Harry, Tony the Wop, Spoke Conway, Square Georgie, Birdie, Mutton, Scarface Jock, Long Stan and a few others. But they all knew the war would interrupt their criminal activities. Hill even put himself up for the RAF, claiming he had the genuine intention of serving king and country, unlike a lot of other London villains. He later insisted he'd made provisions for the fact that his pay in the RAF would be low, having responsibilities to his wife and recently widowed mother, as well as all the 'knockers' and 'tappers' who needed looking after on a regular basis, not to mention the families of his blokes who'd been banged up.

*   *   *

After World War Two was declared in 1939, race tracks were shut down virtually overnight. The authorities presumed the race gangs would break up but the exact opposite happened and many criminals switched to point-to-point racing, where there was hardly any police presence. The outbreak of war also sparked a flourishing black market, as people's basic morals faded and once-honest folk bought their goods 'off the back of a lorry'. No wonder criminals were soon reaping a golden harvest.

Blackouts in the big cities provided heavy cover and that meant even more spielers opening their doors. There were also dusky, badly lit clubs inhabited by prostitutes, where fake whiskey was sold at rip-off prices. On pavements and alleyways outside, women offered themselves in the pitch-dark by waving torches. Then there were the teams of touts swarming onto the West End's street corners to flog every sort of dodgy item to any mug who happened to be passing. London was turning into something more akin to a Wild West frontier town, with off-duty soldiers from all over the world invading the West End on their days off.

Soon another war emerged, between the race gangs who'd been forced to quit the tracks and the mobsters already in place in the West End. Spielers were at the centre of the fiercest battles. Groups of men would enter the club of a rival gang, beat up the occupants and wreck the premises. The police would then arrive on the scene and close the place down, leaving more business for a rival firm. Out on the blacked-out streets, fights with chivs were commonplace. Fists were a weapon of the past.

When Italian fascist leader Mussolini declared war on Great Britain, Soho really felt the full impact. Scores of Italians were interned, and the streets of the West End were wiped clean of many of the gangsters who'd ruled the roost up until then. Italian premises were stoned by vicious mobs.

Meanwhile, Billy Hill was trying to pull in as much cash as possible before his call-up papers arrived. And it was this financial pressure which got him involved in his most glamorous, high-profile job so far. In the heart of Hatton Garden, the 'gold district' on the edge of the City of London, Hill had been tipped off about gold bullion which was taken out of a specific jeweller's store every morning at 11am by two guards. Hill and one of his boys, Posh Duke, decided to take a look. (Duke was so called because he was tall and aristocratic looking, spoke all 'la-di-da' and, in Hill's words, "dressed like a Christmas dinner".) After three days of observation on the store, the gang struck. Hill knocked both guards over the head and escaped with £5,000 worth of gold bullion.

Hill then gave a lot of thought to the best way to make a living while the world was at war. He knew there would be huge demands for certain products. While the man on the street was struggling to make ends meet, the rich were continuing to live it up in the best restaurants, hotels and clubs, and so the black market was going to thrive.

He put it perfectly in his autobiography, when he wrote: "Make no bones about it, I did not pose as a patriotic citizen, breaking my neck to do my bit while at the same time hiding like a frightened rabbit behind a maze of complicated laws for the privileged who collared well-paid and reserved occupations."

For Hill adored the black market and its lack of principles. "It was the most fantastic side of civil life in war-time," he later boasted. "I did not merely make use of the black market. I fed it."

By the end of 1940, supplies of everything from whiskey to washing up liquid were in short supply. A classic example of Hill's wartime initiatives came at a West Country services depot which stored bedding. In one well-organised raid using a lorry, Hill's gang managed to steal most of it. Sheets usually costing a fiver a pair were banged out for two a quid.

Next was a warehouse filled with fur coats, which Hill and his boys emptied in a matter of minutes. They had so many that he stored some at his flat in Camden Town, then sold them at a knockdown £6 each, ridiculously cheap. He insisted he did it because he wanted the less well-off to get the benefit of his 'expertise' too. But of course, Hill was exploiting a desperate and cynical population.

Then there was whiskey. Numerous small-time hoods were distilling their own lethal versions. Hill reckoned he was above such unsavoury activities. As he said many years later, "I liked to think that if I was crooked, at least I was bent in an honest way. I sold only real whiskey. Good stuff at that."

Hill's gang constantly looked out for any whiskey storage facilities, after which a raid was quickly organised and it was stolen by the barrel load. He sold each barrel for £500 a time, never ceasing to be amazed by how much money some things could fetch on the black market.

When butchers told Hill they were desperate for sausage skins, he was even able to fix his own price – £500 a barrel, the same as whiskey. He had no idea if it was an accurate reflection of their true value but no one complained, so he guessed he wasn't being *that* greedy.

Hill was personally raking in £300-£400 a week from the black market, and later claimed that, throughout this period, he was still waiting for his call-up papers to arrive. Many believed that Hill eventually bought his way out of serving king and country, but throughout his autobiography he insisted his papers simply never showed up.

Back then, during the early years of the war, Scotland Yard's Chief Inspector Peter Beveridge had taken over command of the Flying Squad. Alongside him was the soon-to-be-legendary Ted Greeno, who'd eventually be hailed as the best murder investigator the Yard ever had. Greeno also happened to be one hell of a 'thief-taker'.

One night, Beveridge, as was his brazen way, was having a drink with his old enemy Billy Hill in a Camden Town pub, when the Scotland Yard supremo told Hill, "It's got to be put on you sooner or later. Make the most of it while you can because when I feel your collar, you're going to stay nicked for a long time."

Hill was careful not to even smile when he heard such remarks. He knew that if he did, Beveridge would take it even more personally and come after him even harder as a result.

"Well, guv'nor, you can't blame me for everything. I've got to earn, and you've got to catch. What you havin'?"

Greeno was an even more thorough investigator and never seemed as kind-hearted as Beveridge, which made Hill even more wary of him. He was the kind of policeman who'd stand there and carefully weigh up his enemy, making no pretences about being a friend to Hill. This was a serious business to him. If Hill offered Greeno a drink, Greeno would invariably reply, "I don't want your drink, I want your body. Well locked up in a good peter. But I'll buy you a drink any day. Maybe I can buy you enough to make you talk. Because, if I nick you, you'll be glad to talk fast and plenty."

Despite his contempt for the police, Billy Hill always tactfully addressed such officers as 'Mister' and knew only too well that he needed to watch his back very carefully. Out on the streets of London, he often tumbled unmarked police cars, sometimes as many as three, taking it in turns to shadow him. One time the Yard even employed an attractive woman police officer to follow Hill. He seriously thought about chatting her up and offering her a drink, but decided against it in the end, shaking her off his tail with ease.

FIVE

During those wartime years, Billy Hill began venturing more and more onto the mean streets of Soho, despite the heavyweight gangs who still ran the place. Sometimes he and his mob would creep into the West End, fully armed in case of a clash. He saw it as a matter of pride that he should walk the streets unimpeded. In any case, he and his boys had plenty of money to burn and enjoyed hitting the nightclubs and spielers of the sleaziest square mile in Britain.

Many thieves from outside London had also begun invading the centre of the capital. New drinking clubs sprang up to meet the demand. The new breed of criminal – created by the wartime black market – also liked to show off his wealth by dressing his wife or girlfriends in expensive jewellery and clothes.

Every Monday, Hill and many other young gangsters dressed in Savile Row suits congregated in a club in Archer Street, with their wives or mistresses. He later described the scene as "similar to a day out at the Ascot races". Some of Scotland Yard's finest also popped up in the club, to have a look at the opposition.

Hill himself was brimming with so much confidence by this time that he didn't fear going anywhere in London. As he later explained, "I was on my way to becoming the top screwsman in the country. I had the most loyal and the smartest mob behind me, and anyone who wanted trouble only had to knock on my door. My closest friend, a well-sharpened knife with a five-inch blade, never left me. It remained there, resting in my breast pocket, ready to chiv the first man to take a liberty."

London during the war was a strange place. The blackouts, plus a depleted police force, simply increased the opportunity for crime and helped turn the West End into a roaring square mile of activity. Women from all over Britain flocked there to sell their bodies on street corners, or in hotel lobbies, bars and clubs. As Hill would recall, "Good-time girls became brazen tarts, ordinary wives became good-time girls. Small-time tea leaves [thieves] turned into well-to-do operators." In the netherworld of pubs and clubs, of spielers and dives, you were assessed by two things: the amount of money in your pocket and your connections on the black market. A pair of nylons could buy a woman's body, a diamond ring could buy her for life – or as long as you wanted her.

London was teeming with people who, until the outbreak of war, had only ever heard of the city from train timetables. Many of them were in the forces, en route to somewhere else to fight in the war. They were of all colours and nationalities, all creeds and classes.

But despite the great wave of patriotism which swept the nation, gangsters were definitely a breed apart. For that reason, Hill and his compatriots liked to stick to clubs where the entrance form was a file in the Criminal Records Office of Scotland Yard. One afternoon, Hill was in a club when two young tearaways – including a particularly vicious young hoodlum called Jimmy Emmett – started beating the life out of one of Hill's brothers and an old mate called Dodger Mullins, a master screwsman then in his sixties who'd served more porridge than most. Hill was outraged at what was happening and steamed straight in armed with his "little friend", a chiv. "I gave one tearaway my favourite stroke, a V for victory sign on his cheek. Then I cut the other monkey to ribbons," Hill later recalled.

No one turned a hair in the club as the fight continued into the gents' toilets. The two young hoods eventually crawled out on their hands and knees, according to Hill's later testimony. Hill's opponent, Emmett, was a loose cannon who could have started a fight in a room full of nuns. He was later jailed for shooting an innocent passer-by outside the Café de Paris, while the Queen and her sister, Princess Margaret, were inside.

Hill takes up the story: "Emmett was what we call a bit of a slag, just a small-time tearaway who tried to make himself big by the use of a razor or a shooter. That night, poor old Dodger was really gone over. He had head injuries and more cuts than enough. My brother was cut too. If you let anyone take a liberty with you in our game it soon gets round, and in no time every smalltime tearaway wants to have a crack."

Hill took a particular dislike to Emmett, and later went looking for him to mete out more punishment. He even suspended all his robberies to take the time off to find "that slag". Emmett went into hiding when he heard Hill was on his tail, but it only took a couple of days for one of his boys to track him down. Emmett was spotted in the Paramount Dance Hall in Tottenham Court Road, so Hill rounded up Strong Arms, Odd Legs and Square Georgie and headed over to the West End with another gang member, Nosh Abie, at the wheel of their drag.

The moment Hill spotted Emmett emerging from the dance hall, the boys got out to have a word with him. Emmett was with another man, who spotted Hill. They made a run for it, but Hill and his mob soon caught up with them and gave them a real good hiding. Emmett was smashed about the head and striped with a chiv for good measure. His mate got a good kicking as well.

With blood streaming from his face, Emmett tried to dash

across the road but ran straight into Hill's car just as Abie was moving off to pick up some other gang members. The car knocked Emmett flying and then ran right over him. Hill later claimed it was a genuine accident, although Emmett was convinced to his dying day that they had tried to murder him. But whatever the truth of the matter, Billy Hill had just sent a very clear message to the rest of the London underworld not to cross him or face very dire consequences.

As he later recalled, "My chiv was never far away from my hand, and I used it good and proper. To such an extent, I might say, that London's underworld began to think a bit when I got around."

Emmett and his mate even went to the police to file a complaint against Hill for attempted murder, but when he was put in an I.D. parade he wasn't picked out. They'd no doubt reached the conclusion it would be suicidal to pursue the case.

This sort of flare-up occurred with increasing regularity on the streets of wartime London. One night, Hill accidentally chivved his old Australian pickpocket friend, Norman Smith, when they were confronted by two thugs armed with iron bars. Seeing his right hand had been badly cut, Smith screamed, "I'm doomed. I'm doomed. I'll never be able to buzz another pocket."

"Shut up," growled Hill. "If I hadn't cut your hand, accidentally though it was, the other monkey would have cracked your nut open with that iron bar. Thank me for saving your life."

As always, Billy Hill was convinced he was in the right.

And in the middle of all this criminal chaos, Hill noticed that the police were taking an ever closer look at him. Besides being regularly tailed on foot and by car, he now believed his telephones were being tapped. He was also being regularly pulled in for I.D. parades, even for jobs he wasn't involved in, although he was never once fingered.

Even so, his next raid would be on a jeweller's shop in Belgravia. Long Stan, Tosh, Big Jock, Harry Ryan and Hill made their way to the location in a stolen getaway vehicle. It was just after dark and the shop was locked up, but they fiddled around with the locks to give the impression they were locking up. In fact, Hill had a Stillson wrench literally up his sleeve, with which he then proceeded to wrench off the shop's padlocks.

As Hill was working away with his wrench, two bobbies on the beat appeared on the opposite side of the street. The team walked off around the corner to wait for them to move on. But after half an hour the coppers were still there.

Hill then went to a nearby telephone box and rang the fire brigade, alerting them about a supposed fire in Belgravia, opposite the jeweller's shop. Within minutes, fire engines were appearing in the street from all directions. The two policemen then ran to where the fire engines had stopped, as Hill and his team went back to work.

A few minutes later they were in the store, helping themselves to handfuls of gold and silver. Outside, the fire brigade and a crowd of curious passers-by were so engrossed by the blaze that never was that they didn't even notice what was happening in the jeweller's across the street. Then Long Stan knocked a glass shelf down with an awful clatter, and someone in the crowd spotted what was happening in the shop, yelling, "Bandits! Police! Murder!"

Hill, holding his wrench menacingly in his hand, dashed straight out of the shop, followed by his mob, heading across the pavement to their getaway car. First to the vehicle was Big Jock, who accidentally locked the car doors as he got in. As the rest of the team struggled to open the car, the two policemen headed straight for them.

By the time they finally got in the car, Hill was furious with Jock but kept his lip buttoned, except to say, "Let her have it, Harry. Give her a push." One end of the one-way street was blocked by fire engines and crowds, so they had no choice but to drive the wrong way up it.

Hill takes up the story: "It was a miracle we were not bashed head-on again and again. Then, when he got to a busy roundabout, he suddenly swerved the car round opposite the traffic, so we were still driving against the traffic. But at least he reached the West End quicker that way."

Another job done. But Billy Hill knew he was skating on thin ice.

*   *   *

On the morning of 20 March 1940, in a job which earned Hill and his team headlines in the national press, two of the gang drove a small maroon car onto the pavement and straight into the doorway of Carrington's Jewellers, at 130 Regent Street in the heart of the West End. The only problem was that they knocked over the store commissionaire in the process, nearly killing him. Moments later, a big black sedan rolled up containing Hill and another gang member, who smashed both the main windows with a car jack and grabbed thirty rings worth £6,000, before leaping back into the car which covered its first two hundred yards while still on the pavement.

Hill was later picked up by the police and put in yet another I.D. parade, but wasn't picked out. It was a similar story a couple of days later, when he and his team hit Attenborough's jeweller's in Wardour Street, Soho. This time they got away with £9,000 worth of gems. Within a day, witnesses failed to pick Hill out of yet another I.D. parade.

He and his gang were getting increasingly daring with each raid. In New Bond Street, they hit yet another jeweller's, but this time

Hill didn't even bother getting out of his car. He simply reached out from the vehicle's sun roof, smashed the window of the shop, reached into it and grabbed £11,000 worth of 'tomfoolery'. Hill was on a seemingly unstoppable roll.

Each time Hill waited for the call from the Yard, pulling him in for yet another I.D. parade. But he was finding it all rather irritating and extremely inconvenient. He took all this intense police interest as a warning that he needed to try something different, to find an area of crime the Yard would not connect him to. It was around this time that he decided to concentrate on cash-only jobs.

Hill realised high street banks were far too well guarded to be easy targets, but he fancied the idea of hitting some post offices. He knew that a busy sub-post office usually had between £3,000 and £5,000 in cash, stamps and money orders. So he got himself a Post Office guidebook and looked up all the local branches on the outer ring of Greater London and the Home Counties. Hill would soon come to pride himself on averaging a three-fifths increase in profit from the original takings of every Post Office robbery.

One of his right-hand men at this time was Odd Legs, who later went on to find criminal notoriety as part of the team who tried to pull off a £1 million gold bullion robbery at London's Heathrow Airport, in 1948. In many ways, Hill was training Legs up to be his ears and eyes, to think just like him. The gang also included Tosh, the brilliant lock picker, driver Harry Ryan, Jock Wyatt and Patsy Fitzherbert. They were the hard core, although Hill had dozens of others he could call on if and when required.

Soon he and his mob were relieving post offices of an average £3,000 a week in a series of carefully planned raids. Once Hill had selected a target post office, Tosh would find a skeleton key which would open it.

Hill knew that the best time to hit a post office was in daylight hours on a weekday, after all parcels had been collected. The object was the green bags that were brought in and out, as they always contained cash.

During the war years it was easier to pull off this sort of robbery at night, because windows were all blacked out No police patrols could look through them and no lights showed on the outside. Hill usually had a man on the door throughout such raids, just to be on the safe side. Inside, the main aim was to locate the post office safe and crack it at high speed, sometimes using gelignite.

Occasionally Hill and his gang simply took the safe with them, and opened it later in more secure surroundings. But usually it only needed a bit of levering from his favourite peter cane, made from the half-shaft of a car. Hill also had specially made safe-rippers, which were like a huge tin-opener, while his gang brought specially made safe-trolleys, identical to those used by safe manufacturers, in which they'd wheel the safe out of the post office and haul it into the getaway van.

Hill prided himself on not panicking, and his ability to wriggle out of a tricky spot was remarkable. One time he and his gang got into a post office with a fake key, only to discover that a newspaper vendor had set up his stall while they were inside trying to break into a safe. Hill calmly asked the vendor to move because they were bringing some heavy gear out. The man happily obliged, and Hill even bought some papers off him at the same time for good measure.

Not only did Hill pull in many thousands of pounds in cash each week from the post office raids, he even kept the savings stamps and bought books to put them in legitimately from the Post Office, selling them off at a profit.

As word of Hill's involvement in the Post Office raids swept the

London underworld, yet more villains asked to join his mob. One such character was known as Bob the Fitter, who turned out to be an even greater wizard with locks and keys than Tosh. He claimed he could fit any lock with the first six keys he chose from his chain. Hill later said he never once saw the Fitter fail.

Bob the Fitter was a very unusual character in others ways, too. He didn't smoke or drink and he never went with women. But most important of all, he didn't mix with other villains. In fact, Hill was convinced the Fitter didn't know any criminals other than him. And in the suburban street in northwest London where he lived, the Fitter was known as an ordinary, respectable citizen. Hill later revealed that the Fitter only had one vice – photography. He spent all his spare money on new cameras and equipment and even had a penthouse studio built onto his own house, which he boasted was the best equipped studio in Britain. The Fitter even had a straight job, which made it even harder for the police to nick him unless he was caught red-handed. He rarely went on actual jobs with Hill and his boys. Instead he'd join them at the location of the target premises, establishing which key was needed for a specific lock before heading off home to find it.

The Fitter was also a man of few words, but Hill was scrupulously fair and he always got his share of the takings from every job. As Hill later explained, "He deserved it. It didn't matter what lock you put up to him, he was always able to master it within a few seconds. Locks to him were like diamonds to Oppenheimer." The Fitter did have a stroke of bad luck though, when one of Hitler's bombs fell on his house and wrecked the photographic studio, his pride and joy.

Meanwhile, the Post Office was growing increasingly frustrated by Hill and his gang. Their special investigations squad had his flat in Camden Town watched, and they even started trailing his wife, Aggie, although Hill had long since trained her on how to get rid of a tail. All his mail was read before it got to his home and they set up a tap on his phone. But Hill considered the Post Office detectives to be amateurs compared with the real police.

One night Hill spotted them tailing his car, so he drove around and around Regents Park. Eventually his tail ran out of petrol. Hill then pulled up next to the PO car. "Good evening," he said. "Had a nice time? Good night." Then he drove away.

Hill's take on the Post Office raids during the war years perfectly sums up his attitude towards career criminality. "Frankly, I don't blame me for nicking so much of their gear. I blame those who are paid to look after it. After all it is public money, which pays their wages, and the public should insist that they earn them. I earned mine."

Aggie wanted him to take a rest around this time, and for them to enjoy a holiday together, but Hill simply bought her presents to stop her nagging and went back to what he knew best. Tired and overworked, Billy Hill was pushing himself into a dangerous corner.

On 26 June 1940, he and his boys, Ryan and Square Georgie, headed to Conduit Street in the West End to pull off a jewel robbery. The heist itself went well, although Hill and his crew had to threaten the staff in order to get the 'tom'. However, their getaway car conked out just as Hill had jumped in with a bag of stolen gems. The team leapt into Georgie's escape car, which had been used to block the street, but that stalled and they were left with no choice but to escape by foot. By this time, the police were running in their direction and a huge crowd had gathered.

Hill headed into an office block as the gang split up and ran in all directions. When he got to the top of the building, he looked down and saw that hundreds of people had gathered to watch the police pursuit of the robbers. Hill then went back downstairs, and tried to pass himself off as an office worker to one policeman. It seemed to have worked, but then someone in the crowd shouted that Hill was one of the robbers, and he was arrested after a scuffle. Georgie and Harry were also both nicked.

Hill pleaded guilty to conspiracy and got the maximum sentence of two years. The others got three years for stealing and receiving the two stolen cars. Hill considered this a good result, as he knew only too well that they could have been convicted of robbery with violence, which potentially could have earned them each a life sentence.

So now it was back to Chelmsford Prison. He wasn't too bothered as jail went with the territory. He got himself a cushy job as prison barber and made friends with a young hoodlum called Frankie Fraser, who'd just started out on one of the longest and most notorious careers in British criminal history. Hill and Fraser improved the prison's appalling cuisine by having stolen food brought in by bent screws. It wasn't all misery inside prison, at least not for a big-time operator like Billy Hill.

SIX

Back home in Camden Town, Aggie accepted her husband's fate even though she was heartbroken. Hill knew in his heart that it was always the women and children at home who suffered the most. As he later recalled, "There wasn't much I could say to make it right. I felt a bit of a fool in some ways, and I promised myself there and then that I wouldn't get nicked again."

But that didn't mean he had any intention of giving up crime. As he admitted, "Going straight for the likes of me was as likely as the devil being canonised." Instead, he looked on his two-year stretch as an occupational hazard. "There was nothing to do but swallow it and make the best you could of your time."

Hill saw himself as entrenched in crime. Crime was his life and he couldn't ever imagine *not* being involved in it. "I was no more a straight person than Capone. Screwing, banditry, robbery and thieving was my business. I didn't know any other business," he would write in his autobiography.

He also believed he was at war against authority, and especially the police. He looked on his relationship with the law as 'sporting' to a certain degree, but as he later explained, "Lots of people think modern detectives are magicians like Sherlock Holmes and Sexton Blake. They're nothing of the kind. They're ordinary blokes who've got an ill-paid job and who often are expected to work far too hard. My business was to fox them and outwit them. I'm not saying it was easy to do that. But I am saying that I did get the better of them lots of times. The same as they often got the better of me. And, so far as I was concerned, it was the best man who won every time, and no hard feelings."

Back at Chelmsford Prison, Hill came across many screws from his earlier visit. They welcomed the charming master criminal back as if he was an old boy returning to his former school. They liked Hill because he never gave them any trouble, which made their job easier. They also knew that he was loaded and knew how to talk their language.

Hill recruited one screw to be his 'workman'. He paid him £4 a week which, tax free, was almost as much as his straight wages. The tame screw ran messages in and out of prison on Hill's behalf, so that he could continue running his criminal enterprises from inside.

When Hill got out of prison early for good behaviour, in late 1941, he found to his delight that his gang was still very much intact, and that serving time had actually enhanced his reputation in the underworld. As far away as Scotland, criminals contacted him to ask for help in selling stolen goods. One team from Edinburgh got on so well with Hill that they started consulting him before carrying out certain jobs, as did another gang from Manchester.

Back home in Camden Town, everything seemed the same as before he had gone away. Aggie had spruced the place up for his return, and Billy enjoyed his home comforts. "It was good to sit back in an arm-chair again and put my feet up in front of a fire," he later recalled.

Hill's boys had made sure there was plenty of food on the table for his missus, including fresh eggs and butter, things you couldn't get with rationing cards. In his autobiography, Hill talked in detail about that first day back at home. "I knew that, for my first night home, she didn't want any of the boys around. She always did treasure those first nights home of mine. Seemed funny sometimes to see her sitting there not saying much, flittering about putting a cushion right here, straightening a flower there, and asking me for the millionth time if I wanted a drink or a cup of tea."

Hill later insisted he would not have minded if his wife had found a lover when he was inside prison, or even if she'd hit the bottle. But this was largely because he had been playing away from home throughout his marriage, and was trying to alleviate his own guilt. His fame inside the underworld had made him a big catch for other women. His wife undoubtedly suspected this and clung closely as a result, making sure she was irreplaceable to him. On the business front, Hill's team began stealing "decent motors" to try to avoid the mechanical problems which got him nicked the last time. These cars would then be carefully serviced and maintained, stored in lock-ups until the day of the robbery in question. Hill had the black market as a 'bread and butter' source of income, although the really good profits came from the screwing jobs. So Hill and his gang started hitting those sub-post offices again.

* * *

Wartime Britain suited Billy Hill in many ways – although there were inconveniences, like the constant risk of being stopped by police on routine checks for misuse of petrol, which was being strictly rationed. He solved this by sometimes borrowing a hearse from a local undertaker pal, which the police always waved through all roadblocks. By this time he also had a special garage where he took all his stolen safes, so they could be blown open in a safe environment.

Hill then decided it was time the gang got themselves a safe house somewhere out in the countryside, so they didn't have to drive back into London after each job. He knew he needed to find a property with a tame owner who'd keep quiet if he was paid a handsome rental fee. Gang member Strong Arms Phil was so taken by the idea that he suggested the whole gang move to the countryside like evacuees, until Hill pointed out that they'd all stick out like a sore thumb.

Hill eventually heard of a dream place near a big air base at Bovingdon, Hertfordshire. It was being rented by a London businessman contact, but the man was prepared to sublet it for a tenner a week. It even had a huge barn with double doors, which would be perfect for storing vehicles. Better still, the barn partly concealed the main house from the road, so that it was possible for Hill and his boys to live there for weeks on end without being noticed.

Hill also found there were several routes one could take from London, which made the house even more ideal. For the remainder of the war years, that huge barn was often filled to the brim with anything in short supply: whiskey, clothing, towels, sheets, furniture, foodstuffs, silks, tobacco, jewellery and petrol.

He frequently stayed overnight at the four-bedroom house and came to enjoy the country air and scenery. Hill and his boys even went out on country drives to some of the local pubs. He later said it was probably the nicest house he'd ever stayed in.

Hill eventually lost count of the number of safes that were blown open at Bovingdon. "The figure must have run into hundreds. Some of the boys called it 'Hill's Home for Hungry Hoisters'. Others called it 'Billy's Bovingdon Bunhouse'." It was well known throughout the London underworld that he had a hideout, but no one ever realised exactly where it was. Hill kept it a closely guarded secret, because he knew one of his rivals would either raid the place or tip off Scotland Yard.

Hill also didn't like his boys being flash with their cash, because that was how trouble usually flared up in the underworld. He blamed a lot of it on drink, as he had decided years earlier to knock his own consumption of alcohol on the head. As he later explained, "Drunks are mugs. And they're usually unpleasant mugs at that." Despite frequenting clubs and pubs, Billy Hill prided himself on always being in control, which was why he rarely touched alcohol anymore.

*　　*　　*

By 1944, deserters had become much better organised and many now held fake identity cards. All kinds of coupons were stolen and then reproduced in huge, well-organised rackets. Poles, Czechs and French-Canadians joined up with Brit villains on the run, and many used guns. When one man was refused admission to a West End restaurant, he pulled out a pistol and was only captured after a chase by Flying Squad officers.

Teams of racketeers were doping greyhounds at tracks up and down the country. Businessman were being lured to houses by the promise of big deals, only to find themselves bound, gagged and robbed. Country housebreakers targeted properties on virtually a nightly basis. The war had definitely shifted the balance of power in favour of the criminals, while the black market helped the underworld focus on the community at large.

Before Billy Hill's criminal ascendancy, most thieves couldn't get near the West End without permission from the notorious Sabini brothers. Hill liked to think that, during the war years, he'd really opened things up, as he was feared by many and respected by all.

And Hill would often take the law into his own hands. When two of his boys backed out of a Soho club because another notorious gang were there in force, Hill concluded it was a dangerous climbdown which could be interpreted as a sign of weakness. So he decided to pay this particular club a visit on his own.

He was initially refused entry at the door, until he threatened to come back with his boys and bomb the premises. When he walked in there was only one woman in the club, and she ran out after she saw him. When he turned around the only man there had scarpered as well, leaving him entirely alone in a club full of booze. Then the telephone rang. When Hill answered it the manager was crying on the phone.

"Please, Mr Hill. Please leave my club. I want to come back to lock up. I can't do any business with you in there."

"Come back and get me out," Hill shouted down the phone.

"Come on. Come and enjoy yourself."

"Mr Hill," pleaded the manager. "Please, please go away and let me have my club back."

Hill laughed down the phone. "You're only round the corner," he said. "Come on, come and have a drink with me. You know, on the house. It won't cost you."

Eventually Hill left the club, with its lights still blazing and the door wide open. He later explained, "I had scored my point. No rubber was ever going to turn my boys out."

Hill always looked back on those wartime years with great nostalgia. Often, he and various associates would drive down to Brighton on the south coast for a day out. One time, he was with his boys – including Odd Legs, Bimbo, Dodger, Patsy Fitzherbert, Mutton, Square Georgie, Ginger Andy, Nosh Abie, Strong Arms, Horrible Harry, Bert the Long Reach, Wide Gaiters, and about twenty other cronies – to have a chat about a number of imminent jobs.

Then completely out of the blue, one of Hill's police adversaries, Detective Inspector Bob Higgins of 'the Sweeney', walked into the same pub in Brighton. As Hill later revealed in his autobiography, "Since he had nicked most of us at one time or another we knew him rather well. There was a bit of a hush as he walked in. A copper doesn't go lone-handed into a boozer full of villains, unless he wants a villain, as well as a drink. So, in the event of a drink being of some importance to him, I said, 'Hello, guv'nor. What you going to have?'"

Higgins accepted Hill's offer of a drink and then looked around the pub in silence. None of his boys uttered a word, either. They were waiting for Hill's cue. He knew something was up but he was determined not to appear bothered, asking Higgins, "Well, what's it all about?"

Higgins took a deep breath and then launched into a speech: "I've got to take you back to the nick, Billy. Sorry and all that, but there it is. You've been sussed for a blag job and you've got to stand up in the parade. Tell Dodger and Odd Legs that they're sussed as well."

Hill knew something was amiss, because he hadn't done any blags recently. He concluded that Plod was putting on a bit of a show, and had decided to try and pin him and his boys for something they weren't even connected to. Hill looked on it as a mere inconvenience. He'd have to go down to the nick yet again, only to be let out a few hours later. It was a routine he'd become very familiar with.

Hill agreed to co-operate with Higgins, but asked him if it was alright for them to have a final drink before departing. Higgins had known Hill since he was a kid and Higgins was a uniformed constable, so both knew they couldn't con each other. Higgins agreed to wait outside the boozer for five minutes for Hill to emerge.

Neither Hill nor his two gang members were picked out at the I.D. parade at Tottenham Court Road police station, and they were released in time to catch a cab back to Brighton for another drink with the boys before closing time.

Whenever Hill had similar brushes with the law, he saw it as a warning to change his tactics. As he later said, "It's no use standing still and saying that times are good. Time is the only thing you gain by standing still."

Hill was already uncrowned king of the north London underworld, thanks to his unparalleled success. But there were some loose cannons who fancied having a crack at his title. He could no longer pop into any boozer for a quiet drink on his own. He needed his own team of minders on duty all times of the day and night.

And wherever Billy Hill went, trouble seemed to follow. One night he was in the Butcher's Arms, on his manor in Camden, when a huge fight broke out. As Hill later recalled, "Glasses, broken bottles, chairs, pieces of furniture, razors and knives were flying about like paper in the wind."

But Hill's biggest worry was that he was drinking with a woman who was the wife of one of his boys, George the Burglar, who was on the other side of the pub. Hill managed to duck one punch and didn't even retaliate. Then someone smashed him over the head and he couldn't stop himself from steaming in. He slashed one man down the face from his temple to his chin. As George the Burglar moved across the bar to reach his wife, he got in the way of Hill and also suffered a slash from his chiv. Two of Hill's other boys got chivved in the fight, while Hill and George grabbed his wife and managed to get her through the fighting mob to a waiting car. Hill never did explain why he was with George's wife, or whether the injury he inflicted on George was actually carried out to protect him from a jealous rage.

But Hill got into increasingly violent fights at this stage in his life. A few weeks later he was glassed in a pub for no apparent reason. Hill recalled, "It stuck there like a dart in a dartboard. I pulled the glass out of my face with one hand and my chiv out of my pocket with the other. Then I got to work doing a bit of hacking and carving. I don't know how many blokes I cut that night. I didn't care. When you get a jagged glass shoved in your face you don't bother about counting the blokes you chiv. You just hack away until your knife gets blunt or the others swallow it."

Meanwhile, as a professional criminal he was making a small fortune working as a fence, as well as organising robberies. One time he got offered three thousand clothing ration books by a small-time villain who couldn't handle the volume. Hill reckoned he could get £3 per book so he offered the other man £2. The deal was agreed on the spot and Hill handed over £6,000 in readies, but then the small-timer failed to deliver the ration books. Hill was furious and decided to steal them all from the other man. But he didn't actually know where the books were, so he got one of his boys to tail the man. When that failed, Hill decided it was time to have "a little chat". He and his boys followed him to a well-known pub and walked in to find him drinking with a bunch of other small-time hoods. Hill didn't really want any trouble with other gangs, so he got one of his boys to tell the man he was urgently wanted outside.

Hill's boys then pulled their car up in front of the pub. They even placed a big box in the front seat, so that the man would have no choice but to get in the back. But he was highly suspicious when asked to "step outside". Hill's gang member insisted there was no trouble, but said they were in a hurry. The man – Hill called him 'Chummy' in his autobiography – then got in the car and was driven around the corner, to where Hill and another gang member, Wooden Jimmy, were waiting in another car. Each of them sat either side of Chummy, and they all headed off to the country house in Bovingdon, Hertforshire.

Chummy insisted to Hill that the coupons didn't actually belong to him, but to a friend. Hill didn't give a monkey's toss. He just wanted the deal to be sorted out. Chummy then insisted he didn't know where the coupons were stored, but Hill had had enough of playing games. He and his mob arrived at Bovingdon at about ten that night, and spent the following four hours torturing Chummy. They eventually dumped him in a ditch in St Albans in the early hours of the following morning. Wooden Jimmy was so concerned about the state of their victim that he insisted on driving back to the ditch, and putting fifty bob (two and a half pounds) and some cigarettes into Chummy's pockets. "Poor bastard," explained Jimmy. "He's got some guts. Might as well see that he gets home all right."

Hill got the coupons that night and was a grand richer before noon the same day. He saw the torturing of Chummy as an essential part of his work. It was vital that the rest of the London underworld realised that Billy Hill was as hard as nails when it came to business.

Not long after "sorting out" Chummy so brutally, Hill decided to carry out a job which could potentially have been the biggest robbery of his career. It involved the theft of insurance and savings stamps from a printing works in High Wycombe, Berkshire, to the west of London. They were regularly picked up by two postal workers and delivered to the local railway station, where they would be distributed around the country.

Hill had his own boys tail the two men in their van from the H.M. Stationary Office in Harrow, over to High Wycombe, and then to the station. He quickly worked out a very precise record of their movements, even noting that the men stopped at a High Wycombe café where they would take it in turns to go in to eat. Hill had also been told by inside sources at the Post Office that the van could be carrying as much as £7 million worth of stamps.

He then took over all the surveillance work himself. One man created much less attention than two, and he didn't want anyone in his team to know the final, precise details until he was ready to involve them. Then Hill's source inside the PO at Harrow told him the van was to be loaded to virtual capacity within the next couple of days. It was only then that he brought in his boys and briefed them. But he'd later claim that one of the gang got drunk that night and blabbered about the job. "He did not tell the law or anything like that. He just boasted about the size of the job. As soon as word got around one of the underworld grasses went straight to the law. It was my turn then to learn from loose talk." Hill knew from his own police sources that two of Scotland Yard's finest – Sweeney detectives Bob Lee and Bill Judge – were watching the job very closely. "That was enough for me," he later recalled. "I can't say I knew Lee that well. But we all knew a lot about him. He's not the sort of man anyone can afford to mess with."

So Hill called off what would have been the biggest robbery in British criminal history thus far. He was bitterly disappointed, because he knew his status as the country's number one gangster would have been confirmed for life. Hill tried to put a brave face on it and was determined to find an equally lucrative job. "It would have been nice to have had a seven-million tickle, but there would have been the bother in getting rid of the gear."

Hill found himself in something of a vacuum after that one massive job was called off. Smaller blags seemed like an anticlimax, even though he continued to organise them with seeming impunity. One day he gathered up Odd Legs and Big Jock, and they picked up one of his special drags to carry out a lunchtime job that promised to deliver at least £5,000.

It involved knocking a postmaster on the head in Islington, north London, and then grabbing bags of money from him and the girl who escorted him. It seemed simple enough. Everything went according to plan for Hill and his boys until they jumped

into their getaway vehicle. A lorry driver had seen the entire
robbery and drove straight at Hill and his mob in their getaway
car. He crashed into them head-on. Hill and Odd Legs managed
to make a run for it from the wreckage. Big Jock – who had been
the cover man, standing nearby – would never have been nicked if
he hadn't run away, alerting the police who then grabbed him.

Hill and Odd Legs were later arrested and identified by the
lorry driver. They pleaded to be given the cat of nine tails in return
for short sentences, but because Odd Legs had a weak heart, the
judge, Recorder of London Sir Gerald Dodson, refused because
the cat could only be given to all of the defendants or none. So Big
Jock and Billy Hill got four years apiece and Odd Legs copped a
three-year stretch.

This time, Hill's new home was to be Dartmoor Prison, a much
bleaker prospect than Chelmsford. As he later wrote: "If ever
there was hell on earth, this was it."

SEVEN

Victory in Europe Day, London, May 1945, was unforgettable for the citizens of the capital. Street parties were held in every neighbourhood and effigies of Hitler dragged onto the streets for massive bonfires, which filled London with clouds of thick, black smoke. Residents proudly hung out bunting and Union Jacks. Even pianos were hauled into the streets for a good old fashioned knees-up. Streetlights came on for the first time since the Blitz, five years earlier. Fireworks exploded in the moonlit sky as searchlights danced across the horizon to celebrate the end of the war on the continent.

However, this new spirit of happiness and freedom meant little to Billy Hill, as he remained under lock and key in Dartmoor.

In the West End, the gangs maintained their grip on the centre of London. The war had even introduced the Italian 'springer' knife in place of open razors and chivs. The springer was a blade concealed in a metal or leather handle which was released by the touch of a knob. It then sprang out, a thin, double-edged stiletto. In Soho, protection rackets flourished while soldiers of all nations crowded into the capital after VE Day, with money to spend.

After the war, a lot of London crooks returned to their former trades, such as smash-and-grab robberies, safe breaking, car stealing and just about every petty crime imaginable. More violent armed robberies soon began occurring on a regular basis. Petty criminals were more frequently using loaded firearms, and the police started to fear London was turning into the Chicago of the thirties.

In December 1945, two thousand Metropolitan Police officers swamped Soho, checking the papers of everyone they came across in pubs, cafés, dancehalls and gambling clubs. The following month, checkpoints were set up on all major roads leading in and out of London, plus all the Thames crossings between Tower Bridge and Hammersmith. Police hoped to round up some of the twenty thousand deserters reckoned to still be on the run. All it really did was flush out a few small-timers, while the big-time criminals continued climbing the ranks of the underworld.

Practically every commodity was still in short supply after the end of the war. Printing paper, pepper, ice-cream powder, paraffin, textiles, cigarettes, petrol – you name it. But food itself yielded the biggest profit. The government's rationing system restricted the use of certain foodstuffs in the home, but not in restaurants. Owning a restaurant was virtually a licence to print money, if you could get the meat. Black marketeers scoured the countryside, buying up broken-down horses which would later be served up as choice rump steak in high-class establishments.

The London underworld, in those early post-war days, was an ever-shifting nucleus of people moving backwards and forwards across the capital. The West End thrived because there was a need to enjoy oneself, even after wartime. But now drugs, blackmail and confidence tricks performed on rich old ladies could be added to an already potent mix.

*   *   *

It was in 1946 that another up-and-coming star of the underworld, Jack Spot from the East End, decided he wanted to take over the racetracks and start up a few West End spielers. Spot knew that, in the north of England, local mobsters ran the newly reopened courses at a profit in a similar way to the Sabinis in earlier years. Track officials were even dishing out pitches themselves to bookies.

Back down south, Spot and his mob focused on the royal race meeting at Ascot where some of his most hated enemies, Little Jimmy and his Islington gang, were trying to take over the hallowed turf. They'd already grabbed all the best pitches on the free side at Ascot, and threatened to clear Spot and his team off if they made any attempt to move in. "So my pals and I decided to do the clearing instead," Spot later explained.

Spot completely saw off the Islington Boys from the race-tracks by early 1947. Then, with his own boys and the considerable support of his allies in the Upton Park and Ilford gangs, Spot decided to widen his powerbase by spreading his net across the entire nation's racecourses.

Spot had even seen off the King's Cross gang, led by bookie Harry White, a curious, round-faced fellow who sent his two daughters to Roedean, England's most expensive school for girls, yet was renowned for cutting anyone who dared get in his way. But when Jack Spot began boasting around town that he was the new 'King of the Underworld', Billy Hill soon got word of it in Dartmoor Prison. He wasn't best pleased. Hill had run with the idea of he and Spot cultivating each other to a certain degree, but was only doing it so he could "keep his enemy close" – as was so often the way of the underworld. But he certainly didn't want Spot jumping onto his throne.

*   *   *

While he was in 'the Moor', Hill did his best to keep his spirits up. Naturally, he spent a lot of his time thinking, and remembered back to his days in Wandsworth Prison. In there at the same time had been two American gangsters, Sammy Kleinz and Jack Goodman. They'd come over to show their British 'cousins' how it was done, and had ended up nicked. While in Wandsworth, awaiting extradition, both of them had got on famously with Hill and taught him a lot of the tricks of the trade.

Kleinz kept banging on to Hill about how all his small-time jobs would get him nowhere in the long term. Goodman even added, "If you're gonna be bent, get as crooked as a corkscrew, and then give yourself a few more turns on top. Don't play at it, son, get busy and big time."

The Americans even mentioned the financial advantages of kidnapping. And they weren't talking about holding the children of wealthy parents to ransom. As Kleinz explained, "You see, anyone can take a stick and screw a jeweller's gaff. Any mug can go in and blow a peter with gelignite. But that ain't got no finesse about it. No polish. You know what I mean! To get by in our game you've got to be original, new, ahead of the brains all the time."

The two yanks explained to Hill how easy it was to watch employees or managers of jewellery shops and wait for the opportunity to steal their keys. But if they were kidnapped, said the American gangsters, then they could not cause any problems. Sure, they should be carefully looked after, but the kidnapping side of it was strictly business.

So while Hill kept a low profile in Dartmoor, he began working out a method to put all that advice to practical use as soon as he got out.

*　　*　　*

Hill's faithful wife, Aggie, was there waiting for him when he got out of Dartmoor. She had come all the way down from 'the

Smoke' to greet her husband. Hill's later recollection seems to sum up his feelings towards her by then: "I did not want to drag her all the way down to the Moor to meet me when I was released. But there she was like a piece of furniture when I walked in. 'Hello,' she said. 'How are you?' 'All right,' I replied. 'How're you?'"

Aggie had moved into a much classier flat in north London. When Hill got there he was a bit taken aback by how the curtains in the new place were all frilly, and the bed was brand new. Even the carpets were clean and there was a pure linen tablecloth. Aggie cooked him a mutton stew, and Hill said it tasted better than anything he'd had since being sent down.

Hill knew that Aggie had been hurt by him in many ways. He explained it very clearly in his autobiography: "You see you don't get sorry for yourself in my business, and, as I say, once you know you've got a lagging to do, the only thing to do is settle down and get on with it. But she'd had to live all alone all the time I was away. It must have been hard on her. The loneliness is tougher for her than it is for her mate; and there's nothing quite so tough as loneliness."

Aggie hadn't changed much since they'd got married, though she'd put on a bit of weight. But whenever Hill was sent down, she'd move back in with her own family and spin a yarn about how he'd left her. When he got out she'd announce they were getting back together.

Within twenty-four hours of getting home from Dartmoor, it was as if Billy Hill had never been away. He got himself another place to use for "business purposes" and returned to the boozers where he'd meet his mob. While Hill had been inside, Strong Arms, Teddy Odd Legs, Ginger Andy and Tosh had all carried out jobs for the firm. Hill had kept in close touch with all his team through a tame screw, and the boys had grafted hard enough for their boss to have £5,000 waiting for him in the bank when he got out.

Hill decided to "tread water" as far as his rival, Jack Spot, was concerned. So he gave him a wide berth, deciding instead to "open up" a few sub-post offices. Hill knew a man whose job was to inspect safes and maintain them in good working order. He wasn't well paid, so Hill greased his palm with ease. Now he could keep himself amused by breaking into one post office every ten days. As each job brought in an average of two grand, it wasn't a bad little earner.

*   *   *

Over at his country hideaway in Bovingdon, many of Hill's black market goods were stored in the huge barn. He reckoned on making at least £500 a week from a Post Office parcel racket alone, in which he intercepted the post. "Variety really is the spice of life," he later quipped. He remained convinced that if he stuck to one type of job the police were sure to eventually catch up with him.

London had changed enormously while Hill was in Dartmoor. The war had ended and attitudes had softened, but the post-war crime wave was nearing its peak. Hill perfectly summed it up when he later said, "It seemed that any and every Tom, Dick and Harry had turned to crime." Hill also knew of at least six hundred American deserters in the capital, and then there were the thousands of other Allied renegades. They all needed bent ration cards and identity cards.

In early 1947, the *Daily Express* thundered across its front page, 'MASTER CRIMINALS RECRUIT DESERTERS BY BRIBES AND THREATS'. Then it went on to state, "One of the biggest difficulties confronting the authorities is the highly organised industry built up by the major criminals to facilitate the deserters avoiding capture," adding, "Crime is on the march in Britain today, boldly and violently. It is double what it was in 1939, and the evil grows by 10,000 cases each month."

The *Daily Express* seemed to be at the forefront of the so-called war against crime. A few days later one of its top journalists breathlessly reported, "It is a new West End I have seen as a reporter. It is a London of gambling schools on the pavements, secret markets where thousands of pounds change hands in currency deals; where the best blends of whiskey are bought by men in uniform at prices which makes last week's black market seem childish . . . it is a London of big money. Within shouting distance of a spot where Eros may soon stand again I have seen men pull out fists-full of pound notes, and do public business in the streets. Provincial criminals have smelt the boom in London, and have come helter-skelter to cash in before the D's get cracking . . . guns, revolvers, and tommy-guns sold well over the week-end . . . There are more guns on the black market than there is ammunition to fit them . . . sovereigns are being sold in the streets . . . furtive new clubs are springing up."

The post-war crime spree had caught the attention of the most sensationalist newspapers. They were soon predicting bloody battles between teams of crooks and Scotland Yard, where Sir Harold Scott had just taken over as Commissioner of Police.

'CAR BANDITS TELL POLICE "STICK 'EM UP'" screamed the outraged *Express*.

Hill read all these newspaper stories with great interest, sensing it was time to start making some contingency plans. He was convinced that the police remained heavily outnumbered by the criminals, and that it was impossible for them to keep up with the outbreaks of crime, but he knew they were going to try much harder from now on.

Then, in the middle of dozens and dozens of robberies and

smash 'n' grabs, Hill was suspected of turning his hand to the very crime that those American gangsters had schooled him in all those years ago. Kidnapping.

Hill never actually admitted involvement in this controversial crime. And in his 1955 autobiography, he hid behind the news stories, particularly an account of a kidnapping in the *Daily Express*, which stated, "About 100 C.I.D. men swooped on London's West End last night in search of the men who were concerned in the kidnapping on Tuesday evening of a Mayfair jeweller's manageress and the theft from the shop of jewels valued at £18,425. All main roads out of London were guarded and cars and their drivers were watched."

In the police's eyes, it was an extremely disturbing development. Scotland Yard detectives said the robbery was in the category marked 'Technique 100 per cent'. It emerged that the victim, Mrs Irene Coleman, had been snatched near her home in Belton Road, Tottenham. She was bundled into a car, her safe keys were taken, and she was bound and gagged. An hour later she was dumped, still bound, on the roadside on a lonely part of Hampstead Heath, where she was found by three Air Training Corps girls on their way back to camp. Within twenty-four hours Mrs Coleman had told her full, dramatic story to the newspapers.

Hill always refused to confirm or deny his involvement in the kidnapping, but branded it "the perfect crime" in his autobiography and admitted it was the forerunner of many other similar crimes. Meanwhile, the Yard were pulling in virtually every known criminal in the capital for questioning – except, of course, Billy Hill. They set up roadblocks between London, the south coast and even routes to the north of England. Pubs, clubs and vice dens were raided in Soho. Literally hundreds of people were brought in for questioning. Hill kept well clear of the West End by remaining on his home manor of Camden Town.

Back at the Yard, top detective Bob Stevens was wondering why no one had even brought up Hill's name in connection with the kidnapping of Mrs Coleman. Eventually, word reached Hill that Stevens wanted to see him, so he called the Yard and asked for his home telephone number. It is a measure of Hill's influence that he got the details without any objection from the detective's colleagues.

Stevens wasn't so pleased to get a call from Billy Hill in the early hours. But what next happened between the two adversaries provides an intriguing insight into the respect between the two men.

"I hear you want to see me," Hill said to Stevens rather meekly. "You?" the detective yelled. "Who are you? I don't know who you are."

"I'm Billy Hill," he replied. "You know, the villain."

Hill then heard a gasp on the phone, before Stevens shouted into the mouthpiece: "Who the hell do you think are, Al Capone? You be at my office at nine o'clock in the morning. And sharp."

"Yes, Mr Stevens," responded Hill and the line went dead.

Hill turned up at Savile Row nick as instructed, on the dot of nine, and got what he later referred to as "a right going over".

"I suppose the police have got their job to do, and we don't begrudge it to them or envy them. But they ought to have known that I was not going to tell them anything about anybody. They ought to have known it was a waste of time. Then, when they got fed up with talking to me, they stood me in the identity parade." Ten minutes after the usual failure to identify him, Hill was picked up outside the station by one of his boys and driven back to Camden Town.

Hill wasn't bothered about the pull because he was confident the law had nothing on him. And branching out into the kidnapping business would certainly prove very profitable. Hill used a character called the Lemon Drop Kid as a 'creep' at the time. Lemon's game was to creep into offices during lunch hours and steal whatever he could lay his hands on. He was such a cool customer that Hill recruited him to do some more serious work. This involved keeping watch on the manageress of a jeweller's shop in the West End.

Less than a week later, a black sedan pulled up alongside her as she walked along the pavement and she was bundled in. As Hill later admitted, "Before she could shout 'Oi!' she was enjoying a nice ride round the houses. We did not harm her, merely opened her bag and took the keys."

Hill later claimed he showed the woman mercy by offering her a cigarette and promising not to hurt her. But he admitted she'd been so scared that she couldn't talk. Eventually, Hill and his boys nicked £9,000 worth of jewellery from the shop, and then drove her home and let her go. Hill conveniently avoided the whole issue of physical threats when he wrote his autobiography ten years later, and described the kidnappings as if they were the same as pickpocketing. But the Yard were alarmed by the rise of kidnapping in the capital, and there was a genuine fear that someone would be very seriously hurt or even killed.

But none of this bothered Billy Hill. He seemed oblivious to the terror his latest crime wave was causing. His obsession was cash and he didn't really care how he got his hands on it. When one of his boys heard about a European refugee who'd smuggled thousands of pounds worth of jewellery into London, he had the man tailed for days before he and his boys pounced on him in the street. The man put up a hell of a struggle.

As Hill later confessed, "It took more than half an hour to cut that bodybelt away from him. He would have been more sensible if he had given it over. It would have saved him a lot of trouble. There's not a lot of room in any car for fighting, and when the bloke in front has got to keep his mind on driving, hooting and hollering only makes things awkward."

Hill and his gang eventually got away with £17,000 worth of diamonds, but their refugee victim was seriously injured. Hauled in by the police to take part in yet another I.D. parade, as usual Hill wasn't picked out.

Hill and his boys also followed a Knightsbridge jeweller all the way to his home in Surbiton, on the southern edge of London. But the jeweller sussed out what was happening and, when Hill's mob tried to grab him, began screaming and shouting. One of the gang knocked him unconscious and they took him to a safe house in north London, while his shop was ransacked. Hill and his mob eventually got away with £6,000 worth of jewellery, but the beating they inflicted on their victim made the authorities doubly determined to bring them to justice.

Hill continued to delude himself that he was in no danger of murdering anyone. "We used as little violence as possible. And, providing the person kidnapped did not pick us out on an I.D. parade there was nothing anyone could do in the way of nicking us." What he never openly admitted was that he made sure that any potential witnesses were intimidated so heavily that they wouldn't dare identify him or his gang.

As word of Hill's new criminal activities spread, he began getting even more tip-offs from all over the country. One of his most successful jobs occurred in Leeds, where he and his team raided a house with the specific intention of grabbing a wealthy jeweller and then ransacking his store.

But when Hill broke into the property he found the man and his wife fast asleep. So he grabbed the keys to the shop from a jacket, headed for the premises, emptied it of £25,000 worth of gems and then coolly returned the keys, without having woken anyone up. As he later recalled, "I don't know what that jeweller thought when he opened his shop safe the next morning. There was not the slightest sign of breaking and entering anywhere. We did hear from the Leeds team that the police did not actually believe the old boy. I hope the insurance people did."

Hill adored such challenges. Like the time he decided to creep on a wealthy bookmaker, whose mistress had spilled the beans about how much cash he kept in his safe. Hill knew most of the money had come from black market deals, so the bookie couldn't even scream to the law if it was stolen.

Hill persuaded the mistress to have sex with the bookie and make sure his trousers, with the keys to his office and safe, were in another room. He took his time to set up the robbery, and, on the day in question, he and his gang watched from a car outside the bookie's flat until the mistress gave the signal for them to move. Hill got hold of the keys, copied them and then put them back. A few days later they broke into the flat when it was empty, only to find that the keys didn't fit the safe.

Hill knew there was at least £20,000 in that safe, so he wasn't going to give up that easily. He went back to the mistress and got her to repeat her performance. But the same thing happened again, so Hill went back to the girl a third time. This time he took a specialist locksmith with him and measured the keys to within a thousandth of an inch. Hill ended up copping a £22,000 fortune in cash, and he later claimed that the bookie never found out how the money came to be stolen.

* * *

Hill's ascendance of the criminal ladder meant that only the best things in life were good enough for him now. He wore forty-guinea suits, handmade shoes, shirts and ties made of the finest silk, priced at six guineas each from Sulka's in Bond Street. Demand for black market goods still continued to far outstrip ordinary purchases. Clothes, jewellery, whiskey, silk and nylons remained in big demand. And Billy Hill was still the man to provide them.

"All I had to do was take a stroll round the West End and I was literally besieged by people wanting to buy almost anything from a pair of nylon stockings to a fresh salmon or shoulder of good smoked bacon." Up in Hertfordshire, the Bovingdon hideout was constantly packed tight with bent gear, thanks to a relay of cars bringing goods back and forth to London.

Meanwhile, Hill and his mob continued with screwing jobs on post offices across London and the suburbs. Usually, all the safes were taken to Bovingdon where they could be safely blown apart, and the system was fine-tuned to bring in a fortune every week.

Even the police started referring to Hill and his gang as 'the Heavy Mob'. As a direct result of their crime wave, bigger and better safes were being manufactured. (Hill was mightily proud of this fact.) And the centre of London continued to be jam-packed with demob-happy servicemen, loaded with money which they flung around the West End like tickertape on Broadway. Hill also noticed that new faces in the West End were popping up all over the place. It had him particularly perplexed, because most of these duckers and divers seemed to be making a living without even trying.

Hill and his mob had by this time returned to all their old criminal enterprises, with impunity. The Yard still suspected they were behind many of the capital's crimes, but they never discovered where they stored their gear and, despite continually putting tails on Hill, they never even got remotely close to unravelling his empire. Sometimes he was so cocksure that he'd call the Yard and tell them to call their surveillance off.

EIGHT

Billy Hill remained supremely confident. He believed he was the top dog in London and now made a point of warning off his rivals. On what Hill christened 'the night of the long knives', in early July 1947, he let the opposition know he had an arsenal of weapons ready to use at any time. As Hill would sum it up, "I had reached the point in my career when it was all or nothing." (The original Night of the Long Knives, or 'Operation Hummingbird', had been a purge that took place in Germany in 1934, when the Nazi regime executed at least eighty-five of their own for political reasons.)

Hill saw off all his rivals by sending a thousand men onto the streets of London that night, to prove he was the most powerful criminal in the capital. The reality was that there were a few scuffles between small-time villains, but in fact there weren't many criminals even remotely interested in taking on Hill's boys.

By the following morning, Billy Hill had crowned himself Boss of Britain's Underworld. And there were few brave enough to disagree. But having a reputation amongst the criminal fraternity didn't guarantee a get-out-of-jail card.

A few days later Hill was visiting one of his mob, Stuttering Robo. Ten minutes after he'd arrived, two cozzers came knocking on the door and nicked Robo for a warehouse break-in. Hill would claim that the coppers took him along as well, "just because I happened to be sitting there."

Hill was taken to Tottenham Court Road police station, where he was charged with Robo for the warehouse job. As he recalled, "I felt choked. I never did mind being nicked for something I had done, but to get picked out for something I hadn't done was as much as flesh and blood could bear."

When Hill got bail he felt that he'd finally had enough. "I decided to go on the run, to leave Britain for ever, while my crown was barely resting on my nut."

He was outraged, claiming to have been fitted up in the hard-nosed crime war waged on the streets of London. The Yard naturally denied framing Hill, but there's no doubt they were more than capable of planting evidence whenever the fancy took them. They were desperate to put all the top villains away and didn't really care how they did it, just so long as they got such characters off the streets.

Back at home in Camden Town, Aggie wasn't happy about her husband facing yet another stretch inside prison. Hill didn't blame her. "The surprising thing about it was that she had stayed with me for so long. It was not as though we had any kids, or a family. Why should she stick with me?"

But still, Billy and Aggie tried to work out the best way to escape London, before the police caught up with him again. Hill began to seriously consider going abroad. He knew he'd miss his friends, but also recognised that maybe it was time to cut and run. In some ways, the beleaguered Hill saw himself as a strange kind of Robin Hood outlaw-hero. "I was always a thief, a bandit, a screwsman. But I was always a good 'un. I went about my business in a proper way. I made no bones about being what I was. I never took liberties with anyone. For instance, I never striped anyone who was not doing me."

Before making a move abroad, Hill needed to pull off one last big job. He'd heard about an RAF officer who was flogging off thousands of stolen parachutes. So Hill and his mate, John the Tilter, dressed up as policemen and tailed a lorry load of parachutes one night. Eventually they forced the lorry to stop in a lay-by. Three men in the lorry made a run for it across some open fields, and Hill even went through the charade of chasing them so it looked more realistic. Then they drove the lorry straight to their hideout at Bovingdon. There were twelve hundred and thirty parachutes in that cargo. Hill and John the Tilter netted £9,225 from one night's work.

This gave Hill enough cash to sort out all his travel costs. He wanted to surprise the London underworld, even telling his rival, Jack Spot, that he'd be setting up a chain of spielers on his own because he didn't want to step on Spot's toes.

Hill knew someone "high up" in the diplomatic corps, who could get him and his wife out of the country. Despite the fact that it took most people about three months to leave in those early post-war years, his contact fixed him up with a passage to South Africa almost immediately. The airline ticket was bought just a few hours before takeoff, so that no one caught wind of his departure. So in the early hours of a Sunday morning in late April 1947, Billy Hill boarded a Stratocruiser at London Airport, bound for Lisbon.

Even though Hill used his own name, no one even attempted to stop him. He arranged for Aggie to go to Canada to stay with relatives, until he got settled in South Africa. The flight to Portugal was delayed because of bad weather, but within a week of hugging his wife farewell in London, Hill was booking into the Elgin Hotel in Johannesburg.

As he later recalled, "The sun was warm. The air was fine. I was feeling fit and well. The fogs and stink of the Big Smoke were thousands of miles away. So was Scotland Yard."

The very next morning, as Hill was taking a stroll around the city, he noticed a poster promoting a match featuring well-known British boxer Bobby Ramsey. Hill immediately headed for the gym where Ramsey was training. That night, Hill and Ramsey visited some of the city's nightclubs, including the Stork Club whose proprietor was a man called Arnold Neville, said to be South Africa's big-shot gambler and gangster. Hill also met a character called Sammy Abinger, known throughout the South African underworld as 'the Black Jew'. Abinger told Hill that Neville was the Boss of Bosses in SA. Virtually no one could place a bet without greasing his palm.

Hill wasn't impressed though, and took an instant dislike to Neville, a thirty-two-year-old former all-in wrestler who depended on a fearsome reputation as a bully. Neville was well over six feet tall and weighed in at seventeen stone. It was said that he had many of the Jo'burg cops in his pocket.

Word that London crime boss Billy Hill was in the city soon spread through the underworld. Hill soon got approached to run a spieler in Jo'burg by Abinger. Hill put up half the money and, within twenty-four hours, premises had been found above a restaurant in Commissioner Street, in the city's downtown district. It was called the Club Millionaire, much to the irritation of Arnold Neville, who didn't know Hill was connected to the new club now on everyone's lips.

Neville even sent for Hill to ask him to help him break up the club, in exchange for a big payment. Hill chuckled to himself when he realised Neville didn't know he owned the club himself, and politely turned down the offer. But Neville blew a gasket when he discovered Hill was working with his enemy, Abinger. Within days he was threatening to wreck the place ahead of its first night, which was to be the following Sunday.

Hill sent word back to Neville that he was welcome to try. He knew only too well that the challenge was sure to end in violence. Then Neville made a very big mistake. He let Hill know that if he left Abinger, he'd make him his lieutenant on a generous wage. Hill was outraged that Neville would think he'd even consider an offer to work *under* him.

Jo'burg's underworld was soon buzzing with rumours of a clash between the two crime lords. Hill thrived on the tense atmosphere and made sure he assembled quite an impressive posse. They warned him that Neville was a big-timer who could cause him a lot of aggravation. But most other criminals hated and despised Neville, which undoubtedly fuelled Hill's decision to take him on. He reckoned that if he could face down the South African villain he'd have the place to himself.

Hill later claimed to have befriended a newspaper reporter in Jo'burg, who supplied him with a revolver. The journalist supposedly hated Neville and told Hill, "Do yourself a favour and use it. In any case you'll most likely need it before you're finished."

Hill greased a few palms to make sure he knew all about Neville's movements, and then went ahead with his plans to open the Club Millionaire. Besides the gun, Hill also had knives – but not a chiv like he used in London. His weapon of choice this time was a huge hunting knife.

On the opening night, Hill paid Bobby Ramsey to wait on the door of the club in case there was trouble. At around midnight, one of the workers from the Millionaire came running back from Neville's Stork Rooms to say the Jo'burg crime boss and his mob were on their way over. Hill's club was heaving with customers, curious to see the notorious London gangster and to rub salt in Neville's wounds.

So, with revolver in hand and tough guy Ramsey alongside him, Billy Hill waited at the door for his latest enemy to show up. It didn't take long. As Hill later explained, "There were eight of them, led by Neville. As they approached us in the street I aimed my gun right at them."

At that moment Ramsey shouted, "Don't, you'll kill 'em," and knocked Hill's arm as he fired. The mob scattered like scared rabbits in all directions. Hill and Ramsey chased them, Hill firing right into them with absolutely no regard for life.

An armed policeman nearby did nothing to intervene, disappearing without uttering a word. When Hill eventually caught up with Neville he pulled out his hunting knife, which he used to slice at the South African's head. Neville's scalp was lifted clean off, almost as if a strong wind had blown off his wig. "He went down like a stuck pig," Hill would boast. "Bobby grabbed my knife and slashed at his buttocks as he was falling."

Eventually Hill heard a police whistle blow in the distance, as crowds of people began gathering around the wounded gangster. Hill and Ramsey retreated to the club to resume their business. Neville was taken to hospital by ambulance. He remained unconscious for two days. As the *Rand Daily Mail* reported it:

"Mr Arnold Neville, the former wrestler, of Highland Road, Kensington, was given nearly 100 stitches in the Johannesburg General Hospital early yesterday morning after being attacked outside a city night-club. His assailants slashed his head and buttocks with razors and his condition is serious. It is alleged that shots were also fired during the attack. At about 1:30am Neville and two friends were standing outside the nightclub when there was an argument. Blows were struck. Two men drew razors and one a revolver. Neville's friends retreated. When Neville attempted to break away, he was knocked to the ground and slashed. Later, Neville stated, he heard the firing of bullets."

Less than an hour after the attack, Hill rented a car and drove with one of his workers through the night to Durban, where he booked into the Waverley hotel under an assumed name. Hill's employee was arrested back in Jo'burg, after he returned to the city with the hire car. He spilled his guts to police and admitted where Hill was, after detectives pretended Neville had died and that he would be held accountable.

Less than twenty-four hours later, Hill was asleep in his suite in the Waverley when his bedroom door was "suddenly bashed clean off its hinges". Six plainclothes men rushed in with guns drawn, ordering him not to move or they would shoot. They then ripped the room to shreds, looking for Hill's gun.

Hill was thrown in a cell at the local police station, clamped in leg irons so that he could hardly walk. He was appalled at the conditions. For the following three days, he was kept locked up while he awaited a magistrate's agreement to transport him back to Jo'burg.

The floor was Hill's bed and he had one blanket, though a native African, accompanied by a warder, brought him in three meals a day. After three days the Commandant of Police told Hill that C.I.D. detectives were coming from Jo'burg to fetch him. The Durban magistrate signed the order for his transfer, and two heavily armed cops took him over. They replaced his leg irons with handcuffs on both wrists.

Hill claimed one of them then said to him, "We've heard all about you. We know you're the tough English gangster. If you try anything funny we'll let you have it." He later admitted he had no doubt they meant every word.

After getting into the first-class compartment of a train for the twenty-two-hour journey to Jo'burg they became more reasonable. One of them even produced a bottle of brandy which they all shared. Typically, Hill insisted on buying bottles of whiskey and brandy to reciprocate the toast.

In Jo'burg the police tried their hardest to get a confession, but

Hill was a past master at avoiding that sort of trap. He hired a top lawyer called Harry Gross, so when the police threatened to keep him in custody for days before a proper bail hearing, Gross immediately made a couple of calls and the case was brought forward to that afternoon. On the way to court, Hill agreed to tell his brief the truth about what happened. Even when he admitted he had thirteen previous convictions to his name, Gross still claimed he could fix things.

In court Hill cut a strange, dapper figure with horn-rimmed specs and a very conservative two-piece suit. He spoke softly and politely and made a point of sounding almost hesitant. He used no gesticulations and never raised his voice or overemphasised anything. As Hill later admitted, "This was my own natural disposition. It was also part of my game as well. After all, anyone can shout and holler. Anyone can hoot and bawl."

Hill's modestly low-key performance enabled Gross to appeal to the court, "Look at this poor young man. Just look at the man this gangster Neville accuses of attempting to murder him." Hill got out on bail of the equivalent of just £75, which he paid in cash before walking out of court.

Up until this moment, the South African authorities had no idea of Hill's previous offences back in Britain. But he knew it would only be a matter of time before his fingerprints were sent over to London. Initially, he was determined to fight the case against him and stay in South Africa. But he soon concluded it was better to book an air ticket back to England, via what were still known back then as 'the colonies'. Three days later he landed in Cairo, where he booked himself into the Heliopolis Hotel.

Back in South Africa there was outrage when it was discovered that Hill had done a runner. In Jo'burg, Bobby Ramsey and a Hill employee called Harry Snoyman stood trial. The *Rand Daily Mail* reported:

"Robert (Bob) Ramsey, a twenty-four-year-old London-born boxer, and Harry Snoyman, a twenty-year-old clerk, appeared before Mr J.H. Nolte in the Johannesburg Magistrate's court yesterday on charges of assault with intent to do grevious bodily harm. William Charles Hill, aged thirty-six, who should have appeared with them on a similar charge, was not present during the hearing. His bail of seventy-five pounds was estreated and a warrant issued for his arrest."

Ramsey and Snoyman were accused of assaulting Neville's sidekick, Dirk van Loggerenberg, by cutting him in the face with a knife or similar instrument, and also of maliciously assaulting Neville. Both pleaded not guilty. The court heard how they started fighting with Neville and five other thugs in the street outside Club Millionaire. The prosecution told the jury, "Everyone was punching each other, and guns and knives were flying, then two shots were fired."

Ramsey ended up with five months in prison for assault, his bail fixed at the equivalent of £250, pending appeal. Snoyman got three months for common assault. Ramsay's appeal was later dismissed and he was deported.

* * *

By now, Billy Hill was back on the familiar streets of London, able to move around with ease as the police didn't know he was back in the country. He moved out to East Ham, just beyond the East End, and set up a new headquarters. Billy Hill Inc was far from insolvent. When Jack Spot heard the news, he just shrugged his shoulders and told one associate, "Well he'll have to start all over again, won't he?"

In many ways, Hill was glad to be home amongst familiar faces. He was technically on the run, but the Yard didn't seem to have received even a whisper about his reappearance. Naturally, he went straight back to work. As he later wrote, "An idle man is a dangerous man, and all I wanted was an industrious life."

Raiding jewellers for their safes and getting back in with all his old cronies, Hill steered well clear of all his old West End haunts. And just two weeks after arriving back in London, Hill later claimed in his rather self-serving autobiography, he was offered an incredibly lucrative proposition by one of his chief snouts. A communist agent wanted Hill to break into a safe at a certain London embassy and steal some documents for him. The fee would be a minimum of £100,000, worth probably £5 million today. It was more than Hill had ever nicked on one job in his life. When Hill described this in his book he seemed to be implying that a Soviet agent wanted him to steal documents from the US embassy. It is entirely possible that Hill may have embellished parts of the story. As Britain's first real celebrity villain, certain incidents seem to have been intended to make him appear like a hero of the Free West at the height of the Cold War. However, other indications given to this author suggest there was some kind of an approach made to Hill, whatever the eventual outcome may have been.

Anyway, Hill agreed to meet the agent, who turned out to be what he later described as "a slimy individual", but suspected the deal was too good to be true. But those magic words "one hundred grand" were enough for him not to turn his back. Then the agent happened to mention there would be another £100,000 in readies in the same safe where the documents were stored. He even said he had an inside man in the embassy to provide vital information. The only snag was that there was an armed guard patrolling the corridors near where the safe was stored.

But Hill wasn't put off that easily. He got together his finest team, including Terrible Ted, Square Georgie, Odd Legs, Wide Gaiters and Horrible Harry. Hill had already been told the safe weighed about half a ton, so the boys got together their heavy gear, including steel rollers, a safe trolley, big peter canes and even some jelly, in case they had to cut open the safe on the premises.

The team travelled to the job in a shooting brake vehicle, equivalent to an estate car and big enough to transport the safe. It was parked around the corner from the embassy. The inside man let the team in through a basement door and quietly led them to the strong-room, where he gave them the keys and then disappeared. Five minutes later, Hill and his mob, working in complete silence, were wheeling the safe out when they heard footsteps. Hill and Terrible Ted pushed themselves hard against the wall, unable to get back into the strong-room as the safe and trolley were blocking the entrance. The remainder of the team remained inside.

Hill takes up the story: "So Terrible Ted and I pushed as hard as we could into that concrete wall hoping against hope that the fool of a sentry would not hear us breathing or even see the whites of our eyes in the darkened corridor."

His free hand slowly and silently drifted down towards the pocket that contained an automatic pistol. "If this guard was armed, and if he was the sort of armed guard I had heard about, it was likely that he would shoot first and talk about it afterwards. I was determined that I would get the first shot in, if only to settle his hash and permit our escape."

As the footsteps echoed from down the corridor, Hill held his breath so tightly "that I thought my heart had stopped beating." His hand gripped the gun so firmly that it was a miracle it didn't go off in his pocket.

As the guard approached, his shadow became increasingly distinct. The cloth of his uniform brushed past Hill's naked hand as he remained flattened against the wall. Then a voice said in broken English, "You are making too much noise. Do it quieter."

Hill let out a sigh of relief and wiped his sweaty brow. The embassy guard was another spy. By the time this had sunk in, the guard had already headed off around the corner.

"Come on, boys," Hill told his men. "This bloke's on our side. He's with us. He's one of them. Let's go."

It took another fifteen minutes to get the half-ton safe out into the street and into their estate car. Within another half an hour they had it hidden away in one of Hill's numerous London lock-ups, to be taken up to Bovingdon.

On arrival back at his new East Ham HQ, Hill was greeted by the original snout on the job and the commie spy. Hill was furious that the man now knew where he was based. But the snout whispered to Hill, "He said he'd kill me if I didn't bring him here."

The spy demanded the documents be brought to him there and then. Hill tried to explain that opening the safe was a complicated procedure and didn't just take five minutes. In any case, they were planning to take it to their country hideaway to blow it open. The spy insisted on accompanying Hill and flashed his automatic, just to prove the point. Hill was so outraged by the threat that he decked him with one swift right-hander to the jaw. The agent fell down on a sofa like a sack of potatoes.

"Grab his shooter," Hill barked at Odd Legs. Then he turned to the stunned agent rubbing his chin on the sofa and said, "If you want the paper you'll have to come down to the country with us while we get to work on the safe. But I warn you, we're not going to work on it tonight."

So they took off to the countryside in the shooting brake. Hill had no idea if the spy was a genuine trained intelligence agent, but he made sure the man hadn't a clue where he was being taken. He also had one of his blokes watching him throughout the night, while the agent was locked in a room and told to keep it buttoned.

The following day, Hill and his team started work on the safe. It took more than a couple of hours to strip it open but there was only about £72,000 in it. Hill then grabbed the all-important documents, which were all in a foreign language. The commie spy's eyes lit up and his hands reached out to grab the paperwork. But Hill had other ideas. "Oh no," he told the agent. "We must know what these are all about before you get them, mister."

The spy was outraged. Hill told him that it didn't matter. He wanted to know what he was selling first, and if they thought it was worth more than £100,000 they would hold onto it. It was a typically risky strategy, but Hill had a feeling he might be able to earn even more money out of this particular caper.

Hill then ordered Odd Legs to look after their commie friend while he returned to the Smoke to get the papers examined. He set off with Horrible Harry at the wheel and headed straight to Soho, to find someone who could translate Eastern European languages. Eventually, Hill established that the documents detailed the activities of anti-communists in another Iron Curtain country. They also included plans for the sabotage of various government installations in cities in that same country. Hill claimed that his translator told him, "If the Communists get these papers about a thousand people will certainly be killed by the Communists. That's why the Communists want those papers. It's a dead give-away to the whole set-up."

Then Hill made a remarkable and heroic decision – or so he claimed in his autobiography, some years later. "I wasted no time. I burnt the papers there and then."

Back in Bovingdon, Hill played the agent like a true professional, who pleaded with him for the papers and promised to get him that £100,000 fee.

"Where is the money?" asked Hill.

"I promise. I promise like a true Russian that you will be paid."

"All right. All right," said Hill. "Let's have the dough then."

"But I have not got it with me. I promise."

Eventually, Hill later insisted, the spy gave up trying to force him to hand over the papers. As Hill would later claim, "Well, we got the £72,000 out of it. We did a little in at least prolonging about a thousand anti-Communist lives. And that Commie spy was never seen or heard of again." Projecting the image of an underworld James Bond, Hill claimed that the spy was probably killed by his bosses for failing to get his hands on those papers.

Billy Hill was in many ways sitting pretty now, with his share of the £72,000 from the embassy job. He felt tempted to try his luck somewhere else in the colonies, but, when he remembered what had happened in South Africa, he realised his heart still belonged to London.

NINE

By this time the police must have known Hill was back in the capital, but they had still failed to locate him. And as was the case before he went to South Africa, he was being inundated with offers of jobs from other villains.

Eventually he decided on a huge job put up to him by a businessman from the North. He claimed there was £35,000 in his business partner's safe and, since they had fallen out, he wanted a piece of it. On Hill's first trip to Manchester to speak to his informant, Hill also fell in love with a nightclub hostess called Connie. He would keep the affair secret from Aggie, but admitted to one of his boys that he was smitten.

Back in London to prepare the raid, Hill and his boys loaded up a wartime ambulance they sometimes used for such jobs and headed back up the A1. They'd been warned the safe might weigh a ton, so a sturdy old ambulance was ideal transportation.

Horrible Harry was sent in ahead of the team to break in. Luckily for them the owners were away, so he immediately let the rest of the gang in. The six-foot safe was resting on a pedestal, so Hill and his boys had no choice but to knock an entire wall down to get at it. Once they had it loose they sat it on rollers and started pushing it towards the front door of the house. The ambulance was brought round to the front of the house and backed up to the front door. Two hours after starting the job they had the safe in the back and were on their way back down to the Smoke.

Hill and his gang used a drag car about ten miles ahead of the ambulance to warn about any possible roadblocks or other dangers from the police. Occasionally the car would turn around and meet the ambulance on the road, before continuing its scouting journey ahead.

About ten miles outside the town of Litchfield, in the Midlands, the ambulance broke down because the one-ton weight of the safe had broken its back axle. Hill and his boys pushed the ambulance to the side of the road, and gang member Sam Ferryboat Feet volunteered to watch it while they continued their journey to London to find a new pick-up vehicle. The next day they brought a furniture van back up to Litchfield and transferred the safe into it. Then they headed back to the Smoke while Ferryboat and Horrible Harry tried to get the ambulance repaired.

Two days later, the safe was finally opened at the country hideout in Bovingdon. It was found to only contain £9,000, but Hill didn't complain. "You win some. You lose some. And we still got a few bob out of it so we didn't really mind."

But the big money jobs were "fantastic tickles", and one of the easiest was a safe belonging to a textile business magnate who'd been shooting his mouth off in the wrong company. Hill and his boys turned up one night at the man's house, brandishing fake police warrants to search the premises.

The family pleaded with the 'police', but they insisted on going ahead with the search. So with all of them in one room 'under interrogation', Hill and two of his other boys opened the safe and found £65,000 in hard cash. Meanwhile, his 'officers' had tied up and taped the family. After Hill and his gang had departed, the textile businessman went to the police but claimed he'd only been robbed of £2,500. The rest obviously came from illicit means.

* * *

Hill's presence in London only came to light when one of his team let slip in a pub one night that he'd organised the theft of four hundred and twenty-six cases of genuine Scotch Whiskey. Now the police knew for sure that Hill was back, although they still couldn't fathom out where he was based. They'd taken it for granted that he'd be in the West End, and never thought of looking for him in suburban east London. For when Hill did pop 'up West', he was careful to keep a very low profile and never overstay his welcome.

As the country started slowly recovering from the waging of war, Hill found that the continent beyond the English Channel was opening up for him too. One French mobster called in his help after his gang stole a safe which they couldn't open. Hill was intrigued, presenting himself at a disused airfield in Sussex where a private plane was waiting to whisk him across the Channel. Eight hours later he was safely back in East Ham, with £800 in his pocket.

His long suffering wife, Aggie, had by this time returned from Canada where she'd moved many months earlier. She went straight back into a flat on the old manor of Camden Town, but Hill had to avoid the place like the plague because he knew the police had it under observation. Meanwhile, he moved his northern conquest, the nightclub dancer Connie, into a flat in the West End. Aggie visited Billy in East Ham frequently, although she was far from happy when she heard rumours about his other women. Aggie was also worried he would be picked up by the police at any moment and sent away again.

However, Hill was convinced he could remain on the run if he set his mind to it. As he later explained, "I thought to myself, why should I give myself up when the going was so good? Why, it was possible for me to go on like this for years."

Meanwhile, Hill was flown over to a French city in another private plane to do a 'jelly job' on a safe. But the resulting explosion was so loud that he and his team abandoned their target and made a run for it across the rooftops. His partner on the job, Bimbo, was nicked by the local gendarmes and got eighteen months. Hill knew it had been a close shave, and made sure that Bimbo was supplied with tobacco, food and newspapers to make his sentence more bearable.

In fact, Hill always made a point of looking after any of his boys if they got banged up. When his old mate John the Tilter went on the run to Australia, after almost being nicked for a massive forged petrol coupons scam, he and his family never once went without. That was how Hill instilled such incredible loyalty in his gang. If they had to go on their toes or face a long stretch, then he would at least make sure everyone survived.

In the case of John the Tilter, he went to extraordinary lengths to make sure he was not betrayed by his girlfriend, whom Hill believed would grass him up, given half a chance. He even organised a complex series of letters to give the impression the Tilter was in America, rather than Australia. But then the Tilter contacted his girlfriend in London, and she immediately shouted her head off to the police. Within hours the Yard were seeking his extradition from Australia, and he ended up with a three-year sentence.

Back at home, Aggie kept urging Hill to go see the police and resolve the international fugitive status he'd earned by walking away from charges in South Africa. She even promised that, if he'd give himself up, she'd happily wait for him all over again despite the presence of Connie in his life. So Hill straightened out all his affairs, made sure that everyone would be looked after while he was away, and then walked up to Savile Row to give himself up.

He eventually went for trial on the job he'd originally been nicked for with Stuttering Robo, before going to South Africa, and got a three-stretch in Wandsworth. "It wasn't so bad when you came to think of it," Hill later recalled. "By now I knew the smell of Wandsworth. Even the bugs which infest the place knew me when I returned. They as much as said, 'How are you?' at the first bite."

In prison, Hill decided that once he'd served his time he'd reform his mob and see off the rising threat of Jack Spot. He would later dub his newly formed gang "the best mob I ever had," and reckoned on characters like Slippery Sam, Bullnose Bertie, Billy the Long-Reach and Iron Jemmy Spike queuing up to join him. As he explained, "There wouldn't be a safe in the country we couldn't go for and get. Our speciality was going to be post office and bank safes."

*　　*　　*

Many of Billy's boys came to see him inside Wandsworth. Being as it was in London, it was easier for him to continue running his empire. He got himself a tame screw and, apart from not being able to make appearances up West, very little was changed by his incarceration.

Aggie also came to see him regularly, and yet again he was amazed by how she handled it. "Didn't seem to change her a bit," he later recalled. "Waiting about for me to come out again. But it wasn't very satisfactory seeing her behind that perforated glass screen in the visitor's room of the nick, and bawling my lungs off trying to tell her that everything would be all right once I got out."

Hill assured his wife that he had committed his last crime, in an attempt to keep her happy. There was a lot of other stuff he wanted to tell her about, but he decided it could wait until his release.

But then he had other things on his mind. A new Criminal Justice Act had come into force while he was inside. The part that worried him was that anyone with three previous convictions for the same type of offence could now be sent away for a period ranging from eight to fourteen years. Hill summed it up perfectly when he later wrote, "And with it went so little remission that most men who got that lot would serve every day of it before they got out. It meant that a bloke aged forty, in the prime of his life, could be sent away until he was fifty-four. So I made my mind up that I had seen the last of the inside of the nick. And I meant it." Hill reasoned there was now no need for him to stick his neck out anymore. He knew he could earn a good living without actually going out on any more jobs. Even now, from inside prison, he was about to mastermind probably the most notorious crime of his career.

In the summer of 1948, Heathrow was being constructed to replace Croydon as London's main airport. Extremely valuable cargoes were stored at the airport overnight, and one of Hill's boys had an inside contact who let them know when the next big shipment of valuables was en route. Hill's preparations for the job were so meticulous that he even got his boys to join special guided tours of the airport, to case the joint.

Then bulky parcels were sent from Ireland to test the lorry delivery system. Sammy Ross and another member of Hill's team, Franny Daniels – both licensed truck drivers – found they could gain access into the inner precinct of the customs building to pick up parcels without an official pass. In fact, Daniels and another notorious villain, Teddy Machin, had until then been part of Jack Spot's mob, which helped fuel rumours that Spot was involved in the robbery.

Then word came through that a bonded warehouse inside the airport perimeter was taking delivery of £380,000 worth of diamonds and a further £280,000 of cash on the night of 24 July 1948. Hill's team rapidly devised a plan to dope security guards with sedatives in their coffee. Then ten raiders – all wearing nylon stockings over their faces – would follow a single torchlight to the customs shed where all the loot was stored.

But someone on Hill's team grassed them up. By 11pm all roads leading to the airport were under surveillance. Thirteen Flying Squad detectives lay in wait in the customs shed and ten more were hiding in a van round the back. As Hill's team crashed in, a bloody battle ensued. Two of Hill's mob – Billy Benstead and Spot's old crony Franny Daniels – turned around and scarpered. Teddy Machin, the other villain with Spot connections, escaped by jumping on the back of a moving truck on its way out of the airport compound.

The remaining robbers were marched off to waiting black Marias. They were all convicted and received up to twelve years' imprisonment. On the underworld grapevine, many were saying that the airport job was grassed up by one of Jack Spot's henchmen, annoyed that he hadn't been involved in the robbery. Ironically, Spot did indeed try to take some credit for the attempted Heathrow raid, although he played no part in it whatsoever. He was even more infuriated when he later found out that two of his team were involved. Still inside prison, Billy Hill didn't actually mind Spot taking some of the heat off him. He was quietly chipping away at Spot's powerbase, even from within his prison cell in Wandsworth. When two of Spot's sidekicks got out of jail they immediately transferred their allegiance to Hill. Another heavyweight criminal called Billy Benstead had already crossed the pavement to Hill's mob.

In any case, Spot was considered to be 'the racecourse man' while Hill was regarded as the clubs man in the West End. Yet Spot deluded himself into believing that he was the senior of the two gang leaders. Hill held his peace, as he believed that Spot would eventually fall on his own sword.

* * *

In the East End of London, two teenage twin brothers were hitting the front pages of the local newspapers thanks to their skills inside the boxing ring. In the winter of 1948, Reggie Kray, already champion of Hackney, won the London Schoolboy Boxing Championships. Within months he was South Eastern Divisional Youth Club Champion and the London ATC Champion. Meanwhile, brother Ronnie had fought his way to the Hackney schoolboy and London junior championships, plus a London ATC title.

But even more significantly, Ron and Reg were an up-and-coming pair of young hoodlums, who would soon run their own mob of thugs. The twins were so notorious in the East End that they'd been barred from most of the cinemas and dancehalls in the area. Ron and Reg would even proudly announce that they kept choppers, machetes, knives, swords and other weapons under the bed they shared at their parents' tiny terraced home in Vallance Road, Bethnal Green, a hardnosed district where gang fights flared up virtually every night.

The London underworld grapevine went into overdrive when the twins – aged sixteen – got involved in a fight using bike chains and coshes outside a dancehall in Mare Street, Hackney. The police nicked them for grievous bodily harm on three people, but they were later acquitted at the Old Bailey. Ronnie then boasted how he'd purchased his first gun before he'd turned seventeen, and that he fully expected to shoot someone "sooner rather than later". The Kray twins were steeped in violence and paranoia. Even before they went to bed each night in the family home – known as 'Fort Vallance' – they'd place newspapers around the floor, so that they'd hear the rustle of the papers if an intruder entered the bedroom.

The Krays were immensely proud of their strong right arms and made sure they were always available as musclebound minders to the highest bidder. The more chilling twin, Ronnie, would spend hours sharpening his cutlass blade on oil spread across the doorstep of their home. The teenager relished swishing his blade through the air, as his face contorted with venom while he imagined beheading his enemies. One time Ronnie even turned to his brother and said, "Can't you see how that would stop them? Half a dozen blokes come at you and then BINGO! the first one gets his head cut clean off his shoulders and it rolls on the floor. Wouldn't that make 'em run!"

Meanwhile, other gangs of up-and-coming young hoods started to emerge on London's criminal horizon. In Brixton, south London, two mobs attacked each other with razors and glasses in a test of strength "to see who was boss". They all shook hands afterwards, although it took four buckets of water to clear the blood from the floor. Incidents like this happened with increasing regularity across the capital. Billy Hill knew only too well that he needed to keep an eye on these up-and-coming characters.

*   *   *

When Hill saved the life of a screw by intervening after south London hard-man Jack Rosa attacked him, he got six months off his sentence. Rosa was later paid £5,000 in cash, and many presume the whole incident was set up in order to get Hill an early release.

Hill finally walked out of the imposing cast wooden gates just before dawn on a crisp autumn day in 1949, to be greeted by his cigar-chomping underworld rival Jack Spot, who had specially driven to Wandsworth in his flashy white Cadillac Eldorado and waited for him. Spot was hoping the two of them could work together, but Hill wasn't so keen, especially since he still suspected Spot of grassing his team up on the airport job.

Spot later claimed in his autobiography that Hill was close to middle age, penniless and looked "as thin as a pickled herring" at the time of his release. Spot also said he offered Hill the chance to oversee his London spielers. Hill knew he needed time to get back on his feet, so he was grateful for any money-making opportunities – although he had no long-term intention of dancing to Spot's tune.

Jack Spot had certainly made inroads into the West End club scene. As Sammy Samuels, who ran small Soho clubs from the thirties to the sixties explained, "The gaming clubs and the drinking clubs in and around Soho were meeting places for the fly-boys, the screwsmen and the tea-leafs, the hustlers and the sharpers, and while on the one hand the club guv'nor can do without their custom he cannot keep them out of the club. They are part of the set-up. And they often brought with them info about new criminal opportunities."

Soon Hill was re-establishing his own clubs, as he later explained, "These places didn't have names and committees and all that stuff. They just started and the word got round that there's a game on. The customers ranged from regular villains to tearaways to every kind of person from titled aristocrats down to cab-drivers and waiters. Our game was not to trim mugs who wanted to play for some sort of thrill. There was no need for that."

Billy Hill's occasionally violent habits greatly bothered Jack Spot, even though they occurred away from his spielers. One time Hill slashed the face of a pimp who was trying to force his lover Connie back on the game. The first Spot heard about the incident was when Hill phoned to ask him to check out the hospitals to see what condition his victim was in. Spot took it upon himself to personally persuade the pimp not to grass Hill up to the law, although he was furious that Hill's personal life had encroached into 'the business'. Cracks were already beginning to appear in the so-called partnership between these two London crime overlords. So within months of Hill's release from prison, his gang of thieves were dominating London's boomtown West End alongside Jack Spot's mob of bruisers. They ran protection rackets, took their cut of gambling revenues and channelled all their power to ensure their own survival. But all was not so rosy beneath the surface. Hill told one associate that Spot was "becoming insecure and a bit jealous of me."

Spot later insisted he should have had Hill "seen to" when he had the chance, as their tentative partnership was far from perfect. But for the moment they could continue crushing the smaller gangs with ease. Many West End traders did not trust the police, or had something to hide, so they turned to Spot and Hill for protection instead. The two men even recruited a strong army from the Elephant, south of the river, including such notables as brothers Lennie and Jimmy Garrett, and Bobby Brindle, to back up their number one heavyweight henchman, Johnny Carter.

Billy Hill wanted to maintain real power and influence, and not just by flexing his muscles. He adopted an image as a pristine gentleman, often dressed in immaculate handmade suits with a fedora to match and a cigar protruding from his mouth. Hill wanted to run the underworld as if he was the head of a legitimate corporation. While the West End was booming, he was operating numerous protection rackets and using his power base for one main purpose – the survival of the status quo. In this sense he really was a businessman, drawing his profits from a monopoly and only becoming dangerous if he felt his empire was threatened. Hill even set up regular gatherings of his boys at the Royal

Lancaster Hotel in Bayswater, where he'd sweep through the hotel's double doors with a hefty sidekick in front, checking out the place. Then he'd saunter through the lobby still flanked by bodyguards, two of whom were well-known boxing professionals, before settling in the bar for a conference with 'the chaps'.

But it was the police who were Hill's most important 'boys' at this time. In Soho, spielers were usually tipped off by police for a fee as to when a raid was due. Hill would then get "a few mugs" in that day so regular customers escaped arrest. Soho's brothel-keepers were also helped by police who offered to 'adjust' certain evidence at a price. The payments covered what an officer might say in evidence relating to a police raid.

Hundreds of Soho basement clubs were tolerated thanks to their unofficial contribution to police funds. Uniformed policemen in Soho received up to £60 a week in bribes, the average PC's wage set between £9 and £11 a week by this time. Even in the courts, evidence was frequently 'cooked' to benefit the accused. Details of previous convictions were often suppressed on sentencing, so that defendants were fined rather than imprisoned.

*   *   *

In his later autobiography, Billy Hill gave Spot the name 'Benny the Kid' in order to avoid any legal problems. But there is no doubt that, after Spot picked Hill up outside Wandsworth on that crisp autumn day in 1949, Hill had already become disenchanted with him. He even believed that Spot's friendliness was just a façade.

In Soho, Hill had already started taking a 'tax' from many clubs, bars and spielers in exchange for his protection. He certainly didn't want other criminals, Jack Spot included, soaking up his special tax by leaning on his clientele.

Hill also greatly enjoyed working a scam in which he would

open a spieler and nominate one of his 'workmen' to stand in for him in case of problems with the police. His job was to say he was the owner and to be prosecuted for allowing gambling on the premises. Hill would then pay his fine and all his expenses, and give him a bit on top for his trouble. This all meant that if the law tried to suggest the owner had previous criminal convictions, he could stand up and say no. It also meant the fine would be considerably less, and the premises wouldn't lose its licence.

Amongst Hill's best spieler customers were the foreign-born pimps who always had plenty of readies. Many of them would drop hundreds of pounds on cards, but he was weary of the Maltese and Cypriot ponces. "Few regular villains will stand any nonsense from them. They are despised in the underworld, but if they wanted to gamble their dough away in my spielers, that was all right. If I didn't take it someone else would, so I let them."

Hill also insisted the West End became a quieter, more respectable place after he returned from prison, although this was disputed by many others. But then trouble only ever attracted the attention of the police, so it made sense for him to keep a low profile.

He did purchase one drinking club with a notorious reputation from a colourful local character called Mrs Holder, who was earlier convicted of stealing £35,000 from a member of the aristocracy. The club attracted ponces, thieves, blackmailers, pickpockets, burglars, male and female prostitutes, and all the general scum of Soho. Hill later said he spent the first two weeks throwing the dross of the West End down the club's two flights of stairs.

Then a character called Freddy Ford came into Hill's life. Ford was approaching eighty years of age and had a record as long as your arm. He'd made a stack of cash in his time and was renowned as something of an egomaniac. Ford kept banging on about opening a spieler that would be the Monte Carlo of London, so Hill obliged by going into partnership with him. Ford proved the perfect partner, not clever enough to work out that he was being robbed blind. But the spieler didn't last long as the police raided it three times in two weeks. It was simpler and cheaper for Hill to open up elsewhere.

Still in Soho, Hill went into partnership to run a spieler in Dean Street, with two Greek criminals called Chris and Charlie. It was soon known as one of the toughest clubs in the West End. Located in a dimly lit cellar underneath a shop, Hill often had to yell his lungs hoarse to be heard and keep order. He later recalled, "It was like the tower of Babel; shouting, bellowing, hooting and hollering. Money was at stake. Big money. Sometimes grands at a time. There was no time for ceremony. A word out of place and the only cure was to get out the cosh, use it, and then continue the game."

Hill usually had Strong Arms Phil alongside him for protection at the Dean Street spieler. The place was packed most nights, largely because of the pull of Billy Hill's name. Hill was often up two or three nights on the trot without any sleep because business was so good. Some regulars were the scum of the earth, while others were the household names of the British aristocracy. Film stars came for a spell. Bankers, bookmakers, businessmen, burglars, thieves, taxi drivers, waiters, all crowded around the tables, yelling for a chance to lose (or occasionally win) some money.

The heavyweight villains who showed up at the club were a veritable who's who of the underworld, many of whom had worked for Hill in the past: Sid the Burglar, Bear's Breath, Soapy Alec, Fat Jock (a 'dipper'), Blueball, Kipper Johnny the Spiv, Alec the Poof (a ponce), Oggie Bishop, Akinlulu (an African), Tony the Wop, Italian Alec and Chuck-a-Dummy Maxie. As Hill explained of the latter's sobriquet, "Chuck's game was to throw a dummy when the game was warm. Then while they were all fussing around the unconscious man an accomplice would get round and try and nick the loot."

Other regulars included notorious London burglar Taters Chatham, Paddy the Creep, Flannel Foot, Little Hymie, Banjo, Fido, Sly Boots, Tom Thumb and Bananas, the club barman.

The club in Dean Street was open from eleven at night until five or six the following morning. The stakes ranged from a nicker to a 'monkey', although the average bet was between a tenner and a score. Big players, however, bet in fifties and centuries, and people like Taters would put as much as £200 on each go.

*　　　*　　　*

It was around this time that Hill's northern girlfriend, Connie, disappeared off the radar, to be replaced by a girl called 'Gypsy'. Phyllis May Blanche Riley was working behind the bar of one of his West End clubs. Her nickname was said to have originated when she ran away from her East End home and joined a band of gypsies. Gypsy had been hired out as a prostitute by a Maltese pimp. She had a fiery temper and was known to have physically attacked Hill on numerous occasions. Hill had even chivved one of Gypsy's pimps, Belgian Johnny, and then had to bribe him not to tell the police about the attack.

TEN

The early 1950s were highly profitable for Billy Hill, who reckoned he was single-handedly keeping the peace in the West End. "Visitors and strangers must have found Soho a rather dull place with no running gang fights and feuds," he later recalled. "And so-called crime columnists were certainly feeling the draught when they had no 'inside dope' to stick into their columns all about Soho and the West End."

As usual, he was on the lookout for new business opportunities. He'd heard that war was virtually breaking out in nearby Trafalgar Square between lowlife photographers who hassled tourists to take their pictures. So he popped down to Nelson's Column to talk to a character called Tommy Bird, who was edging in to take over the entire business. Hill told Bird where to get off, and installed five men employed by his younger brother Archie in Trafalgar Square. From that moment on, according to Hill, "the public got value for their money without being molested".

Then two gangs of outsiders began taking an unhealthy interest in the West End, the Fraser mob and the Carters, both from south London. They started by wrecking a couple of Soho clubs, with one man seriously wounded by a broken glass in his face. Before the law could investigate, Hill was called in to sort it out. As he later explained, "It seemed that both these mobs were creeping into the West End, and when they had a few drinks the usual trouble broke out. If this glass incident had been let go any further, it was more than likely both mobs would have met right on my manor and had it out with guns."

Hill always claimed that he effectively stopped the gangs feuding, although a short time later Carter was banged up for two years for causing grievous bodily harm. Unfortunately for him he was sent to Wandsworth, where some of the Fraser mob were also locked up. Carter got a hiding and was then transferred to another prison to prevent the feud reigniting.

But other mobs were taking a closer look at the West End. A character called Ginger Randall, from Shepherds Bush in west London, decided to take on the remnants of the old Sabini mob, originally from Clerkenwell but dominant in Soho. Randall and his boys came across one Sabini gang member at New Cross dog track and battered him beyond recognition. This sparked the threat of all-out war, with the Sabinis and Randall's boys arming themselves with guns and knives and searching London for each other.

Hill heard about it and stepped in to try and sort things out. He let it be known that, if they didn't both lay down their arms and settle it all in a peaceful manner, then the police were to be let loose on them. It was a drastic, uncharacteristic threat by Hill, who wasn't exactly good friends with the police but knew he needed to bring the situation to a head. Hill agreed with Jack Spot that they should both go and see Randall and his team in Shepherds Bush, while Spot would go to the Angel to get hold of the Sabini mob. Both men also agreed to tell all the major faces in London to meet them, all tooled up, at a specific West End pub on a certain night.

Then Hill went in search of Randall. He eventually tracked him down to a boozer called the Warwick Arms, in Notting Hill, west London. Hill walked into the pub alone, having made sure

Hill's dapper appearance dated back to when he was still in his teens.

Borstal boy Billy Hill with a young lady friend.

These young London gangsters of the early 1930s almost resemble their Chicago counterparts. Billy Hill is the second from right.

Hill stored stolen booty in the barn of his country 'run-in' in Bovingdon, Hertfordshire, throughout most of the 1940s.

The classic Billy Hill pose, in his favourite fedora and mackintosh.

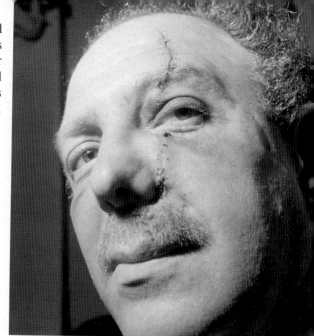

Hill's underworld rival, Jack Spot, was marked for life after Hill's boys attacked him outside his London home.

Hill proudly shows off his 1955 autobiography, *Boss of Britain's Underworld*, at the Soho launch party for the book.

Hill with the Kray twins, Ron (right) and Reg, at his home in Tangier, 1966 – shortly after Ron had killed George Cornell.

The gravestone in the City of London cemetery, Manor Park, east London, that marks the final resting place of Billy Hill.

some of his mob were amongst the customers, and went straight up to Randall.

Randall looked at Hill doubtfully, his eyes darting up from Hill's handmade shoes to his face, then sideways to his men. Hill knew Randall was trying to put on a show of strength. Randall knew that, since Hill and his boys had taken over from the Sabinis, they had made their peace and were now on talking terms with them. Hill could tell that Randall thought there was some kind of double dealing going on.

Randall and three of his boys eventually agreed to leave the pub with Hill. Once outside, they handed him their Lugers and Webleys. He put them in the boot of his car and locked it, taking them to a boozer in the East End.

Randall and his three men almost fainted when they walked into the pub half an hour later. In the saloon bar were more than two hundred members of Hill's mob, tooled up and ready to go to work. They stood about in groups of twos, threes and fours, talking amongst themselves. One or two quietly nodded in Hill's direction as he walked into the bar. The only real evidence of a threat was in their eyes. They followed Hill and Randall from the door of the boozer to the bar where they stood and ordered their drinks.

Randall's hand shook as he picked up his glass of beer. Hill then turned to Randall and said quietly, "Just look round. You know many faces here. Some you don't. Well, just look closely and give your eyes a treat. You think you've got a mob that's useful! Well, take a good look at this one. It's mine, and each man's a killer if he gets upset."

The atmosphere inside that pub changed even more drastically when Jack Spot walked in, with Sabini and three of his boys in tow. Hill later said in his autobiography, "I thought I noticed a sort of involuntary movement towards us at the counter, as though the mob were closing in on us as Benny [Spot] walked towards me, followed by Black [Sabini] and his team."

Hill told Randall, "There's only one guv'nor round here and that's me. If any of you fancy your chances you can take your pick, but remember this is what you're up against. Now shake hands on it and call it a day."

Randall and Sabini shook hands. Then they each bought a round of drinks for everyone in the pub.

Never before had so many villains assembled under one roof outside of Dartmoor Prison. Hill later claimed it was the last real gang meeting ever held in London. "From that night we never had any trouble with gang warfare. There hasn't been a gang fight since, and while I'm guv'nor I'll see to it that there won't be."

*   *   *

In the summer of 1951, Billy Hill and his ex-hooker lover, Gypsy Riley, joined Jack Spot and his pretty young wife-to-be, Rita, on holiday in the South of France. Rita and Gypsy instantly detested each other, which then caused friction between Spot and Hill. "Rita thought Gypsy was a loose woman who'd bed Spot the moment her back was turned," one old east London villain later explained. "But actually Gypsy had a heart of gold."

Despite the tensions, Hill adored the good life on the French Riviera. The sun softened his chiv scars and helped him forget the awful stench of Wandsworth Prison. Hill knew that his relationship with Spot was far from easy, but he tried to laugh it all off as "a touch of woman trouble". Shortly after returning from the Med, Spot promised Rita he'd begin "easing off" on the day-to-day running of his empire, although he wanted to ensure that no one – particularly Billy Hill – thought he'd gone soft.

Just before his wedding to Rita, Spot even leaked a story to the *People* columnist Arthur Halliwell in which he implied he was "going legit". In truth, he was trying to keep Rita off his back and had no intention of walking away from his life of crime. It seemed to Hill that Spot was trying to have the best of both worlds. In any case, he considered himself to be the man in charge, and saw Spot's behaviour as yet more evidence of his weakness.

Hill remained in his element in London's clubland. He continued meeting and greeting new contacts and was always on the lookout for "new investments" to put his money into. He was financing and organising robberies much more successfully than Spot ever had.

*   *   *

Twelve men arrived separately at a flat in the West End at midnight on 21 May 1952. They knew they were to be part of a team of blaggers, but nothing more than that, until Billy Hill entered the apartment and told them the assignment. Two hours later, at 2am, a man dressed as a postman walked through the gates of the main London post office, in Eastcastle Street, just a stone's throw from the Old Bailey, on the edge of the City of London. He nodded at the men at the gate and headed towards a group of vans near the sorting office.

The man picked out one of the vans, lifted the bonnet and broke a wire that disconnected the alarm, which could be started by the driver if he was in trouble. Then he walked calmly out of the complex, got into a car and drove away. He went to a phone box where he called the others at the flat to report that his part of the operation was complete. He too had no idea about the other component parts of the job.

Soon after 3am, two stolen private cars with false number plates were handed over to the gang. The two cars were driven to Eastcastle Street with four men in each vehicle. They pulled up in a mews on one side of the street and waited.

Then another member of the gang went to Paddington station and watched the Post Office van with the disconnected alarm leave soon after 3:30am. He phoned the flat. At a bomb-damaged garage in St Augustus Street, Camden Town, another gangster parked up a van filled with empty apple boxes covered in tarpaulins. There was a large square gap in the centre of the boxes.

At 4:17am the driver of the mail van slammed on his brakes after a black Riley swerved in front of him. A green Vanguard then pulled up behind the van just as a man jumped out of the Riley and leaped towards the van driver's door, yanking it open. Two more men followed and hauled all three guards out of the van, attacking them with fists and coshes.

The guards were thrown to the ground. The three robbers climbed into the van and slammed it into gear while another villain got back in the Riley. The rest of the team jumped into the Vanguard and headed off with the other vehicles into Covent Garden, where they took a left into Floral Street. Another car was waiting around the corner in Rose Street. They got in and drove off behind the mail van at high speed.

At 4:32am the van pulled up outside the yard compound in Augustus Street. One man jumped over the gates and unlocked them. The other robber followed the van into the yard while a lookout waited in the street. The mailbags were ripped open. Within half an hour they'd counted £287,000 in cash.

Then a brown van was driven out of the compound into Camden Town Road and south through the back of the City down to Spitalfields Market. Just after mid-day that morning, the van turned into a country lane, ferrying the £287,000 that was shared out between a team of seven, including master planner Billy Hill. Later that same day, Jack Spot went to see Hill, who'd taken a suite in the Dorchester Hotel to celebrate the job. Spot later recalled, "There he was dressed like fuckin' Noel Coward ironing bank notes with his moll Gypsy standing alongside him. Across the room was a clothes line with more notes drying out attached with clothes pegs."

Spot rather clumsily tried to put the word around that he'd helped finance the robbery, because he thought it would bolster his reputation. Typically, Hill decided on a very clever response by handing Spot a few thousand pounds out of the proceeds. It was as if Hill·was saying, *"There you are Spotty old son, have a few bob on me because we've just made a shedload of money."* Spot didn't even bother saying thanks, and left the room moments later. Hill later described that decision as, "The worse thing I ever did." In fact, Spot accepted the money knowing full well that Hill was rubbing his nose in the fact he'd pulled off a brilliant crime. Spot should have recognised it as the ultimate confirmation of Hill's ascendance, but instead considered it the petulant behaviour of an upstart – even though Hill was one year his senior, and already worthy of the title 'Boss of the Underworld'.

By the time of the Eastcastle Street job, Billy Hill was forty-two-years-old, a snappy dresser in handmade suits and obligatory fedora with the brim neatly snapped forward. His hair was carefully dyed and slicked back with Morgan's pomade. Hill saw himself as the managing director of crime, and was determined never to go back to jail again. His passion was making money through other criminals' endeavours.

Clubs, dives, spielers, pubs, hotels, private homes were all kept under constant surveillance by detectives investigating the 'Big Job', as the robbery quickly became known. Naturally, Hill and Spot were hauled in for questioning, but both had good alibis. A £10,000 reward was offered by insurers who later increased it to £14,500, which was chickenfeed compared with what Hill's team had scooped.

Hill couldn't resist bragging about the robbery later. "If you went through the most confidential files at Scotland Yard to find out who planned the greatest robbery in British criminal history, you would come to the conclusion that only Billy Hill could have done it. That's what the Yard thinks. It's what the Underworld thinks. It's what the insurance people think and the banks and the Post Office chiefs."

But then Hill knew he'd never be fingered for the Big Job. Not even Jack Spot would dare squeal on him. Two villains were eventually charged with receiving in connection with the blag, but Hill nobbled the jury and they were both found not guilty. No one would ever be successfully prosecuted for the Eastcastle mailbag robbery.

*   *   *

By the early 1950's, Soho's favoured tools of the trade included razors, knives, broken bottles, revolvers, hammers, hatchets, coshes and knuckledusters. Charing Cross Hospital employed a special staff of medical seamsters to sew up the gaping wounds made by these weapons. Victims seldom complained, but harboured an urge to get even with their attacker. Flying Squad detective Bert Wickstead recalled, "One well known tearaway who was 'chivvied' had a beautiful 'curvature' of the face that stretched from one ear right round his chin to the other ear. He had to have ninety-nine stitches inserted to draw this gaping wound together."

Wickstead's boss, Detective Superintendent Ted Greeno, had Billy Hill and Jack Spot under close surveillance throughout this period. Greeno – who'd first encountered Hill during the war – was well respected by villains, many of whom he'd known for years. Greeno's police career spanned thirty-eight years and he'd been backing horses for thirty-nine: "If I'd not backed so many winners I couldn't have caught so many criminals, because at both sports you need information, which costs money. A man rarely turns informant just for the money, but he certainly does not remain one without it. And usually it was my own money."

Greeno was renowned for a photographic memory, which he claimed could literally card-index ten thousand criminals into his head, supposedly including every major East End villain. Greeno investigated twelve murders and solved the lot, including notorious wartime child killers Gordon Cummins and Arthur Heys. He even rather proudly pointed out, "That one hundred per cent record is even better than my record with Derby winners." Greeno was awarded the MBE in 1949 and was eventually commended eighty-eight times by judges, magistrates and the commissioners at Scotland Yard.

His policing philosophy was very down to earth: "When police officers say, 'We know who did this, but we just cannot pin it on him,' my answer is 'Nuts.' Either they know or they don't, and if they do then their job is to prove it. I was never rough for the sake of it, but when I saw trouble coming I forestalled it. I have given some villains awful hidings. I think if more policemen showed more villains that it is not only the lawbreaker who has strong arms, we would be nearer the end of this age of violent nonsense."

Greeno made a point of trying to pull in Hill and Spot for relatively minor offences, "just to let them know" the police were watching them. On 23 September 1953, Spot was arrested in a West London telephone kiosk with a knuckleduster in his pocket. He was fined £20 for possession of an offensive weapon. When Hill heard about the Spot arrest he tried to turn it to his own advantage by immediately suggesting to other villains that Spot was getting "too close" to certain senior Scotland Yard officers, claiming he'd heard Spot's name thrown into a conversation in a

West End club by another Yard legend, detective Jack Fabian. Hill claimed Fabian had been threatened by three roughs in the same nightclub, and went out of his way to mention Jack Spot. Others on the premises had apparently raised their eyebrows and taken note.

ELEVEN

Billy Hill commanded the utmost respect in the underworld by always looking after the families of gang members imprisoned on behalf of his firm. When they came out of prison he set them up with cash and clothes, as well as a job. Usually they went straight back into his team as a reward for his loyalty. Hill pioneered an intricate circle of criminal associates, who drew weekly wages from his organisation. Generous 'salaries' were supplemented by 'nips' from the clubs, pubs, spielers and car dealers that, willingly, or unwillingly, enjoyed his firm's protection. Nips could be free drinks or gratuitous gifts from a wide range of merchandise. When Hill's boys grew too old for active work on the streets they were found gentler jobs, like running their own pub or managing a spieler. Hill now considered he was the underworld's number one boss. He continued to openly boast about being the mastermind behind the Big Job. And he didn't scotch the stories that Jack Spot had "gone soft" since his marriage to feisty Rita.

Rumblings of tension between Hill and Spot caught the ear of new Flying Squad Chief Superintendent Robert Lee. His officers were in the habit of swooping anywhere in the Metropolitan Police district, if Lee requested a 'chat' with a villain back at the Yard. Lee was credited with turning 'the Sweeney' into the most efficient force of policemen in the world. But probing blags like the Eastcastle van robbery had proved a difficult task. Sending out Wolseleys, Bentleys, Morrises, Rileys, Railtons and secret squad cars to hundreds of locations across the capital had brought no results. So, with Ted Greeno's backing, Lee decided to turn up the pressure on the big boys.

Lee knew Hill and Spot hated each other, and that if he was patient they'd start creating trouble for themselves. Billy Hill's throne was by no means secure. And there were younger, far more deadly rivals on the horizon.

*   *   *

Just after the Kray twins turned twenty, in the autumn of 1953, they began turning up in the Vienna Rooms, just off the Edgware Road. It was a second-floor restaurant which catered for businessmen, criminals and prostitutes, and also happened to be directly opposite Edgware Road police station. Other regulars at that time included Spitzel Goodman, a dapper little character with thick, black wavy hair who'd at one time been manager of Primo Carnera, the Italian heavyweight champion of the world. Then there was a West Indian called Bar who had most of his right ear missing. He'd served seven years for shooting and wounding a club owner who owed him money. No one gave Bar any aggro. He even owned a famous dog called Bar's Choice, which won the Greyhound Derby that year.

Billy Hill and Jack Spot were also regulars at the Vienna Rooms. They both loved chatting to boxers, and later boasted that they'd sometimes persuaded certain boxers to throw fights. Spot claimed he once arranged for a world champion boxer to take a dive in the first round of a title fight. Apart from clubs and spielers, boxing was a huge pull for villains. The fight game traditionally attracted a mixed crowd including movie stars, lords and ladies, MPs, bookmakers, pickpockets, confidence tricksters, former champs, jockeys, football players, cardsharps, nightclub kings and cheque bouncers.

The young Krays were very particularly impressed by one of Hill's boys, Teddy Machin, born in Upton Park in the East End, close to the West Ham football ground. He'd earlier been on Spot's team but then switched sides around the time of the disastrous 1948 Heathrow job. He had jet-black hair and the looks of a film star. He'd had a run-in with one of Jack Spot's gang, Jacky Reynolds, at the Queens pub in Upton Park, and smashed a broken glass into Reynolds' face, disfiguring him. Reynolds claimed that dozens of villains called him up to offer to help take revenge on Machin. But Reynolds refused, insisting he was still friends with him, and that it had just been a drunken brawl which went one step too far. The Krays were impressed by such loyalty.

But it was undoubtedly Billy Hill and Jack Spot who'd made the biggest impression on the twins. "They were the centre of attraction wherever they went. They controlled London as bosses of the underworld," as Reg would later recall.

Spot had no idea that the Krays had secretly been in contact with Hill. To quote Reg's admiring recollection: "[Hill] had a good brain, and this appealed to me. I learned a lot by observing the way he put his thoughts into action."

Hill was flattered by the twins' adulation and sensed they could become very big players in the near future. He believed in nurturing such characters, not antagonising them. He even put the twins to a bizarre test. One day Ron and Reg, their brother Charlie and friend Willy Malone were at the Kray family home, 'Fort Vallance', when the phone rang. Ron picked up the receiver and it was Hill on the line: "Will you come over to my flat quick as poss?"

"OK, Billy," responded Ron. He then told the others, "I think he's got some kind of trouble. Let's get over there."

The twins picked up a gun each and departed for Hill's flat in Moscow Road, Bayswater, with Charlie driving. As he walked in, Ron said to Hill, "What's the trouble? We've bought some shooters."

Hill laughed, left them in the lounge and went into his bedroom. When he returned, he tossed £500 in brand new notes on to the table and told the Krays, "Take that few quid for your trouble and cut it up between you. I was only testing. I wanted to find out if you would get here fast or if you would blank the emergency."

It was a turning point in the Kray twins' relationship with Hill. They undoubtedly wanted him to stay at the top while they learned the tricks of the trade. Shortly afterwards, however, they beat up a doorman at one of the many clubs under Hill's protection. Instead of being furious, Hill commended the twins, chucked a few more quid at them and announced that he owed them, because the owner of that club would never dare to stop paying his protection money.

As Reg Kray later recalled, "To me, Bill was the ultimate professional criminal. I like to think that in some ways I have come close to emulating him, but in many other ways he stands alone. There will never be another Billy Hill."

At their favourite haunt, the Vienna Rooms, the Krays continued to make their mark. Regulars at the club included dozens of prostitutes, led by a big blonde called Kate, whose Maltese ponce so upset them one night that they robbed his flat, "because we don't like pimps."

The Kray twins were already showing their potential as a deadly duo.

* * *

In early 1953, Billy Hill and Jack Spot turned up in separate limos at the Harringay Arena to see British heavyweight Don Cockell fight Toni Renato, the Italian champion. They didn't cross paths until the bar during the interval. Spot hadn't yet confronted Hill with his suspicions that he was trying to usurp him, as he wanted all the key evidence at his fingertips.

Intrepid *People* crime reporter Duncan Webb was also at the fight, and intended asking Spot and Hill if they'd been involved in dozens of lucrative mailbag and Post Office robberies up and down the country. (Days earlier, £10,500 had been stolen in cash from a Brighton to London train.) But at the end of the fight, Spot and Hill bolted for the exit with hats in hand.

Webb just managed to catch up with Hill. "Well," he said, "What's all the hurry? Something on?"

"See you tomorrow," said Hill. "Be at the end of a phone. I might have something to tell you."

Webb was a classic old-fashioned snoop who started as a cub reporter on the *South London Press* in the thirties, where he'd showed a great aptitude for crime stories. After war broke out, Webb served in West Africa before being invalided out in 1944. He then worked at the *Daily Express* before moving to the *London Evening Standard*, where his obsession with crime didn't prove popular. Webb eventually joined *The People*, edited by Sam Campbell, a keen follower of headline-hitting investigations. By this time Webb was so obsessed with crime that he even assembled dossiers on crimes he hadn't covered and offered them to the police.

Webb's love life even had a criminal element, thanks to his romance with nightclub hostess and murderer's wife Cynthia Hume, whom he eventually married. He publicly exposed the Maltese Messina brothers as the main pimps of Soho in a hard-hitting investigation for *The People*. That article attracted the interest of Billy Hill, who was delighted by the exposé. Webb would soon be writing frequent and highly sympathetic articles about Hill himself.

Webb's attitude toward law and order was profoundly ambivalent. On one hand he nurtured numerous senior Scotland Yard officers, while he also helped promote the almost mythical status of the Heavy Mob and gang leaders like Hill. Webb described Hill as, "A crook, a villain, a thief, a thug," but then added that he was "a genuine and a kind and tolerant man".

Webb didn't care if Hill manipulated him, just so long as he got a headline to blast across *The People*'s front page. And Webb knew that bigmouthed Jack Spot had lost control of his empire.

Small incidents began occurring. One robbery planned by Spot was delayed at the last minute because one of the team never turned up. A number of such crimes were soon cancelled or postponed. Spot's income was plummeting. He noted how some of his more unreliable men were soaking up his angry outbursts before walking straight out on him for a job with Billy Hill.

Spot monitored the newspapers more closely and noticed how many robberies were still being successfully committed by other gangs. Then the *The People* came out with a series of articles in which Hill described himself as 'The Boss of the Underworld'. The articles were sensational, featuring headlines such as 'I'M THE GANGSTER WHO RUNS LONDON'S UNDERWORLD', in which, "Billy Hill tells he took over London's underworld with guns and chivs." Hill even claimed he was about to leave the underworld in an article headlined, 'I'VE MADE MY PILE SO I'M QUITTING.'

Other villains and the police took it all with a very big pinch of salt. They knew what a clever operator Hill was, and how he was using his pet reporter, Duncan Webb, to send a few messages out to friends and foes.

Hill was quoted as saying, "My word is law in the jungle. Today there isn't a single crook or hoodlum with the guts to challenge it. Those who did cross my path when I was battling my way to the top all bear the same ugly trademark – a long chiv scar across the face."

Then he told Webb, "So where do I go from here? Frankly, I haven't made up my mind. For the moment let's say I am content to enjoy the Riviera sunshine. And why should I worry?"

Jack Spot later admitted he should have closed up shop the moment he saw the first *People* article on Billy Hill. Then, as if to prove he was still a big cheese in the underworld, Spot tried to assemble a safe-breaking team for a major bank heist. But once again the villains pulled out at the last moment, before walking out on him altogether. At Spot's Soho office, fights were regularly breaking out between his henchmen. Within hours of each punch-up, they'd quit and more often than not walk 'across the road' to join Hill.

At the racetracks, Spot suspected one of his most trusted henchmen of betraying him to Hill. Each week the man's returns from bookies dropped, and he was making all kinds of excuses about problems in collecting protection money. Dozens of bookies had fallen behind with their 'dues' to Spot's organisation, but the man snapped back, "You can't treat people like dogs. Not these days you can't. You can't threaten. You have to compromise."

Spot then heard that other villains were laughing behind his back, saying he'd been stitched up like a kipper by Hill so he ordered his number one henchman, Moisha Blueball, to help him show the underworld he was still someone to be reckoned with. With Spot's boys Sam and Mugsy in a second car behind them, they headed to the northwest London suburb of Hendon, where lived a bookie who'd refused to pay Spot protection money. On arrival, Sam and Mugsy knocked on the front door before barging past the woman who answered. Moisha and Spot, still in the back of their car, heard a high-pitched scream. Spot turned to Moisha and declared, "There's only one way to make a man toe the line. Let him feel the keen edge of a razor."

Spot's boys emerged from the house with the woman screaming after them, "They've killed him! Murderers!" Spot grinned, tapped Snakes on the shoulder, and off they went. Then he turned to Moisha, hunched in the seat next to him. "You'll find everythin' will be different now, Moisha, me old mate," Spot said, almost light-heartedly. "All that bastard needed was a little incentive to pay up."

That 'incentive' turned out to be a couple of stripes across his backside with a chiv, leaving the bookie with an uncomfortable memory of Jack Spot every time he tried to sit down.

Meanwhile, back in Soho, Billy Hill shrugged his shoulders when he heard the news. He knew what Spot was up to, but he wasn't bothered by it.

Then Spot became paranoid about his loyal lieutenant, Moisha. He wondered if he was still up to the job. Or maybe Moisha was preparing to break away and join Hill, just like all the others? His fears were growing virtually by the hour. He also confronted one of his formerly most trusted fences, an old fellow called Chester, who was now refusing to handle anything from Spot's mob.

Spot barged into Chester's West End office with one of his henchmen, grabbed the old man by the arm and scraped his own diamond ring along the top of his £1500 antique mahogany desk. Hill smirked when he heard about all this. He knew that such incidents could only be good news, as they diverted Spot away from the day-to-day running of his criminal empire.

*   *   *

Racetrack bookmakers – usually minor crooks – were by this time making a fortune. And at those not so well policed point-to-point races, they took even more liberties. It seemed that just about any villain could go to a meeting, stand on a couple of boxes beside a post with a bookie's name on it, and start writing the odds up on a board. However, these so-called bookmakers still had to pay other crooks for permission to use the 'site', plus the chalk and even the water to wipe the board clean between races.

Billy Hill's hardman pal, 'Italian' Albert Dimes – already known as the 'King of the Points' – ran a classic version of this type of protection racket. Dimes' criminal record went back to 1941, when he was involved in the killing of another crook called Harry 'Little Hubby' Distelman at the Old Cue Club in Frith Street, Soho. At the time Dimes was sidekick to the psychotic Babe Mancini, who'd splattered the ceiling with blood while stabbing away at Distelman with a dagger. Dimes escaped with a caution for unlawful wounding.

Dimes was a master at finding dim bookies and placing bets with them just after the end of a race. His right-hand man back then was a fearsome character called Prince Monolulu, a broad-shouldered six-foot-four man with redskin feathers in his hair. Monolulu had a reputation for providing the racing world's greatest tips, which he flogged for a very healthy few bob at a time.

Dimes also organised bare-knuckle boxing bouts at racecourses like Epsom. One Derby Day, he oversaw a fight to the death between one of his boys and a 'pikey' (gypsy) on a strip of field close to the track. Genuine racegoers were barred from entry as the two scrappers tore each other to shreds for a £500 prize. Many thousands of pounds changed hands in bets.

Back in London, Dimes had his finger in other pies, including a tame doctor who exempted people aged eighteen and nineteen from National Service. He was also renowned for getting what were known as dockers' tickets, or books, sold on for a fee. These enabled anyone to work in the docklands, loading boats and

WENSLEY CLARKSON

barges. Dockers' wages were vast compared with most similar jobs, despite the working hours being relatively short. Dimes also used dockers to help steal items like jewellery and watches before they could be cleared through customs.

Albert Dimes was an independent operator with a very astute brain – just the sort of character Billy Hill liked to have on his side.

* * *

Hill always later insisted that his position as Boss of Britain's Underworld was confirmed by the way he sorted out Ginger Randall's feud with the Sabinis ('the Big Meet'). "The Big Meet put the final seal on my authority over gangland, and its propaganda value throughout the entire underworld of Britain was incalculable."

Hill also remained a master at changing tactics in order to confuse his enemies at Scotland Yard. He even ditched his countryside 'run-in' at Bovingdon, which he believed had outlived its usefulness. In its place he opened new offices in the West End and the East End. "From these two vantage points I found that I could keep a fair control over the various enterprises I now governed. My personal fortune was substantial, so I was able to buy my way into certain legitimate businesses, which brought back to me a safe and secure return."

Hill acquired a toy business and several licensed drinking clubs plus various bookmaking enterprises, all of which yielded substantial profits. He also continued to go out of his way to make sure there were jobs for the boys.

TWELVE

Even beyond London – in cities like Manchester, Liverpool, Leeds, Glasgow, even Dublin – Billy Hill's name had become a byword for criminality. Many visited Hill for advice, or to tip him off about jobs, both in Britain and on the continent.

But in the background was the spectre of the Big Job, the 1952 mailbag robbery which loomed over everything he did. As the pressure mounted on the authorities to bring the robbers to justice, Hill began to feel the pressure. His spielers were raided on a virtually nightly basis and his wife, Aggie, suggested that maybe it was time for them to move abroad. She'd also heard all about her husband's other women, of course – especially Gypsy, whom he'd taken on holiday to the South of France with Jack Spot and his wife.

Hill assured Aggie he couldn't be arrested because he'd long since stopped carrying out robberies himself. But still she told him, "Get out while you can with a clean pair of hands. If you go on with this game you're bound to lose in the end. You can't win. No one's ever won."

He didn't blame Aggie for her attitude. She was now forty-two, the exact same age as him. For more than twenty years she'd stood by him through thick and thin, but hadn't fully realised just how committed he was to his empire. Many of his oldest mates were in prison because of crimes they had committed on his behalf. Their families had to be looked after, and the boys themselves needed constant supplies of snout and decent food.

Even so, Aggie relentlessly tried to make her husband begin a new life, even though she knew he had a mistress and other women dotted around town. Then one day she confronted him with a stark choice – it was either her or them. She would not wait for him anymore if he got banged up again. "Billy, if you can't make the break now you've still got the chance, then the best thing for us is to part," she told him. "You go your way and I'll go mine. But I want you to understand that if we do part I'm free to do as I please."

Aggie's attitude had undoubtedly hardened because of his close relationship with Gypsy. But Hill was actually rather relieved. "I didn't seem to care very much when she left me. It was a bit of a relief in some ways. I know, deep down inside me, that it was a relief of my own conscience, and that I was the weaker one of the two."

Hill let Aggie keep the Modernaires Club, the most prestigious place he owned, and bunged her handsomely with cash every now and again. He even bought her a little poodle dog called Chico. But, despite putting on a brave face, he was upset by the split and decided to take off for a holiday to North Africa.

Hill travelled to Casablanca, Marrakech, Algiers, and then across the Mediterranean to Monte Carlo, followed by a stay in the famous Carlton Hotel in Cannes. Then it was back to Tangier before slipping across the water to Gibraltar. Hill adored travelling, as he made clear in his autobiography. "I ate food I had never heard of, met people who were actually kind as well as educated, who were friendly although they were loaded with gelt. Then I came back home."

Hill returned to London more than a month later, completely

refreshed and determined to expand his empire. He began getting a lot of approaches to begin a debt-collecting agency. Many gamblers had debts running into the thousands and Hill knew there were vast amounts of money to be earned. He charged a fee for taking on the job, plus a percentage of every debt recovered.

Hill later claimed in his autobiography that he was then approached about something altogether more sinister – murder. Some of his boys wanted him to turn the job down. But he reckoned there was a way to earn from it without necessarily committing an actual killing. He began with a £300 charge just for considering the job, which involved bumping off another man's former business partner. Hill managed to squeeze out another £200 in 'consultancy fees', and then told the client the risks were too high but he was keeping the money to cover 'legitimate expenses'.

It was a typical Hill scam. He couldn't see any harm in setting up a highly profitable 'Murder Incorporated' business, as long as there were no actual murders committed. Hill later claimed numerous irate husbands came to him about their wives' lovers. Hill and his boys would then oblige all sides by having a "homely sort of chat" with the man in question. "What, in fact, we were doing was preventing stupid idiots from doing desperate acts for which they would have been sorry afterwards."

One such classic case was also that of an angry husband. Hill's trusted new henchman, 'Mad' Frankie Fraser, gave the target a "slap or two" and then told the man to walk around Brighton in bandages. Hill was later said to have received £5,000 for the so-called job. Hill claimed that, during 1952 and 1953, his mob undertook three hundred such contracts on behalf of Murder Inc.

A classic example of Hill's power and influence came in June 1953, when champion jockey Sir Gordon Richards was the victim of a burglary. The raider got away with many items, including a gold cigarette case presented by King George V and golden spurs awarded by *Sporting Life*.

Hill was outraged that such an esteemed hero of the turf should fall victim to a 'screwing'. Hill even used the furore surrounding the Richards burglary to sound off about the so-called "respectable face of crime", telling one newspaper, "To break into harmless Sir Gordon's home and nick the things he treasured most was worse than a blagging." For Billy Hill actually believed he was more 'respectable' than a normal, everyday blagger – which may seem a bit rich, considering his background.

Hill put the word out on the criminal grapevine that he wanted all the missing items returned. His personal involvement was enough to have the desired effect. Within a few hours, the cigarette case and the golden spurs, plus a gold pencil and gold powder compact belonging to Lady Richards, had been handed in at the Yard. Hill happily paid over £300 to the criminal associate who arranged for the safe return of Sir Gordon's stolen property.

Thanks to the Richards case, Billy Hill now had a reputation as the underworld's master fixer. A few weeks later he was approached by a well known businessman who'd had £30,000 worth of jewellery stolen from his home. The problem was that it wasn't insured, so the businessman offered Hill £3,000 for its safe return. Hill worked out it had been an inside job and sent a further message out on the grapevine. Within less than twenty-four hours all the stolen jewellery had been returned. When the businessman was a little slow in paying up the reward, however, Hill kept some of it "on account". The man eventually paid up in full.

But big trouble was never far away. When one of his younger gang members, Slip Sullivan, virtually cut the ear off a Maltese villain in a fight sparked by a complaint from Hill's girlfriend, Gypsy, it almost provoked a vicious war on the streets of Soho.

Sullivan ended up with his throat cut by one of the Maltese's minders, an all-time loser called Tommy Smithson.

Hill knew he was expected to respond on behalf of his boy Sullivan. He put the word out that he needed to have words with Smithson, who – realising he'd severely wounded one of Hill's boys – got scared and went to ground. It was one of Smithson's own bosses, George 'Maltese Joe' Caruana, who fingered him to Hill. As Hill later said of his informant, "Maltese Joe will finger anyone for a fiver. He's that type."

Smithson was eventually tracked down and taken in the firm's shooting brake to a safe house in Regent's Park. Hill later claimed in his autobiography, "He knew he was on the spot, but now I come to think back on it, he had guts, that Smithson. He didn't murmur, didn't scream. Even when we cut him he took it like a man. That was after we relieved him of two shooters. Word had gone round that he was coming to look for me with a Sten gun. So we were well prepared."

Eventually an ambulance was called and Smithson was taken to a nearby hospital. He'd lost five pints of blood and was put on the critical list. When Hill heard the news he warned his boys to expect the worst. The police sent word that they would stop at nothing to arrest those responsible if Smithson died, pointing the finger of suspicion straight at Hill and his gang.

Back in hospital, Smithson refused to name his attackers to the police. As Hill marvelled, "Even while he was breathing what he thought was his last he didn't sing." Eventually Smithson made a recovery and commanded the utmost respect from Billy Hill, who even helped find him work.

But Hill's next big problem came in the shape of a character called Freddy Andrews, who hailed from the same north London manor. Andrews had served a long sentence for cutting an American soldier during the war and had also played a role in the murder of a coal merchant called Alfred Ambridge at his Kilburn home in April 1941.

Andrews liked to shoot his mouth off when he was drunk and had a habit of slagging off Billy Hill to anyone who would listen. Then he began turning up at one of Hill's West End clubs, shouting about what he was going to do to him. In the end, Hill decided something had to be done to Andrews.

A few days later, Billy turned up on Freddy Andrews' doorstep in Camden, and striped him with a chiv when he answered the door. "So long, Freddy," was all he said after lashing out. Andrews went to the police; Hill was charged with grievous bodily harm with intent. He eventually found himself standing in the dock in front of the Recorder of London, Sir Gerald Dodson, who'd sentenced him to his last three spells in jail.

But then Andrews had a change of heart, and told the court he could not recognise Hill as the man who had chivved him. The jury were obliged to return a verdict of not guilty, but Dodson was furious and told them "either the witness does not want to remember or he is afraid to remember". Hill didn't care. As he walked out of the court a free man, his boys gathered round to offer words of congratulation. Even Andrews stepped up to say hello.

At the Modernaires Club, Aggie rounded on Hill after his acquittal and pleaded with him to give up crime. He told her to shut up. His tone implied that he was still angry with her for leaving him. As he later admitted, "I felt like a rat for talking to her like that." Then he put his arms around her shoulders. "It's all right," he said softly to her. "I'm here, that's all that matters."

But Aggie wasn't impressed. "That's all you worry about. You're here. Hah, you're here! That's it. So long as you're all right, everything's all right. Yes, I should have thought of that twenty years ago. I should have done this and left you where you were even before I got hurt."

Hill tried to make her keep her voice down in front of his boys. But Aggie didn't care who heard and carried on laying into him. "You can go away and get lost for all I care. It's been nothing but worry, worry since I've known you. Why don't you leave me alone? Why don't you go away on your own and let me live my life?"

Then she burst into tears. Hill later said he couldn't handle her reaction and left the club. They'd been apart for months already, but her public outburst made him think about the real implications of their separation. He then got one of his boys to take her a bunch of flowers, plus an envelope with a monkey in it. He knew she was better off without him.

"The dull sort of passion with which I had loved her was no longer throbbing inside me. It had been replaced by a loyalty, a strong feeling of friendship. Then I knew. It wasn't me she loved any more. It was what I had represented to her. The hope and the prospects. I knew that any love she had had for me I had worn away through the years. The years during which I had climbed out of the slums of Camden Town to reach the zenith of financial riches."

Billy went back to the apartment he now shared with his fiery lover, Gypsy, and decided that maybe it was time he looked for pastures new. He had it in his mind to leave the country for a while, to try to come up with some new scams.

But just before he departed, a character called French Toni popped into Hill's New Cabinet Club. He had a proposition that involved a job in the Mediterranean. There was a guaranteed fee of £50,000, and it sounded as if there was little or no risk of arrest. But this wasn't about robbery, Toni explained. Hill's mission was to bring the respected Sultan Mohammed V of Morocco back to Tangier from exile in Madagascar – where he was living with a dozen or so wives after being replaced by the immensely unpopular new Sultan, Mohammed Ben Aarafa, whose reign was perceived by many to be illegal.

Hill was intrigued but highly suspicious. For starters, French Toni was nothing more than a Soho spiv with a few vague connections in France. When Hill nailed him down on the money, he was told he'd be paid in US dollars. Toni also claimed that the main reason Hill had been put up for the job was that if he turned it down he'd keep his mouth shut.

Two nights later, Hill and French Toni were ushered into a stucco-fronted mansion in Belgravia by a butler. Hill immediately noted down the locks on the street door in case he decided to get a team to come back and screw it. He even glanced around the walls to see if there was any sign of a safe.

Then a man with a strong French accent and a big diamond ring on his left hand bounced into the room to greet 'Mister Eel', as he called him. Hill was introduced to five other men in an upstairs room and the plan was outlined to him. "As he was rabbiting away I was thinking a bit fast like as to how I could get out of Madagascar, break into wherever this Sultan geezer and his broads were kept, nick him, and then get him all the way back to Tangier without being tumbled."

Hill then pointed out some obvious home truths, like how he'd need a boat or a plane to transport the Sultan back, plus a virtual army of men and loads of weapons, not to mention a hefty cash advance to set things up.

Then the man with the diamond ring – who Hill called 'Big Rock' – outlined the financial side of things. He told Hill he'd be paid a total of $250,000, plus a guarantee of "perpetual sanctuary" in Tangier for the rest of his life. Hill calculated what the payment would be worth in sterling – £84,000 – and said it wasn't enough. He wanted £100,000 or it was no deal.

Big Rock explained the request to his five other colleagues and then agreed to £100,000 plus £25,000 expenses. He offered half before the job, with the rest of the cash paid upon successful completion of the mission. Hill demanded a minimum advance of £10,000 before he'd properly consider the job. The foreigners eventually agreed to his request, and he said he'd take two days to think over the job.

Initially, Hill thought he'd just take the £10,000 and then pull out. But the more he considered it, the more he began to reckon he really could pull it off. He and two of his most trusted lieutenants, Patsy Murphy and old prison pal Franny Daniels, decided to use international smuggling as their cover. It was well known that the Moroccan government ignored such criminal activities, which had been an accepted part of life in Tangier for many generations. In fact, the proceeds from smuggling allegedly provided much of the financial support for many of the population.

Hill liked the sound of it but needed a skipper to run the boat, someone who genuinely knew their way around in terms of navigation. He'd also require an engineer. By the time Hill went to bed that night the skeleton of a plan was formulating in his head. He tracked down an old mate who'd just sold his yacht and hired the former skipper of the vessel, a character called Mike Henderson. That evening Hill went back to Big Rock and subbed £5,000 expenses from him on the spot.

Skipper Henderson recommended a Fairmile Harbour Defence motor launch as the perfect vessel for Hill's mission. The former Royal Navy launch was driven by two powerful diesel engines and could reach speeds of twelve knots, fully loaded with up to seventy tons of cargo. The best aspect of the boat was that it only needed a crew of six. Henderson soon spotted the perfect vessel in Torquay, Devon. Hill haggled the price down to £2,900 as it needed £1,400 worth of repairs.

Hill then went about choosing his team. Murphy and Daniels

were a certainty. Then there was a young ex-boxer known as 'Stevie the Sledgehammer' who'd recently fought for a major championship. Hill later wrote in his autobiography: "He was a hefty lad in his young twenties and, in my opinion, ready for anything. He was not a crook like me, but I knew he would not regard this venture as being crooked. Political I suppose you could have called it, more than anything else."

Also on Hill's team for this special mission was Square Georgie, one of his oldest mates. He even ended up recruiting his onetime Camden Town enemy Freddy Andrews as an engineer, to sort out the mechanical problems on the boat, although he had no intention of taking him on the actual job.

While Hill was sorting out his team he also came across a fascinating character called Eddie Chapman at the Star pub in Belgravia, where Hill had been drinking his favourite non-alcoholic tipples for a few months. Chapman had been a notorious screwsman before the war, and had actually been imprisoned in Guernsey when the Germans overran it. He was offered his freedom by the Germans if he spied for them, and he duly obliged. Then, after he'd parachuted into Britain, he became a double agent. As Hill acknowledged, "You have to give [Chapman] his due. He even returned to Germany after that and continued spying for them. Then he doubled for us again." After the war, Chapman got mixed up in a political scandal in West Africa; since returning to Britain he'd kept a low profile.

Hill knew straight away that Eddie Chapman would be a key component on the mission to get the Sultan back to Tangier. He spoke French and German, knew all about nautical engines and had just the right kind of personality to fit in with everyone else. In February 1954, Hill went to see Big Rock in Belgravia to report that they were almost ready to embark on their mission. He gave a full account of where the £5,000 advance had been spent and explained the entire rescue plan. Hill intended to go to Tangier to make it known he was in the smuggling game. Then, once the authorities had accepted them as smugglers, they could drift further up the Mediterranean, through to Suez and then down to Madagascar. By that stage the boat would no longer be known as the Fourth Lady – its original name – or be registered under the British flag, which would save a lot of legal complications if anything went wrong.

By the following month of March the ship was ready to sail. Hill had completed negotiations with the Central American republic of Costa Rica to re-register the vessel under their flag, so that British authorities would have no jurisdiction over it. However, when Chapman and Hill arrived to set sail, they found to their horror that the boat had already sailed without them.

The boat hit major storms in the Bay of Biscay, off the coast of Spain, and since its crew – apart from skipper Henderson – of assorted criminals had never been on a boat before, tempers became very frayed. With Henderson gripping tight to the helm as they tossed and turned through the treacherous waters, his motley crew were on the verge of mutiny. The only reason Henderson survived was that the villains on board knew that, if they killed him, they wouldn't stand a chance of reaching dry land.

After the storm died, the waters calmed as they passed Oporto on the Portuguese coast and the crew painted out the name *Fourth Lady* and substituted *Flamingo*. Eventually the razor-edged bows of *Flamingo* cut through the still waters of Tangier harbour.

A few hours later, Hill and Chapman landed by air in the Moroccan city. Hill was so angry with Henderson for leaving ahead of him that the skipper went to the Tangier police to complain of threats. The copper assigned to investigate his claims turned out to be an Englishman called Colonel Watson, in charge of the special branch of the international police force assigned to keep law and order. The city was awash with tobacco, diamond, arms and dope traffickers, political plotters, refugees and fugitives from justice of all shades.

Hill summed it up when he later wrote: "The scores of other mobs who had floundered about in Tangier were relatively boy scouts compared with the potential [the police] saw in our sudden descent on the city." But at least the authorities had no idea of the real purpose of Hill's voyage – until Scotland Yard sent Watson a bulky dossier on the gang.

"The most they could say was that we were a band of robbers and burglars," noted Hill, "that we were suspected of having been concerned with the Great Mailbag Robbery, that we might have been connected with the attempted robbery of £1,000,000 worth of bullion from London Airport in 1947, that I was the guv'nor of Britain's underworld, that Eddie Chapman had been a screwsman and a spy and had got himself involved in West African politics, that Andrews was on the run from a job for which he had been nicked since I had employed him. And they most likely said that we were there to nick whatever bullion or currency notes we could lay our hands on."

Even Interpol, based in Paris, fired off some warning shots about the notorious London criminals now dubbed *Los Bandidos Ingles* by the locals. Rumours flew around Tangier that Hill and his boys would be targeting vaults and strong-rooms. As Hill recalled, "Apparently we'd come to raze and pillage the city of its wealth. No jeweller was safe. No bank would dare open its doors on the morrow. Post offices of all nations were vulnerable to this ruthless band of robbers who had come from the place which housed the world's greatest robbers." The local press even dubbed Hill, "The King of Soho", "The Bandit King of Britain" and "The Great Bandit Who Frightens Scotland Yard". Most damagingly, one paper even dubbed Hill's newly re-registered vessel "a pirate ship".

As Hill described, "In the cafes, cabarets, bistros, restaurants, in the streets and narrow alley-ways, the populace followed us crying out, 'Mister Flamingo. You like a drink. You like nice girls. Plenty dancing. Plenty drinks. All free to Mister Flamingo.'"

Then Colonel Watson paid Hill and his boys a visit. Watson was extremely nervous of Hill, who tried to put the copper at ease by being open about himself and the rest of the gang. Hill claimed he had "got tired of villainy" back in London and had come to the Mediterranean to "undertake a spot of smuggling".

The following day, Watson requested that Hill and his boys visit his headquarters. He asked for them to pose for mugshots and provide fingerprints. Hill knew all their dabs had probably already arrived from Scotland Yard, so he didn't raise any objection.

Then the radio operator and skipper Henderson, both of who'd fallen out with the rest of Hill's boys, disappeared from Tangier, leaving Hill without a captain or technician. "We were in Tangier with not a living soul on board who knew the back end of a ship from the front," Hill later recalled. "I thought to myself, 'never mind.' The sun is warm. We've got a few bob between us. We might as well enjoy ourselves while we're here. Enjoy ourselves? Tangier didn't know what hit it."

THIRTEEN

Billy Hill's boys began getting a little carried away with the relative freedom of Tangier. Many of them started drinking a lot more than was good for them, and spent a lot of time and money on local women. One night Hill's boxer-minder, Stevie the Sledgehammer, went on board the *Flamingo* and stumbled across Square Georgie and the volatile Freddy Andrews, bashing each other to smithereens. Andrews had Georgie on the deck and was belting him very hard with a hammer, blood spurting all over the place. Stevie belted Andrews before Square Georgie got hold of the hammer, and began to bash the life out of Andrews in return. "They all finished up in the local hospital, telling all sorts of stories to try and hush the matter up," explained Hill.

The following day, Hill got two more of his boys over from London and onetime spy Eddie Chapman came up with a new skipper for the boat. His name was Bill Beamish, and Hill immediately fitted him up in some nautical gear he'd bought back in the Smoke.

Meanwhile, crowds of locals would come down to the quay to look at the *Flamingo* every day. One morning, Hill got the shock of his life when two British Navy submarines pulled in alongside his vessel. He was working out the legal fees he'd incur in trying to get bail before he realised they were on a routine cruise.

The officers on the submarines even invited Hill and his boys into their wardrooms for drinks. "God knows what they thought about us, Londoners in charge of a Costa Rican ship in Tangier, and not one of us, except old Beamish, who could tell the difference between a marlinspike and a left-handed spanner."

Apart from the dapper former spy Chapman and Hill himself, they were a motley crew by anyone's standards. There was Stevie, the big lump with a broken nose, Andrews covered in chiv scars, and odd bod Patsy Murphy. Even Hill must have looked a little sinister, with his chiv-marked face and slightly awkward manner.

*   *   *

Hill knew he needed to be active while in Tangier, otherwise the authorities would begin to wonder why he was there in the first place. So Hill and Chapman started 'smelling out' some smuggling contacts. It wasn't a hard task in a city like Tangier. There was no duty on tobacco and there were also no currency restrictions back then. American cigarettes could be bought for five pence a packet and then sold on to Spanish, French and Italian dealers for as much as double the price. With tens of thousands of cartons smuggled out of Tangier every day, it was a massive business. But Hill's main aim was merely to mask the arrangements to bring the Sultan back to Tangier.

When one of Big Rock's associates made contact with Hill, it was to tell him that there were real fears that the appearance of him and his mob had sparked so much interest that the job might be at risk. Hill's main contact was a man called Yustef, a sheik with a penchant for silk robes and manicures. Hill couldn't take his eye off the gigantic diamond ring on Yustef's hand. He warned Hill that the enemies of the Sultan were everywhere in the seedy city of Tangier, and agreed to set Hill up in business with an American smuggler to provide a convincing cover story.

Hill even formed an insurance company while in Tangier called the Anglo-American Fidelity Company, with capital of £70,000. The scourge of insurance companies and banks was now in a legitimate insurance business, backed by an American bank. And just a few hundred yards from his office was his ship *Flamingo*, crewed by the toughest and most ruthless bunch of villains ever to tie-up in Tangier.

It was May 1954, and Tangier was hit by swelteringly hot weather. Hill's main problem at the time was keeping all his crew occupied. As he later explained, "Idle men are dangerous men, especially when they're villains. They were drinking far too much as well." So while he was making plans to smuggle the Sultan back in, he was also trying to launch a few smuggling runs just to keep his boys busy and earn a few quid. He also knew it was good for his mob to get back out on the sea.

Hill also got in with a couple of local smugglers, who lined him up with a hazardous job involving cargo which had to be delivered just off the Portuguese Atlantic Coast. Most Tangier smugglers wouldn't touch the assignment because it was at a lethal drop-off spot called the Balingas Rocks. But Hill saw it as a perfect opportunity to break into the business. It would also get his team off his hands while he quietly got on with making plans for the job that really mattered.

So the *Flamingo* was loaded down to the gunwales with sixty-five tons of American cigarettes. Hill was given an upfront $50,000, the first half of the payment. With new skipper Beamish in command, he watched from the quayside as the *Flamingo* glided out of Tangier under the cover of darkness.

It turned out to be a disaster. Halfway through loading the cigarettes onto a local vessel in the Atlantic, Chapman went on board the boat to collect his money and two Portuguese bandits tried to attack him. He pulled a knife but one of the other men knocked it out of his hand. Chapman shouted to alert the boys on the *Flamingo*.

As soon as Stevie the Sledgehammer heard Eddie Chapman's voice, he and the others grabbed their guns and jumped on board. When they got into the cabin, they saw Chapman just about to give one of the Portuguese a dig. Stevie stuck his shooter into the ribs of the head man, while Square Georgie and Franny waved their weapons in the air. Then Stevie barked at the man, "Come on, you bastard. Hand over the dough, that's all we want." The British gangsters then made the Portuguese count out every note of the fifty grand in dollars that they were owed. Then, after Chapman had packed the lot away, Stevie slung a couple of vicious right-handers at those Portuguese "just for luck". He later recalled, "You should have seen the mess we left them in. Don't think they'll want to do any more business with us again."

After the crew had sorted out their local difficulties, the *Flamingo* almost hit the notorious Balingas Rocks. The motley crew stood on the deck convinced they were about to die, as the *Flamingo* passed so close to the rocks that they could hear the hissing of the sea rushing passed them. They didn't even have time to find the lifejackets. In the end they were saved by the fast tidal race, which shot the Flamingo between the rocks "like grease through a goose" according to Stevie. As he explained, "You know, I saw all my past life in those few minutes. I saw myself as a kid, then as a schoolboy, then I thought of my girl. Blimey, I thought to myself, I'll never even see her again. Then I saw my mum sitting in our kitchen at home, and I knew more than anything else in the world that this was my lot, our lot. I knew it was all over. Then suddenly we were in the open sea being tossed about like a cork. Blimey, I don't care how high we were tossed that night. I wouldn't have cared if we had been turned upside down after getting through those rocks."

Ten days after setting out for the Portuguese coast, the Flamingo motored back into Tangier harbour. When Hill heard the full story of the smuggling fiasco he decided it was time they got on with the real job at hand. His final negotiations with the deposed Sultan's people were virtually completed, and he'd definitely had his fill of Tangier. Hill's gang had been on the piss virtually ever since they arrived and there had been numerous flare-ups between his boys and the locals.

The Spanish were particularly angry with the Brits at that time, because the Queen had been on a visit to nearby Gibraltar, which had greatly upset General Franco. Hill and his boys found themselves having to listen to appalling insults to Her Majesty and Stevie the Sledgehammer was soon back in action, swinging punches at any Spaniard who wouldn't button it.

One night, Hill was so upset by the anti-British insults flying around a café that he ordered Stevie to lay into one particularly noisy 'dago'. As Hill later recalled, "The Spaniard went down like a sack of spuds." But within minutes all hell had broken loose in that café, as the Spanish and a bunch of locals came at Hill and his gang with chairs, tables, bottles and anything else they could lay their hands on. Then the hammers and bits of lead piping came out. Hill ordered his boys to 'swallow it', to keep their guns out of sight and head back to the *Flamingo* immediately. However, that meant fighting a rearguard action all the way down the hill to the harbour and along the dusty, darkened road to the quay where the *Flamingo* was berthed.

Freddy Andrews and Square Georgie were desperate to tool up and have a go back at the Spaniards, but Hill was adamant that every crew member should stay on board the ship that night. He didn't want the law coming anywhere near him before he set sail on the Sultan job.

It turned out to be an inspired decision, because in the early hours a local boy tipped Hill off that the same Spaniards from earlier were planning to set fire to the *Flamingo*. Hill and his boys searched the ship for hammers, Stillson wrenches, spanners and any sort of weapons to use on the Spaniards. There was no moon that night so it was difficult to see any movement from the quayside. They lay flat on the deck in the darkness and waited. Half an hour later, Hill spotted a number of dark figures hiding behind the buildings near the ship's mooring.

Hill crawled over to where Stevie was standing behind the wheelhouse and counted twenty-nine figures out in the pitch dark creeping towards the ship. "Right!" he shouted. "Let 'em have it." Hill and his mob then leapt ashore, hitting out at anything and everyone within reach. The Spaniards fought back viciously with hammers and coshes, their superior numbers forcing Hill and his boys back to the boat where they regrouped before charging into them yet again. Hill once again takes up the story: "It was either them or us, and we knew that once any of us went down the leather would come in and we would be kicked into unconsciousness. Then after that it would have been anyone's guess as to who dumped our limp bodies into the drink."

Out of the corner of his eye, Hill saw a Spaniard bringing a cosh down on young Stevie's head. He immediately knocked the cosh out of the Spaniard's hand. "I thought I heard a bone broken as I struck. The Spaniards were hooting and hollering, but the more they yelled and screamed the harder we hit them."

Eventually the Spaniards were split apart by the viciousness of Hill's mob and retreated. The gang spent two hours washing blood from the deck and gunwales at Hill's insistence, in case Colonel Watson appeared on the scene. Then Hill posted watchmen and turned in for the night. He hoped for a lie-in the following morning but Watson was up early, insisting that Hill and his boys go down to his office.

The only member of the group who spoke French was Eddie Chapman, so he was given an expulsion order to read out to Hill and the others. "Then like mugs we all signed it," Hill later declaimed. When he asked for "a bit of time to get things straightened out", he was told in no uncertain terms that it took immediate effect.

(He did manage to hire a local lawyer, Moishe Cohen, who tried unsuccessfully to get the order delayed, but when he discovered it had been personally signed by the present Sultan's personal representative he quickly gave up the battle.)

Hill immediately ordered Chapman back to the ship to fill the fuel tanks and get in a supply of fresh water. Then he was told by Yustef to sail thirty miles further along the coast, to the Spanish territorial port of Ceuta, where someone would be waiting to meet the *Flamingo*. Within minutes of arriving, an Arab came aboard and gave Hill instructions to go to a specific café in Ceuta the following morning, to ask for a coffee and wait to be contacted.

The following day Hill went to the café and a man introduced himself as Ahmed, telling him in a booming voice, "The message is that you will have to wait until a new plan is formed. Do not stay here in Ceuta too long. It is not good. Go to Genoa. You will find friends and business there."

Back at the boat, Hill consulted Eddie Chapman, who was far from hopeful: "If you ask me, it's all over. I think the best thing is to swallow it and try to cut our losses." Hill was worried because he believed Interpol and the local police where constantly watching them. But Chapman said he didn't believe they'd bother sending ships to sea just to intercept them smuggling.

In the last week of June 1954, the *Flamingo* cruised steadily across the Med from Ceuta to Genoa. Within a short distance of Italy, it dawned on Hill that the local police would probably inform Interpol of their visit. He ordered skipper Beamish to head for the smaller nearby port of Savona. But within minutes of arriving, dozens of uniformed officials were swarming all over the boat. It seemed that the whole of the Mediterranean had been alerted to the *Flamingo* and its crew of vagabonds.

Hill and his boys were immediately ordered not to leave the ship and an armed policeman was put on sentry duty at the end of the gang plank. Then a police car full of Italian coppers raided the vessel, armed with revolvers and machineguns. After they pulled mattresses apart, crawled underneath the diesel engines and even inspected the inside of the steering compass, Hill shared a drink with the Italian police chief in charge of the raid. He eventually saluted Hill and Beamish and departed, but not before he'd ordered some of his men to remain on board.

Hill and Chapman were still allowed ashore that evening, and headed for the luxurious surroundings of the Astoria Hotel. The police followed them throughout, even watching from a doorway as they ate dinner. Hill tried to get his shadow to join him for a drink but he refused, so Hill sent him over a beer instead.

The following morning, Hill got ex-boxer Stevie to put his training kit on and go for a ten-mile run. "That'll show 'em how to tail you," Hill told his young minder. Stevie stepped ashore in his plimsolls, shorts and sweater and started off at a steady boxer's trot with his police shadow – in heavy uniform, carrying his gun – running after him for five miles through the streets of Savona. In the end, the Italian copper was so exhausted he gave up.

Naturally, the English *bandidos* were attracting a lot of attention in Savona, with crowds of locals standing on the quay just looking at the *Flamingo*. Hill later joked that he could have made a fortune charging fees to tour the vessel, but the police wouldn't allow it. Whenever Hill or his boys ventured ashore, they'd be followed by dozens of nosey Italians, as well as an armed policeman.

When Hill and Chapman decided it was time to shake off their police tails, they dived into the doorway of a small hotel and waited behind a palm tree in the reception area. Their two shadows headed straight for the bar, so Hill and Chapman slipped quietly out of a side door and back onto the street. Hill's next stop was Genoa.

The two men jumped on a bus and, once in Genoa, headed straight for the main railway station, which they walked through and out the other end in case anyone had been following them. Then they strolled into the Hotel Londra and ordered a drink. Just to be certain there was no tail on them, the two men then slipped out of a side window of the hotel to continue their journey, hailing two cabs in quick succession.

Their eventual destination was the Hotel Terminus, from where they telephoned their contact on the Sultan job. Five minutes later their contact, who called himself Giuseppe Dominica, walked through the door accompanied by three heavy looking types. As Hill explained, "It was a monumental sparring match for about half an hour. I didn't know what he had to offer us, and I don't suppose he knew our weight exactly."

Then one of the mobsters, an Arabic looking type, explained that Hill and his gang had attracted so much attention in the Med that it would be a waste of time trying to complete the business they'd originally gone to Tangier for. Hill was steaming mad and made sure they knew it. They tried to compensate by cutting him in on a big smuggling operation, but Hill wasn't impressed. He later recalled, "The whole business stank. I knew this was the pay-off. But there was little we could do about it. The man who called himself Giuseppe explained in broken English that they had a small but valuable cargo, which needed to be transported in the *Flamingo*."

Hill knew immediately it had to be drugs, and he'd always kept to a firm rule never to smuggle narcotics. "Sorry," he said apologetically to Giuseppe. "We don't run dope. It's not our cup of tea."

The Arab tried pleading with Hill but he refused, turning to Chapman to signal for them to leave. The Arab said he might have "some other work" for Hill and his boys that wouldn't involve narcotics. Hill told him to get in touch with them in Savona.

Hill and Chapman then took a taxi back to where the *Flamingo* was moored. As they were walking down the quay an armed Italian policeman sprang out on them, although he did not attempt to approach them. At least half a dozen other coppers then appeared from various hiding places as an obvious show of strength. Hill ignored them. He was more surprised by the size of the crowd looking at the *Flamingo*, which now numbered thousands. He and Chapman pushed their way through them all and headed up the gang-plank. They were then told by Franny Daniels that a *Daily Express* photographer had been arrested by the police.

By this time, the Italian newspapers were treating the arrival of the *Flamingo* in Savona as a threat to world peace. Radio and newspaper reporters swarmed down to the quayside. Hill was dubbed 'the King of Bandits' and Chapman 'the International Spy', while the *Flamingo* was renamed 'the Mystery Ship'. Hill and his boys were overnight international celebrities. A TV crew eventually turned up and made a documentary programme about them.

The Italian police continued tailing Hill, Chapman and the rest of the gang morning, noon and night, keeping armed guards on the ship all the time but still searching it at regular intervals. Whenever Hill and Chapman stayed the night in the local Astoria Hotel, their two shadows – christened by Hill as 'Charlie' and

'Aubrey' – had to sleep outside the rooms. Journalists from as far away as America started arriving and other reporters were constantly telephoning from London.

When the coppers swarmed on that boat one morning, one of them secretly told Beamish to inform Hill that Giuseppe wanted to meet him at the same place in Genoa where they met previously. At the crack of dawn next morning, Hill patted his shadow Charlie on the back and, knowing he couldn't speak a word of English, said to him, "Never mind, cock. We're going to scarper again today like we did the other time. Savvy? Yes, no?" Charlie looked puzzled for a moment, then broke out into a huge smile.

Within minutes of reconvening with Giuseppe and the three other hoods, Hill had been offered a few tobacco runs between the Balearic Islands and France. The Arab confirmed the big job was off but claimed that, once the authorities in Tangier had lifted their expulsion order, it could get underway once more.

Just then Giuseppe chipped in to say he would be taking a five per cent commission on all smuggling operations. Hill barked through interpreter Chapman, "Tell him that's all right by me, but no dope, no penicillin, no narcotics." Then one of the 'mobsters' revealed himself to be a lawyer, producing a contract which Hill and Chapman signed on the spot. Giuseppe told Hill his agent would meet the *Flamingo* in Barcelona, and the deal was done.

Hill and Chapman made their way back to Savona, to find Charlie and Aubrey were so furious with them for escaping that they'd stolen a shipment of American cigarettes as punishment. Hill wasn't worried. His only concern now was to set to sea as soon as possible, and to start earning some cash again. Forty-eight hours later, the *Flamingo* was steaming out of Savona harbour as crowds of locals cheered them on. One of Hill's boys even fired off a homemade firework as a fond farewell to the Italians.

Hill decided not to head straight for Barcelona, because he

surmised their visit might spark as many problems as it had in Savona. So the *Flamingo* sailed in the direction of the island of Corsica. Hill took to the island's capital, Bastia, like the proverbial pig in shit. As he later wrote, "It was my idea of Heaven. Nowhere in the world are there such beautiful girls. Nowhere are there such kind people."

The only problem was, as ever, the police. They immediately arrested Eddie Chapman as a spy, and Beamish became so unnerved by the never-ending dramas that he wanted to quit. He was particularly upset about his friend Chapman being arrested, but when Hill's boys pretended they were about to storm the local police station to free him, Beamish got so scared that he retreated to his cabin.

Chapman only stayed in jail overnight, and was released the next morning without charge. Hill then ordered that they set sail for Barcelona. But the *Flamingo* ran straight into a storm and Beamish insisted they head for Toulon, a naval base. Once they were anchored, Hill went ashore and headed off to Cannes for a business meeting, Beamish having assured him the weather would not improve for at least forty-eight hours.

The next evening, Hill was gambling in a plush casino in Cannes when he was told that he was wanted on the phone urgently. It was his faithful minder, Stevie the Sledgehammer. "They've set fire to the ship. It's blazing like hell," he told Hill.

Stevie explained that Hill's old enemy Freddy Andrews had come back on board drunk in the early hours, thrown Beamish down into the engine room and set fire to it. The blazing *Flamingo* was moored between a load of petrol tanks and a French cruiser called *Richelieu*, which made it a potential powder keg. The oil down in the ship's engine room blazed for hours, and when they finally rescued Beamish he was rushed to hospital, telling anyone who would listen that Hill's boys had tried to kill him. He even claimed they shouted at him, "You'll roast alive, you old sonofabitch. We'll show you how to run a ship."

When Hill got back to Toulon he discovered the engine room had been gutted, although the engines themselves did not seem badly damaged. A local surveyor put the cost at £1,000. Beamish claimed he'd been forced at gunpoint to sign a statement admitting responsibility for the blaze, while three of the crew had disappeared completely. Hill knew this was the end of their Mediterranean adventures. He'd even started to wonder if there was a jinx on the *Flamingo*.

Then, to make matter worse, the local police put an armed guard on the ship and refused to allow any repairs until a proper sabotage investigation had been carried out. Hill shrugged his shoulders and returned to Cannes, to think things over. At least he could enjoy some sunshine and win a few bob at the casinos.

* * *

Billy Hill slipped back into London in the late summer of 1954, but made sure that as few people as possible knew he was back in town. He'd seriously depleted his finances while abroad and had numerous criminal schemes up his sleeve, keeping a very low profile at his relatively modest flat in Moscow Road, Bayswater.

On 21 September 1954, Hill masterminded a robbery at the Holborn offices of the KLM airline, where raiders got away with two boxes containing £45,500 in gold bullion after a company lorry was hijacked during rush hour. Hill almost immediately came under police suspicion but was able to prove that, at the time of the raid, he was in the offices of *People* reporter Duncan Webb, recalling a version of his life story as 'Boss of the Underworld' to be published the following Sunday.

In the article, Hill even claimed he was about to quit Soho for good: "I'm not afraid any more. I know now that the law always wins in the end. So I'll talk. I suppose the least I can do before quitting is to tell those young mobsters who want to be like me a few home truths."

It was all classic Billy Hill duplicity. A couple of weeks later he even provided Webb with some details of the KLM raid for another article. Hill was immensely proud of this "brilliant" criminal enterprise, although he was careful not to actually incriminate himself.

FOURTEEN

The sheer audacity of the KLM job left the great British public gasping – not to mention the rest of the world. Even small-town American papers covered the robbery. The copper leading the investigation was the soon-to-be-legendary new head of the Flying Squad, Superintendent Guy Mahon. Hill's old foe, Chief Superintendent Bob Lee, had recently left the Squad to head up the Met's Number Three District.

Ironically, the robbery had taken place on Lee's new manor and he was furious, as were many of the Yard's other top brass at the time. Hill later said that the new commissioner, Sir John Nott-Bower, seemed more interested in London's parking regulations than catching the team behind the raid. "It was the sort of job that appealed to the humour of the British people. Why, the gold didn't even belong to an English firm."

The police finally woke up about forty-eight hours after the raid and rounded up all the usual suspects. They included members of the gang who were nicked for the London bullion job in 1947, also organised by Hill.

Multiple telephone taps were authorised by the top brass at the Yard, and Hill and his associates enjoyed winding them up by laying false trails over the phone. To add to the confusion, the police were inundated with calls from the general public telling them where the gold was hidden. One caller got in touch with the Flying Squad and told them it was hidden in a house in Lavender Hill by a bloke called Guinness. (It was all a grand piss-take, referring to the film *The Lavender Hill Mob*, of course.)

Eventually the law did locate the van used in the raid to nick the gold, plus a couple of sets of false number plates, but nothing else. When Lee and Mahon pulled in all of Hill's mob, they discovered every one of them had an airtight alibi. Two of them were reporting a road accident in Southend when the robbery took place, another was in a club in the West End, and so it went on.

Inevitably the police then went after the man himself. They'd only just realised Hill was back in London after his Mediterranean adventures. So on 27 September 1954, dozens of officers raided Hill's toy warehouse, plus a suite of offices in the East End which he'd owned for years. Hill just happened to be on his way to the warehouse early that morning when he noticed a plainclothes policeman in the street nearby.

He immediately hailed a cab and drove past the building, where he spotted dozens of plain-clothes men hanging around outside. Hill ordered the cabbie to take him straight to his solicitor's office. He immediately made a statement denying any involvement in the KLM job and then accompanied his solicitor back to the premises.

Inside the warehouse the police were ripping open every box, closely examining every toy doll and teddy bear. Hill later put his customary humorous spin on the proceedings: "As they held up the dolls to look at them they murmured 'Aaah,' and as they turned over the teddy bears they in turn grunted 'Oooh.' In the end the place sounded like a blinking zoo with all the 'oohs' and 'aahs'."

In Hill's upstairs offices the police showed him the underfelt of a carpet, and claimed they had found the impression of a heavy box imprinted on it. Hill said he couldn't see it, but they insisted it was there. Then they showed him some wooden chips from a wooden box. As Hill explained in his autobiography, "The implication was that the wooden chips had been torn off one while it was supposed to be in that room. Rubbish! No such boxes had ever been on my premises, and I said so. But they insisted that that is what it was all about."

Hill was furious, insisting to the police that the so-called impression should be immediately photographed, as well as the wooden chips. His solicitor took down a verbatim account of everything that he said. An hour and a half later, the photographer turned up and began snapping away. What followed gives an insight into Hill's devious criminal mind. He was determined to ensure there was no way they could fabricate the evidence.

Hill insisted all the photographs should be taken a second time, but refused to explain why. He then pulled a ten-bob note out of his wallet and placed it on the felt, so the number of the note was clearly visible for the photograph. "Now take it," he told the snapper. "Because with this photograph there cannot be any doubt about where and when it was taken. That's all I wanted to be sure of."

Then he made them do exactly the same with the wooden chip and the ten-bob note. As Hill later explained, "I wasn't going to have those photos confused with any other issue if anything came of it."

After the photos had been taken, Hill told one of the senior officers at the scene, "Now I want to make a statement." The detective's eyes lit up and he stood up and took out his notebook.

"What I want to say is this. If ever the police take me in, I will not and I have no intention ever of making a verbal statement without the presence of my solicitor. Put that down in your book and remember it."

During a search lasting nine hours and utilising dozens of

policemen, not one thing linking Hill to the KLM job was found. The Yard made many more similar raids all over London in the following weeks, but never discovered any trace of the gold. Some years later, Hill claimed the gold bars of gold had been, within hours of the raid, smelted down with copper and silver, so that no expert in the world could positively identify it as connected to the stolen bullion. Then it was buried in the garden of a very wealthy man.

Hill also claimed that, a few weeks before the bullion raid, a KLM airliner had crashed on the mud flats of the River Shannon, just outside the Irish airport of the same name. The aircraft contained a fortune in gold bullion and diamonds, and a couple of villains travelled over from London to take a look but could not get near to the plane as it was so closely guarded. Still they stayed on the job, and followed the precious cargo as it was transported across Europe. It was during their surveillance that Hill's team discovered all about the transportation of the bullion from a bank in the City of London to the Dutch KLM airline's office at Jockeys Fields. They tailed the lorry used to move the shipment and timed every single aspect of their movements. This was the origin of the KLM robbery.

*　　　*　　　*

Not long after the KLM bullion raid, Hill opened yet another club in the West End and proudly announced it as being, "A perfectly respectable place where ordinary people can go and dance and drink." Hill was trying doubly hard to convince anyone who would listen that he'd gone straight.

Billy Hill remained a brilliant manipulator but also continued to inspire great loyalty. He had his own tame lawyer, Patrick Aloysius Marrinan, a well-built, jovial Irishman who'd read law at Queen's University, Belfast, and was even at one stage the Irish

Universities heavyweight boxing champion. Marrinan's legal career had started badly, however, when he was arrested on 15 May 1942, in a Liverpool hotel by police investigating a watch and jewellery smuggling ring.

When the officers began a search of Marrinan's hotel room, they found a suitcase containing hundreds of watches and bracelets and £126 in cash. The following week he pleaded guilty, but it was claimed in court he had been duped and had no idea he was breaking the law. Marrinan was fined £4,500, with the choice of serving three months' hard labour if he couldn't afford to pay the fine.

His offence effectively kept him away from the legal profession for another ten years. He successfully appealed against a rejection by the Bar Council to stop him practising and, in 1951, joined chambers at London's Middle Temple. At first he struggled to makes ends meet, but then he represented a couple of notorious burglars who were close to Billy Hill, and soon his name was circulating in the underworld as that of a "fine brief".

Hill liked the look of Marrinan, who became a regular visitor to his other newly acquired London apartment, overlooking the Thames in Barnes, southwest London. In fact, Marrinan eventually moved into a flat in the same Victorian mansion block, and many believed that Hill paid for it. Marrinan later denied such close connections, but they were regular drinking companions and there is little doubt that Marrinan was dishonest. He was renowned for his ability to pass messages onto criminals while they were in custody.

*　　　*　　　*

By the mid-1950s, Billy Hill and Jack Spot shared a love of the limelight, but little else. Spot disapproved of Hill's relationship with Gypsy Riley, and how Hill had left his wife, Aggie, running the Modernaires Club off the Charing Cross Road, as well as the Cabinet Club in Gerrard Street.

On the racetracks Spot's power and influence had already diminished, thanks to Hill's hard-man associate, Albert Dimes. But for the moment Spot chose not to confront Hill.

Spot had presumed that Hill had been running away when he took off for Tangier earlier in 1954. But Hill never had any intention of moving out of Soho, and saw Tangier as nothing more than a pleasant diversion. For his part, at one stage he had suspected Spot might have organised the fire on board the *Flamingo* to teach him a lesson. Now very much back and settled in London, Hill told his boys he wanted Spot taken completely out of the picture.

Spot was confused and infuriated by Hill's reappearance, and failed to appreciate his new manoeuvres. Hill put feelers out around various London gangs and a number of meetings were arranged in West End pubs. Elephant gang member Brian McDonald recalled, "We all waited our turn. Mine came in late 1954. Hill bought the drinks in the Bath House in Soho's Dean Street, where he'd laid on a tasty buffet."

McDonald's gang – from south of the river – had earlier in the fifties formed a tentative alliance with Jack Spot. The Elephant Boys first established their reputation through a series of battles with other gangs in the 1920s and, by the 1950s, had such a fearsome reputation that many gangs in other districts paid to hire their services. However, most of them came not from Elephant and Castle, but Walworth and Old Kent Roads, Kennington, Lambeth, Waterloo, Blackfriars, Peckham, Camberwell and the Borough.

But not all villains were impressed by Billy Hill's big plans. Jack Spot's old south London sidekick, Johnny Carter, was convinced the gangs would never work together and made his feelings known at another meeting called by Hill. Carter got so infuriated he picked a fight with a couple of rival mobsters, before venting his anger on *Sunday People* crime reporter Duncan Webb – who was Hill's personal guest at the meeting. Brian McDonald later recalled, "Carter gave Webb a nasty tongue-lashing and we all watched as the others tried to steer him away from Webb's table." Carter's anger was directed mainly at the 'ponces' (his word for safecrackers, pickpockets and conmen) whom Hill associated with. He hated the way Hill remained in the background, raking in a fortune while his soldiers took the real risks and often ended up in the nick. The meeting ended with Carter storming out.

Within days Hill approached the Italian mob, still based in Clerkenwell, with a "peace plan" – although the Sabinis were not exactly the force they had been before the war. Once again, Carter blew a fuse when he heard about Hill's manoeuvres and went out of his way to cut Hill's emissary to the Italians, Billy Blythe. The deal then quickly collapsed.

Jack Spot knew what Hill was up to, and it was bothering him deeply. Spot even gave one of Hill's new young tearaways a "right kicking", when he had the effrontery to tell Spot not to show his face at one particular West End club. That same man worked alongside Hill's 'envoy', the fearsome freelance gangster and racecourse hustler 'Italian Albert' Dimes. Hill didn't care if Spot worked out the connection. But predictably Spot, according to one witness, "went fuckin' bananas" when he found out.

Spot and his tinderbox pal, Johnny Carter, then began openly bragging in Soho that Billy Hill was heading for a big fall and they were going to make sure it happened. Hill quickly got wind of the situation and openly recruited a nasty, American-born chiv merchant based in Kentish Town, Scotch Jack Buggy. His job was to get Jack Spot. The cycle of violence was escalating.

Elephant Boys member Brian McDonald later recalled hearing

Spot had been targeted by Hill, just before he stumbled on Buggy lurking outside the Galahad Club in Soho. McDonald explained, "I walked right past him. Buggy pulled a revolver from his overcoat pocket and pointed it at my face. I remember the metallic click as it failed to go off. He fled, but he couldn't outpace me. I brought him down by grabbing the belt at the back of his overcoat."

Word of the incident reached Spot so quickly that he and two henchmen arrived on the scene within minutes. One of Spot's boys then ran a knife down Buggy's face and thighs, the only parts not covered by his heavy overcoat. As McDonald recalled, "The road was busy, so we left him there. In time he limped back to Kentish Town." Over the years, Buggy continued to make a habit of being a nuisance. It wasn't surprising when his body was later found bobbing around in the Channel, off Seaford, Sussex, after he'd been shot – allegedly on the orders of Albert Dimes.

* * *

In early November 1954, Spot met Hill's favourite reporter, Duncan Webb, in a Soho caff and informed Webb he wanted him to write "a story about the underworld" in retaliation for those earlier articles penned through Webb by Billy Hill, after the KLM raid. Webb tactlessly told him he wasn't interested and suggested that Spot go and see the *Sunday Chronicle*. His dismissive attitude infuriated Spot who then told Webb, "If you do anything to interfere with this I will break your jaw." Spot then complained bitterly to Webb about Hill's other big Fleet Street mate, Hannen Swaffer, whom he claimed had made up a story about him in *World Press News*.

A few days later, Webb was lured to a meeting in Soho when someone pretending to be Billy Hill phoned him. It turned out to be Spot, who walked straight up to Webb in the street and told him to come quickly to see the 'injured' Hill. As they got towards Bainbridge Street, Spot turned and punched Webb between the eyes, saying, "Take that, you fucker; I'm runnin' this show."

Spot then grabbed Webb by the lapels of his coat and began shouting, "I'll give you Billy Hill. I'll give you fuckin' Billy Hill." As Webb tried to get away, Spot struck him in the stomach, before missing with another blow.

Webb suffered a fractured arm and reported the incident to the police. When officers called at Spot's flat in Hyde Park Mansions later that day, he told them, "What's it about – that rat Duncan Webb? He's a dirty rat to the police and the public after what he has put in those articles."

Spot was later arrested and eventually admitted causing Webb grievous bodily harm. He was fined £50, plus twenty guineas costs or three months in prison. Spot contested an application by Duncan Webb for damages, which included £140 for a shorthand typist to type his articles while he was incapacitated, £42 for taxis and also medical fees. Damages totalled £732 against Spot.

Meanwhile in Soho, Spot's few remaining henchmen were starting to bicker like kids. Two of his toughest boys, Johnny Carter and Bobby Brindle, had a serious falling out after Brindle's brother Jimmy was beaten up by Carter's brother Nicky. Carter then gave Brindle a stripe down his cheek and shortly afterwards Brindle joined Billy Hill's gang.

In early 1955, Jack Spot tried to have a "friendly chat" with those young tearaways the Kray twins, because he knew they were on the rise. He still had no idea they were in close touch with Hill. The Krays were particularly amused because they'd already decided Spot was not really worth nurturing anymore. Ronnie's head was filled with dreams of gang lordship. He wanted the war between Spot and their real mate, Billy Hill, to worsen, so that he and Reggie could surge through to rescue the underworld. They'd fuelled much of the tension, thanks to a word in the right ears. After Spot left his meeting with the Krays, he told one of his henchmen, "Those two are real trouble. We'd better keep an eye on them."

In February 1955, Hill further justified his title of 'Boss of Britain's Underworld' when a bank strong-room in London was torn open by a gang of highly professional villains. The basement walls were of twenty-two-inch thick concrete and the massive steel door of the safe was blown off. £20,300 in easy-to-pass fives, ones and ten-shilling notes were stolen.

Ted Greeno – still one of the top commanders at Scotland Yard – took personal charge of the robbery investigation. He threw himself back into the groundwork he so adored and headed off to round up the usual suspects. Hill was naturally top of his list. Spot cheekily hoped the outside world might believe he was involved in the job, but he was really seething because he knew Hill was the organiser.

Shortly afterwards, the *Sunday Chronicle* published a series of articles 'by Spot', ghost-written by reporter Vic Sims. Spot insisted he was still the guv'nor of guv'nors, with a duty to make sure that trouble didn't flare up in Soho. Hill read the articles with amusement. Webb had already told him the articles were harmless, and they certainly didn't refer to anything Hill didn't already know about.

Then the Kray twins got themselves nicked for demanding money with menaces. As they were charged at City Road police station, Ronnie Kray made a reference to Jack Spot which sent a shiver up detectives' spines, because they weren't even aware of a connection between the Krays and Spot, let alone Billy Hill.

Ronnie insisted to police that he and his brother had been grassed up by people they'd been 'blacking', which meant blackmailing or demanding money from. Ronnie was also charged with possessing an offensive weapon – a sheath knife. Many years later, the Krays concluded that Spot or Hill might have been behind their arrest. They believed that one of the two had grassed them up, because they wanted to teach the twins a lesson. And their money was on Jack Spot.

*   *   *

In March, 1955, at the Puckeridge Hunt, a point-to-point in Bishops Stortford, held on the same day as the Grand National, Billy Hill recruited a bunch of toughies including Pasquali Papa and Tommy Falco, who'd been working the main race-courses alongside Italian Albert Dimes, by now Hill's number one minder. Meanwhile, Jack Spot had been telling anyone who'd listen that Dimes "couldn't bodyguard a flea".

So in the space of just a few months, Billy Hill had retaken Soho once more and Jack Spot was fading fast. However, the manipulative Krays also claimed they'd been "keeping an eye on things" while Hill was away in the Med, making sure no one got ahead of them.

Then the new police guv'nor of the West End, Superintendent Herbert Sparks, began trying to make a name for himself by cleaning up Soho. Sparks used the new Prevention of Crime Act of 1953 to regularly pull in gangsters whom he thought were overstepping the mark. They were seldom charged with anything, but at least the police could fire a few warning shots across their bows.

Meanwhile, Hill's new top dog, Italian Albert, was making a real nuisance of himself. The tall, gaunt-looking Dimes turned up at a Soho party hosted by a big face in the underworld and then managed to insult Jack Spot's wife, Rita. As she walked past him, Dimes said loudly to a pal, "I'd love to get my hands round that." Rita turned and glared at Dimes, and then told her husband what had just happened. Spot phoned Hill to complain about Dimes' behaviour, but Hill didn't even bother returning the call.

Hill's main priority was building up his number of troops. His recruitment drive included men from west, north and east London, including two of Dimes' favourite tearaways, Battles Rossi and Johnny Rice, who'd once been in the Sabini Gang where he'd used the name 'Johnny Ricco'. Not surprisingly, Jack Spot was growing increasingly attached to his home life. Most evenings he'd leave Soho early and slip back to his apartment at Hyde Park Mansions, to be with his family.

FIFTEEN

By the spring of 1955, Jack Spot was finally waking up to the fact that the Kray twins needed nurturing – although he had no idea how close they already were to Billy Hill. Spot invited the two East End brothers to the flat racing at Epsom, knowing full well that Hill would be there as well. He even gave the twins special pitches of their own, plus introductions to bookmakers who'd work for them exclusively. Hill cleverly kept a distance. He knew from the Krays that they were just playing with Spot, who'd even promised them they could keep a dollar (five shillings) in the pound profit from all takings. Epsom races were a traditional annual outing for many London villains, and whoever controlled the leading bookies' pitches could expect a percentage of the take from every bookie on the course. At Epsom all the villains were on the lookout for a smile, or even a simple brush-off, to see who was on the up-and-up. A handshake implied an old grudge had been long forgotten. Looking away from someone naturally implied the opposite.

The Kray twins later openly admitted they were far from impressed by 'Spotty', and said they only accepted his offer because it might be interesting. 'Interesting' was one of Ronnie's favourite words. "We never had liked Spotty. Never thought much of him," he said many years later.

At Epsom the Krays kept a friendly eye on Billy Hill, who had the number one pitch close to the winning post and was surrounded by minders, including the infamous 'Mad' Frankie Fraser and Billy Blythe, who earlier took a cut from Johnny Carter and was also renowned for a conviction for cutting a Flying Squad officer's face.

The Krays insisted on parking their car close to the pitches provided by Spot. As Reg later explained, "Ron and I and a friend of ours, Shaun Venables, had two or three revolvers in a briefcase hidden away in the car, just in case of any gang warfare."

The Krays might have been relative newcomers, but they were already convinced they could destroy their enemies whenever they felt like it, with many of them present at Epsom that day. One Italian gang member sidled up to Ronnie and told him, "This lot mean business. You two must be stark staring mad to show up here with Spotty. If you want to kill yourselves, there are less painful ways of doing it." The twins laughed and offered the man a drink. When he'd gone, Ronnie turned to his brother and said, "The way these old men worry, Reg. Fair makes you sick."

Billy Hill deliberately and shrewdly continued to keep his distance that day, as racing and betting took second place to posturing. Ronnie Kray eventually settled into a quiet little corner, yawned and rolled over to sleep. A few hours later the Krays collected what was owed to them and drove off, without even a word of thanks to Spotty.

*   *   *

Hill knew that the underworld was on the verge of big changes. Once again, he decided it was time to try pastures new.

In April 1955, in the middle of all the rising tension, he booked himself and Gypsy onto the maiden voyage of luxury liner the *Southern Cross*, bound for Australia. The moment Hill departed,

Jack Spot tried to rally his diminished troops to reclaim what he believed was his territory in the West End. But Hill had very good cover, including his new right-hand man Dimes, who was ready and willing to take on all comers.

Hill would even claim to have secretly closed down his office, sold his home in London and sent his main possessions ahead to Sydney. He also had some letters of introduction to contacts in Australia, including some acquaintances of the Queen's husband, Prince Phillip.

On board the *Southern Cross*, Hill and Gypsy got friendly with three other couples. No one on board had any idea who he was. As he later recalled, "I was just wealthy Mr Hill to them."

Five weeks after the *Southern Cross* set sail, police boarded the ship as it sailed off the coast of Wellington, New Zealand. They had a message from the Australian immigration authorities, refusing Hill permission to visit their country. One of his oldest pals back in Soho had sold the information about his trip to a newspaper, who'd passed it on to the authorities. Hill was also banned from landing in Wellington.

While in kiwi waters, Hill cracked a joke to his fellow travellers about travelling to Australia. "Transportation for life," he called it. But why was he aiming to settle in Australia? As he explained, "In our [underworld] language we are wide boys and the rest of you, people who go straight, are mugs. Well, I have always wanted to be a mug. I wanted to get away somewhere where it is warm, where my name would not mean anything. All the Australians I have met have been pretty broadminded, so I thought of Australia."

As the liner was crossing the Tasman Sea between New Zealand and Australia, Hill and Gypsy joined a group of reporters and kiwi farmers enjoying a holiday voyage. "It makes you sick when you think we have come so far – and then for this to happen," she complained. "If only we had known sooner we could have got off at one of the other places we have called at. Even at Tahiti – wouldn't we, Billy?"

Hill didn't respond, but moments later the couple disappeared off to their cabin on A deck. While all the other passengers would be allowed to disembark at Sydney, they remained onboard the *Southern Cross*.

It was then that Hill encountered Australia's most fearsome policeman, Ray 'Machine Gun' Kelly, head of Sydney's detective force, who came on board the *Southern Cross*. As Hill later explained, "When I heard he'd shot two Australian gangsters in the past eighteen months, I was prepared to treat the guy with some respect."

The two men shook hands, and Kelly said, "Struth, I never thought I was going to meet a guy like you. You're too mild and quiet to be an underworld guv'nor." Kelly advised Hill to stay on the ship and the two men parted in mutual respect. Kelly kept in close touch with Hill and even asked him to give a group of local councillors a tour of the ship the following day, when he was called away on a murder investigation.

After Kelly's departure, newspaper reporters, cameramen, newsreel photographers and radio commentators all swarmed onboard. As Hill later claimed, "No British ship has ever had so much publicity as the *Southern Cross*." At one time, there were seven thousand people clamouring aboard the ship to try and spot the famous British criminal. Hill was even cheered by launches full of harbour sightseers as he leaned over the deck-rail. Boatloads of people went out in the warm late autumn sunshine to see the new twenty-thousand ton ship. And as they caught sight of Hill watching them, they waved and shouted, "Sorry you can't stay!" and "Hard luck Bill!" Hill waved back and then, as the decks began to fill with visitors, went below and slipped into a silk dressing gown, resting in his berth and keeping out of sight.

Hill even charmed the reporters who swamped the ship by offering them cigarettes from his brown leather case. "I thought I would be judged on the present, not on the past," he reflected, insisting he had given up crime long ago. But Hill was resigned about going home. "I've had legal advice and there is nothing else for it," he added.

"It was like being a curious animal in a zoo," he later said of the experience. One of Sydney's most notorious gangsters even came on board the *Southern Cross* to persuade him to get involved in a job. Hill turned him down flat, suspecting he was being set up by the police.

A lot of Australians actually thought Hill got a raw deal, and the couple were showered with gifts from locals including a boomerang, koala bears, and even an orchid for raven-haired Gypsy. All throughout, Billy Hill kept wearing his customary smiling face. He was often to be found sitting in his immaculate, London-tailored evening clothes in the ship's smoking room, supping a fruit-cup known on board as a 'pussyfoot'.

Hill told one reporter, "Life aboard has been pretty slow. Dances, whist drives. No gamblers, though. I am a professional at dice and cards and used to pick up £3,000 or £4,000 a night. The best I could do here was win a £12 'housey housey' pot."

At one stage, Billy and Gypsy got so bored he encouraged her to put on a modelling show for the dozens of newspaper men who'd boarded the liner. Gypsy paraded in £10,000 worth of furs and jewellery for Hill, who said, "You brought them all the way from England so you might as well give them an airing." She even told reporters, "I would like to correct Scotland Yard's description of me. I am five foot four inches and not five foot five inches. I must have had high heels on the day they photographed me."

Just before the liner left Sydney, Hill's new best friend, Machine Gun Kelly, wrote him a note: "I wish you God speed and good luck." He also got dozens of other letters from strangers about a wide range of topics. Some were begging letters, which Hill tore up. Another one was from a clergyman who believed he could cure him of evil and lead him onto the path of righteousness. Hill threw that one overboard. There was even a letter from a man who thought he knew Hill's father "when he was a school master in England". Hill concluded it was someone who simply shared the same name.

As the *Southern Cross* sailed there were at least ten thousand people on the dockside to see her off. Many of them even threw streamers and shouted, "We want Billy Hill!" Hill later claimed he got on so well with the captain and crew that they banned newspaper reporters from cabling stories about him back to London. The skipper also allowed some of his most notorious gangster pals from South Africa to come onboard when the vessel stopped there en route.

Typically, Hill refused to pay another £1,000 for his fare home on the luxury liner and he and Gypsy were forced into a smaller cabin, next to some noisy refrigerators. By the time he arrived back on British soil, he was actually very happy to be home.

Gipsy walked down the gangplank at Southampton Docks wearing a £5,000 mink coat, with diamond rings flashing half an inch across her fingers. Fourteen cases of clothes disembarked with her. But throughout that homecoming voyage, Hill remained coy about his travelling companion out of respect to the long-suffering Aggie.

He also claimed to the pressmen during a conference in the liner's smoking room that he was considering buying a castle in Carmarthenshire for £30,000. "Country life for me," he insisted. "I'm through with town. I want nothing more than a peaceful life." Brushing down his £40 black suit, picking specks of dust off his white shirt, he continued, "Now I realise Britain is the best country, though I had got a bit fed up of it."

So Hill stepped ashore, on the same jetty where he had left for a new life in Australia, thirty thousand miles and just one hundred and two days earlier. And there to meet him, on 10 June 1955, was an entourage worthy of the King of Soho. First, a high-powered limousine picked up Gypsy before another gas guzzler drove Hill – carrying two fat briefcases – to a secret rendezvous in London's East End.

Not surprisingly, Aggie certainly had no plans to welcome her husband home. From her home paid for by Hill, near St Pancras station, she told one reporter, "You see, I heard about that girl Gypsy, who was his companion aboard the liner. I've forgiven him in the past when he was naughty. But this is too much." Though Aggie did assure the reporter she would still remain friendly with Hill.

Hill was given a homecoming party in a Soho club where he sat quietly, chainsmoking, sipping on fruit juice. His abstemiousness underlined how he liked to present himself, the respectable businessman in control at all times. Hill even claimed to one journalist that he had been approached to make a documentary about his life story for "an American commercial TV station".

*   *   *

Over at Ascot racecourse, just after Hill's arrival back on British soil, Jack Spot caught his top man, 'Italian Albert', sneering in his direction. "That geezer's got dead eyes. He's a right fuckin' nutter," Spot told one racecourse pal. "Someone needs to take a pop at him. Teach him a lesson."

Hill's most famous henchman, Frankie Fraser, insists to this day Dimes was never an aggressive man. "But he was six foot two and very powerful," said Fraser. "You'd really have to provoke him before he'd lay a finger on you."

Spot was still deluding himself into believing he had power and influence in the London underworld. In August 1955, he bumped into a fence called Nukey who told him, "Everybody's been warned off you." He informed Spot that his own pals had stitched him up, warning him to forget trying to put together another mob and to tread carefully.

That same morning, Albert Dimes telephoned him. "I don't want you to go away racing no more," he told Spot.

"What the fuck you on about?"

"You've had enough. You been goin' away all these years. It's about time someone else had your pitches."

Spot was virtually spitting blood. He headed over to a favourite Soho club for a drink. He later recalled, "But as soon as I walked in there was dead silence. Everyone looked at me and then looked away." As he walked across the dance floor to talk to one familiar face, he heard others mentioning his name and then laughing behind his back. Spot was about to front up one of the offenders but then decided to leave instead.

He stumbled out of the club in a daze. He began walking across Soho, not even noticing the traffic whizzing by and the familiar faces on the street corners. Then he bumped straight into Nukey again, who told him that Dimes wanted to see him. Spot was furious. Nukey made it sound like he, the great Jack Spot, was some kind of nobody who had to go running to Billy Hill's flunky when he snapped his fingers. Spot told Nukey to tell Dimes to fuck off, and then headed home.

The next morning, Spot was again advised to meet with Dimes, "or else there could be some bother."

Spot was outraged. *Albert Dimes has the impudence, the bare-faced, diabolical impudence to threaten he'd do me up,* Spot thought to himself. He was swelling up with a blind rage. So, on that morning of August 11, 1955, Spot found himself striding through the West End with a worried grimace on his face.

As Jack Spot came out of Charlotte Street, just north of Oxford Street, he bumped into Elephant gang member Brian McDonald on his way to a drinking club in nearby Rathbone Place. Spot gave him a warm greeting and offered to buy McDonald a salt beef sandwich. McDonald reluctantly agreed and, as the pair strolled across Oxford Street and into Soho Square, Spot nodded to some familiar faces. In Frith Street, barrow boys were selling fruit while illegal bookies watched for the police and hordes of shoppers swept along the pavements.

Then Spot noticed Billy Hill's associate, Albert Dimes, walking just a few yards ahead of him. Spot marched straight up to him.

"I want you, Dimes," panted Spot.

Dimes looked Spot straight in the eye.

"You been talkin' big," snarled Spot. "You been spreadin' the word around I'm to come and see you. You been talkin' like a strong-armed guy."

"Take it easy, Spotty," responded Dimes. "Don't blow your top, mate."

Brian McDonald was astonished by what he was hearing.

"You been talkin' too big," repeated Spot, sounding almost like some kind of clichéd Chicago gangster.

"Let's go somewhere quiet and talk it over."

"Don't treat me like a nobody. I've had my troubles. But I'm still a big man. I'm bigger than you'll ever be."

Then Dimes said quietly, but very firmly, "Face up to it, Spotty. You're finished!"

"We'll soon see if I'm finished," yelled an increasingly irate Spot.

Then Dimes repeated, "You're finished, Spotty. What's more,

it's about time you were finished. You've had your day. And this is a final warning. Get the fuck out of here."

At that moment Dimes gave Spot a big shove. It was like a red rag to a bull.

As McDonald later recalled, "He put one right on Dimes's chin. Italian Albert went down like a sack of spuds." As Spot started giving Dimes a few more kicks for good measure, another man, Johnny Rocca, tried to pull Spot away. Then MacDonald stepped in. He explained, "If I didn't, all my respect would have gone with everyone. I jumped on Rocca and we pranced around like a couple of old time dancers, not really wanting to mix it. He kept screaming at me, 'Are you in this? Are you in this?'"

When Spot's hand dropped into his pocket to find his blade, he suddenly realised he didn't have one on him. Those few moments enabled Dimes to hit back at Spot viciously. It was turning into a full-scale battle. Spot later said it was then he felt a blade slice through his arm.

The pair, now locked together, tumbled into a display of vegetables outside the Continental Fruit Store, on the corner of Frith and Old Compton Street. All around them people screamed and shouted. But Spot later said all he could hear was Dimes' heavy breathing as something sharp continued to plunge in and out of him.

Proprietor's wife Sophie Hyams grabbed the scales, made out of heavy cast iron, and hit Spot over the head, splitting his scalp open. By this time, at least a hundred people had gathered outside the Continental Fruit Store.

Spot said he then wrestled the knife from Dimes as they fought inside the shop. Others said Spot grabbed a potato knife and stabbed Dimes a couple of times. It was frantic, life or death. Dimes eventually slumped against the doorjamb, before falling out onto the pavement outside the store. Spot also staggered out, with blood seeping down his trousers. Dimes somehow managed to hail a passing taxi, was helped in by a passer-by and driven away.

At the same time, Spot slithered slowly and painfully down a girder onto the pavement as the crowd continued watching. He was bleeding from his neck, ears and head, and his one hundred-guinea suit had huge chunks torn from it. Spot eventually struggled to his feet and staggered a few yards before slumping into a nearby Italian barber's shop. "Fix me up!" he told the proprietor, in front of startled customers. Spot grabbed a towel and dabbed roughly at his wounds. Then he collapsed unconscious on the floor.

Minutes later an ambulance took him to Charing Cross Hospital.

Police cars raced up Frith Street and reinforcements were soon on their way. Within an hour word had got round all the usual underworld haunts that Spot and Dimes had been involved in a fight. And as the names spread across the West End, people who'd earlier been talking openly about what had happened suddenly lost their memories.

*   *   *

At two hospitals, five miles apart, Jack Spot and Albert Dimes lay badly wounded. Both men were vulnerable to any gangland attempt to knock them off. Spot lay in a bed in the Charing Cross Hospital protected from view by a yellow curtain. Two Yard men remained close by at all times. Spot was barely able to open his eyes and he insisted to the police, while falling in and out of consciousness, that he couldn't remember anything that had happened. His head and throat were swathed in plaster and bandages. He'd suffered a total of nine stab wounds including a punctured lung, just a quarter of an inch from his heart. So much air had seeped into Spot's belly from his wounds that he'd swollen up like a half-inflated balloon.

Over at the Middlesex Hospital, Albert Dimes' forehead cleft had been ripped open right down to the bone and was held together by twenty stitches. His abdominal cavity had only just missed being penetrated and other injuries included cuts to the chin and left thumb, plus a wound on the left thigh.

When Dimes was first told he and Spot were to be charged with GBH, he got so angry that he told the police, "It was Jackie Spot. I'm not prossing [prosecuting]. Spotty does me up and I get pinched. That can't be fair." But later, in an official statement to the police, he would only refer to being attacked by "a tall man . . . I don't know his name. I don't want to kid you, but in the struggle between us I must have cut him up with my knife. If I did use it, it was struggling for my life."

When Spot heard he would also face GBH charges, he told police, "Why only me? Albert did me and I get knocked off."

Billy Hill's tame reporter, Duncan Webb, gleefully celebrated the downfall of 'Jack Spot – the Tinpot Tyrant' in *The People* the following Sunday. He even wrote that, at last, "the mob had discovered what I had known for years – that Spot is a poseur who had got away with it." Webb was out for revenge following his earlier encounters with Spot. Naturally, Billy enjoyed every word of it. In fact, he positively encouraged Webb to write the article.

It became clear that Hill's fingerprints were all over the piece when Webb wrote, "Billy Hill has earned his position as London's Gangster Boss, and by the sheer force of his personality he has kept the peace in the underworld and seen fair play." Spot was once again furious about an article written by 'toerag' Duncan Webb and obviously inspired by Billy Hill.

Meanwhile, Hill and his henchmen took over Spot's pitch concessions at race meetings while the injured gangster lay seriously wounded in hospital.

Scotland Yard feared an outbreak of gang warfare and Soho was flooded with extra police. Traders were better protected than they had been for years. But nothing materialised.

However, across the Thames was a very different story. Battles flared up with alarming regularity between gangs from the Elephant and Castle and Deptford. A lot of the trouble was sparked by thriving street betting. Gangs invaded their neighbours' territory and told bookmakers' runners that, in future, all bets had to be placed with bookmakers sponsored by them.

Back in Soho, the fight between Dimes and Spot meant London's Square Mile of Vice was now perceived as a lawless society where ordinary, decent, law-abiding citizens feared to tread. Jack Spot's attempts to be Soho's peacemaker seemed laughable, and the police were now under pressure to clear the streets of every criminal – including Spot and Hill, or whoever was in command of London's underworld.

In Soho, Hill's outspoken estranged wife, Aggie – still running the Modernaires Club in an alleyway off Frith Street – told reporters, as she waved £2,000 worth of diamonds at them, "You won't find anyone here who knows Jack Spot or Italian Albert. I can only say they are two lovely guys. That's all."

On Monday August 22, 1955, Spot and Dimes appeared at Marlborough Street Magistrates Court to face the charges. They stood together in the dock with three policemen sitting between them. At one stage Spot looked directly at Dimes who didn't even glance back at him. Both men were remanded in custody for a week. The following day in custody in Brixton Prison, Spot was heard discussing the possibility of paying a former Scotland Yard detective £1,000 to appear as a witness for him at his trial.

Shortly before Spot and Dimes' trial started at the Old Bailey, Billy Hill and his sidekick 'Mad' Frankie Fraser popped down to the races at Brighton to visit a wealthy Brighton bookie called Sammy Bellson, the guv'nor of Brighton racetrack and a supposedly close friend of Spot's. They claimed they were collecting money for Albert Dimes' defence and hoped that Spot – awaiting trial in Brixton jail – would get the message about Dimes' immense popularity. Bellson immediately contributed £500 because, as he later explained, "I knew what would happen if I told 'em to fuck off." Later that same afternoon at the races, Fraser was arrested by Scotland Yard detectives after police were told he was about to shoot another of Spot's supporters.

Billy Hill actually proved rather adept at persuading Spot's boys to contribute to Dimes' defence. Faces like Teddy Machin and Jackie Reynolds dropped Spot like a brick. Hill even encouraged them to visit Spot in prison and tell him exactly why they were joining Hill's mob.

Billy Hill's West End headquarters was now deliberately low-key after run-ins with the police. It was above a shabby spieler he ran at the top of a filthy stairway, just off Shaftesbury Avenue. However, Hill still owned two impressive London residences, the flat in Barnes, close to the Thames, and his favourite apartment in Moscow Road, Bayswater, nearer to the West End. Hill had three full-sized poodles in the flat in Barnes, which he and Frankie Fraser often took for walks out onto the nearby common.

Billy Hill remained a man of many contradictions . . .

SIXTEEN

On 19 September 1955, Jack Spot, now aged forty-three, and Albert Dimes, aged forty, appeared at the Old Bailey to face charges arising from the Frith Street battle. Spot's face gave little away as he sat in the dock alongside Dimes. The court heard that, during the fight, Dimes got hold of Spot's knife despite serious injury. Then he was alleged to have done to Spot what Spot had done to him, "namely, to stab him several times." The key was whether the jury felt that Dimes was in lawful possession of the knife, having wrestled it from his alleged assailant.

Judge Sir Gerald Dodson described Dimes as a "strong-arm man" during his summing up. "The inference is raised. Why, on going to interview a strong-arm man, did he [Jack Spot] not arm himself?" Judge Dodson even conceded, "He is entitled to defend himself, and if a knife is being used, he is entitled to turn it on the assailant." As Spot listened intently from the dock, he felt hopeful of an acquittal.

Just over an hour after the jury had retired, they came back into the court and announced that Spot was "not guilty". He leapt up and down in the dock, shouting and screaming so much that the judge snapped at him, "Behave yourself, Comer!"

The following Monday, 26 September 1955, it was Albert Dimes' turn to appear at the Old Bailey to answer the same charges as Spot. Dimes' counsel, Mr 'Khaki' Roberts QC, insisted there was no evidence to go before the jury. "I submit that when a man runs in the street, runs in the shop, runs until he cannot get any further, then it is a grave misuse of language to call that a fight." Mr Roberts also submitted that there was no evidence against Dimes of wounding with intent to cause grievous bodily harm to Jack Spot.

The prosecution then took Judge Glyn-Jones' advice and unanimously voted to withdraw the charges against Dimes. The judge told the court, "From the moment the [Spot] verdict was announced on Friday night, it would be quite improper for a jury to be asked to find him guilty on this charge, especially as all the other witnesses in the other case said the other man was the assailant. It is not for Dimes to prove that he was acting in self-defence. It is for the prosecution to prove that he was not." The judge then said, "I think in all the circumstances, all I can do is to discharge the jury."

So Billy Hill's henchman, Albert Dimes, walked out of the Old Bailey laughing.

Jury members had been put under special police surveillance throughout the two Old Bailey trials, just in case any attempt was made to 'nobble' them. At one stage, detectives noticed Soho gang members hovering near the jurors during lunch-breaks and adjournments. But police never had any firm evidence that they had influenced the jury.

So the world was expected to believe that neither Spot nor Dimes had attacked the other, even though they both had been seriously wounded. Home Secretary Major Lloyd George opened an inquiry into the acquittals, explaining to the press, "There is a need for an inquiry as to whether or not some witnesses were tampered with."

The publicity surrounding the 'fight that never was' showed the great British public that a thriving criminal underworld still existed on their very doorstep. Fleet Street newspapers were incensed that people like Jack Spot and Billy Hill had been allowed to boast of their crimes in the pages of their rivals. Papers who'd failed to secure the villains' exclusive stories tried to turn the case into a moral crusade. There were also demands for more arrests following the internal investigation by Scotland Yard supremo Ted Greeno.

By the end of September 1955, the conventional wisdom in Soho was that Jack Spot was yesterday's man. Many of the up-and-coming new faces hung out at the Granada coffee bar, in Berwick Street, where they also happened to demand money with menaces from the owners.

Old habits die hard.

*   *   *

Jack Spot – who'd been in hiding since his trial – then called up his own Fleet Street friend, Vic Sims on the *Sunday Chronicle*, from a "secret address somewhere on the Edgware Road". Spot conceded to Sims that his reign as King of the Underworld really was over. "I learned that men I had called my friends for years were deserting me in scores. I decided then and there to finish with the game. Yes, I think you can call me the last gangster. Ruthless men think they are now in a position to dominate London's underworld. Most of them have served long terms in prison. Unless the police act quickly, gang warfare on a large scale will soon break out both in London and the provincial cities. For the past ten years, while I was the acknowledged boss of the race tracks, all was peace and quiet. Now anything is likely to happen."

Then Billy Hill's personal spin machine went into overdrive, when his henchman Albert Dimes was lined up to talk to Hill's

People crime reporter pal Webb. Dimes insisted he was nothing more than a bookmaker "who unwittingly led the revolt against Spot and his gang who'd been trying to bleed us white. We bookmakers were showing Spot that we were not afraid of him. So in an effort to show his so-called power, he decided to 'fix' me – with a stiletto."

Then, in a deliberate attempt to wind up his boss's archenemy, Dimes told Webb: "It was Spot's last fling to try to impress the Underworld with his power – so that he could make a come-back. But Spot chose wrongly. He knew I was no fighting man, so he thought I would take it and not hit back. I didn't take it."

Dimes insisted: "The real mobsters of the underworld [meaning Hill, naturally] despised Spot. They said he was no real criminal, but just a cheap slasher." Dimes said Spot had made it impossible for small bookmakers (like himself, supposedly) to make a living. But the most damning accusation came when Dimes claimed Spot was a police informer. "The Underworld was shocked. The 'boys' have a code of their own, and the first rule is that no gangster must inform to the police against another, still less give evidence against him."

Spot was staying in Dublin when he was informed by Scotland Yard that there wouldn't be any further charges arising out of the Frith Street trial. Although there was enough evidence to support perjury charges, detectives had to prove the fight with Dimes had actually happened. This would have been tantamount to a rehearing of the original case.

Meanwhile, Fleet Street continued its campaign against organised crime in London. The public's feelings about such matters were at a peak of indignation, and the authorities felt under immense pressure to prove they were trying to clean up the capital.

*   *   *

On 15 November 1955, Billy Hill poured further salt on Jack Spot's wounded pride by holding a high-profile launch party for his autobiography, entitled *Boss of Britain's Underworld*, as ghost-written by Duncan Webb. Spot hadn't even realised Hill was preparing a book, which was also serialised in *The People* and included elements of the articles written by Webb more than a year earlier. In reality, Hill's 'autobiography' was a self-serving piece of propaganda, moulded to ensure that his reputation as 'Boss of the Underworld' remained intact.

The *Daily Mirror*'s coverage of the book's launch party was summed up by the headline, 'EX-GANGSTER THROWS AN AMAZING PARTY'. Below was printed a photo of Hill enthusiastically kissing London socialite Lady Docker, while her husband Sir Bernard looked on adoringly. In the *Sunday Express*, cartoonist Giles turned the Dockers' presence at the Hill party into a hilarious sketch, featuring bulbous-nosed, scarred crooks like something out of a Damon Runyon novel, alongside their snooty-nosed, high-society guests. The ever-so-posh Dockers later claimed they attended the party without realising the criminal Billy Hill would be present. They insisted they thought the event was being hosted by Duncan Webb.

In her own autobiography, published two years later, Lady Docker recalled of the book launch: "It was a very cramped party in a cramped room. I found myself blocked in by some frightening looking faces whom I could not conceive of as being policemen. Some had stitched scars on their cheekbones, others had cauliflower ears, and there was quite a variety with blunt noses. Nevertheless the first gentleman I was introduced to was Chief Inspector Dimes, and as he was one of them I told myself they were all policemen."

Hill's favourite henchman, Frankie Fraser, insisted many years later that he and Albert Dimes stumbled upon Hill and Lady Docker having sex in a small room just off the main reception area of Gennaro's Restaurant, in Soho.

Naturally, Fleet Street lapped it all up. The *Daily Sketch* ran a picture story on page one the following day, headlined, 'SOHO GANG BOSS NO.1 SCANDAL. PARTY COCKS A SNOOK AT THE POLICE': "There has been nothing like it since the days of Al Capone. It was the most insolent gesture the underworld has ever made."

The *Daily Mail* reproduced the invitation sent to its reporter, concluding with, "A sorry day, I feel, when a gangster's book justifies a gilt-edged invitation." But the *Daily Express*'s William Hickey gossip column described Hill as "courteous and intelligent".

Billy Hill, the newly lauded author, even announced to the press at his book launch that he had broken the power of the West End mobs. But Hill still projected himself as an uncompromising and unapologetic criminal, and people seemed to like him for it.

Spot got hold of a copy of the book, and "went bananas" when he read the following excerpt: "If you stand in any part of Soho at any hour of the day or night you will be spotted by at least six of my men. Walk a mile in any direction and you will pass a dozen. This is the centre of my empire, the district from which I rule the underworld of Britain. Walk up Shaftesbury Avenue and ask the first gangster you see who rules the underworld. If you don't know any, then ask a copper. He'll tell you that Billy Hill is the guv'nor."

Hill referred to Spot in the book as a character called 'Jack Delight' (he never called Spot by his real name, on the legal advice of his publisher): "To give him his due he could have a fight, that Jack Delight. I had to carve him to ribbons before he swallowed it. Then he broke all our codes by going to the law. He had to be given a talking to."

Hill also claimed in his book that he'd stopped two gangsters killing each other by playing the peacemaker. He even presented himself as a hero who'd ensured stolen property was returned to champion jockey Sir Gordon Richards' home, and mentioned the plot to return the deposed Sultan of Morocco from exile in Madagascar.

But it was Hill's proclamation that he was planning to retire, sooner rather than later, which caught the eye of many of his rival gangsters. "I'm on the way out. By the time you're approaching the middle forties it's time to think of retiring. Villainy and crime are a young man's game."

Yet, throughout the book, Hill still threw down the gauntlet to Jack Spot, and anyone else who thought they could take him on. "I am the gangster boss of London, Britain's Public Enemy Number One, if you like. The undisputed king of the underworld. Yes, I ruled the asphalt jungle of Soho as 'Scarface' Al Capone did years ago in Chicago. My word is law in the jungle. Today there isn't a single crook or hoodlum with the guts to challenge it. Those who did cross my path when I was battling my way to the top, all bear the same ugly trademark – a long livid chiv scar across the face."

Spot tried to hit back, but it was feeble stuff. He got Gerry Byrne of the *Sunday Chronicle* to accuse Hill of being "a miserable little character", and ran stories about how Hill's brother, Albert, had allegedly poisoned the pigeons of Trafalgar Square and put green ink in the fountains. Hill was so furious he ordered his boys to make sure Byrne's black Morris saloon was systematically wrecked by 'vandals'.

Scotland Yard detective Bert Wickstead, and many of his colleagues, were outraged that Spot and Hill could find public platforms with such ease. "They dropped their razors and picked up their pens to be the first to rush into print and proclaim themselves 'Gangster King of Soho'," denounced Wickstead. "These villains write books, give press receptions and, thumping their wheezy chests, give long interviews to the reporters telling how they rose to power. Having achieved their immunity from the law by a series of false alibis, bought witnesses, intimidation and fear. One should not be hoodwinked by the vapourings of these mean bullies who for forty years have fashioned their own laws in the belief that they are beyond the pale of the ordinary criminal code."

At the party itself, Hill almost got struck by stage fright as he gave a speech which consisted of a few brief words: "I have written this book as a lesson and a warning to youngsters." He was given a hearty round of applause (by his own mob, naturally). Then a bunch of supposed 'telegrams' were read out:

"Sorry I can't be here. I'm in a Spot. Signed Jack."

"Hope you have a topping time – Britain's No.1 Hangman."

"Hope you send us back our mail van? We miss it – Postmaster General."

*   *   *

Hill knew it was time to finish off any threats to his reign. He commissioned Frankie Fraser to send a final message to one or two of Jack Spot's boys. Within days, Fraser stabbed Hill's onetime boxer pal from South Africa, Bobby Ramsey – who now sometimes worked as Spot's minder – as he was entering a club in Crawford Street, Marylebone. Fraser recalled, "He was with a brass who used to hang out in Gerrard Street. I cut my hand as I was stabbing him." Moments after slinging the knife away, Fraser was arrested.

When both men got to the police station, Fraser claimed he'd been helping his injured victim, Ramsey, instead of stabbing him. The prostitute also told a similar account. Fraser was then allowed to go to hospital to have a few stitches on his own injured hand, and was never charged with the knifing of Bobby Ramsey. Fraser later admitted that Hill paid off a detective to ensure there were no charges.

Spot was so furious that Fraser wasn't charged that he became obsessed with retaliating. "If he'd done nothing, then things would have all died down," Fraser said later. Spot encouraged his latest strong-arm man – a young tearaway called Joey Cannon – to recruit three other men, and gave them guns to shoot Billy Hill and Albert Dimes.

Every Sunday, Hill had lunch in Kentish Town with his estranged wife Aggie. Spot instructed his team to make preparations to hit Hill outside Aggie's home. They then began boasting about the plan in the West End. Hill and Dimes soon heard about it. They grabbed Spot's team and, as Fraser later recalled, "gave them a slap, and explained the facts of life to them". Cannon and the other men bottled out and handed their weapons back to Spot, who knew big trouble now lay ahead.

Hill and Fraser held a meeting at Hill's opulently furnished flat in Barnes, and decided that they needed to punish Spot. Hill gave Fraser a shillelagh to use. Fraser later recalled, "Bill and Albert thought that if I had a knife I might get carried away and kill him. And I might have done because I think he deserved it, getting hold of those four boys and giving them guns."

Spot got a tip that things were about to get very personal, so he went round to Paddington police station to plead for protection. The police refused to help, citing lack of evidence. Spot genuinely feared for his family's safety, and had also convinced himself that others were to blame for his own misfortunes.

By this time, Jack Spot owed money everywhere. His one remaining Soho spieler, in Dean Street, had been forced to close down. He tried to collect money owed to him by various people while at the same time keeping his own creditors at bay. There were no more handmade suits, champagne or caviar.

Fleet Street reported that Albert Dimes was insisting that he and Billy Hill were not after Spot's racing interests, even though he was negotiating with the Jockey Club over new regulations proposed for point-to-point meetings. Dimes claimed he'd been appointed by the bookmakers to represent them, and, in discussions with Colonel Blair, chief of the racecourse personnel, argued that the Jockey Club's plan to charge bookmakers £5 each for pitches was "a liberty".

Fraser later summed up the personal contrast between Hill and Dimes. "Bill was a manipulator, he was made that way. He was jealous of Albert although he would never admit it. Bill wasn't natural like Albert Dimes, although he could be a very charming man if it suited him. He was like a very good snooker player, thinking not of the next shot he's going to take, but of four or five shots after that . . . 'That Albert could be very useful to me, although I don't particularly like him and I'm a bit jealous. Nevertheless he's a good man and I'll keep him for a move or two ahead.'"

Hill showed exactly why he was boss of the underworld when he got into a row with a tough looking, mixed-race Soho character called Tony Mella. When he mouthed off at Hill in a club in Swallow Street, Hill calmly got up and hit Mella over the head with a big glass carafe of water, knocking him clean out and calmly pouring the chilled water over him. It was an impressive performance from Hill, considering that Mella was the younger man and was renowned as a fearsome scrapper.

There was further fallout from the Spot/Hill feud when, in early 1956, small-time villain Tommy Smithson (who'd had a heavy fallout with Hill a few years earlier) was shot dead at a brothel in Maida Vale. Many saw Smithson's death as a warning sign from

Hill to Spot that he should *never* put together another heavy mob. Smithson had also helped the up-and-coming Kray twins set up in a nightclub in Hackney. He was assassinated by a gunman whose two accomplices waited in a car outside the brothel. A Maltese ponce was later arrested for the hit.

Fleet Street was appalled by the Smithson shooting, and started exerting pressure on the government of the day to rescind plans to abolish the death penalty. One newspaper described the slaying as "an almost exact copy of the movies".

Billy Hill and the Krays all turned up for Tommy Smithson's funeral. Hill used the occasion to ensure the twins continued their unsteady alliance with him. He informed them he'd eventually pull out of London altogether to live abroad. Besides property in Tangier, Hill also purchased a villa in the fishing village of Marbella, on Spain's southern coast. The very same stretch of coastline would later become known as the 'Costa del Crime', because of the number of British villains who fled there in the 1970s and 1980s.

Back in London, Hill's estranged wife Aggie was still running his New Cabinet Club, in Gerrard Street, and Hill wanted certain guarantees that she would not be bothered by the Krays.

He also retained interests in a couple of other West End clubs, and claimed he would pop back and forth to keep an eye on his businesses. Hill had tried often enough in the past to head for pastures new, but this time he believed he'd found a formula that would enable him to have the best of both worlds. Spot didn't even merit a mention – although the twins told another associate at the time they were "disappointed" he hadn't put up more of a fight to retain his throne. They'd have loved to see a real bloodbath.

"It's a shame 'cause we'd have liked to have had a right dig at Spotty," said Reg. The Krays kept a close eye on Spot, just in case he tried to put his few remaining troops back on the streets. They agreed with Hill that if he put a foot wrong they'd all come down on him like the proverbial ton of bricks.

By the summer of 1956, the Krays had set up their headquarters in the Regal billiard hall in Eric Street, off of the Mile End Road. The twins were already committing regular acts of extreme violence. They'd taken over most of the East End and were heading west with a vengeance.

SEVENTEEN

Intrepid Scotland Yard detective 'Nipper' Read – the man who would later help bring the Krays to justice – was approached by Jack Spot at the Yard, after he received more anonymous phone threats. Spot had no doubt he'd been targeted by Billy Hill and his boys. He complained to Read that his local police station had refused to help. Read later recalled, "But the evidence was vague." He told Spot the police were "unable to act unless there was more concrete information".

In a bid to defy the perceived threat, Spot tried to lead a normal life. He'd leave his home at Hyde Park Mansions every morning at around the same time, stroll over the road to his barber's for a shave and then head to the Bear Garden bar at the Cumberland Hotel, where he still held court. Despite his problems, Spot made a special point of always being pristinely turned out. Some said it was as if he was modelling himself on his favourite American gangster heroes.

Spot even tried to contact Hill to sort out their problems, but Hill refused to take his calls. For the first time, Spot began questioning the reasons behind his split with Hill. Why, after all these years of peace, had Billy Hill turned against him? Was it pride? Stupidity? Suspicion? Arrogance? Then, as he toured Soho, trying to drum up support, he began to hear more and more about the newfound power and influence of the Kray twins.

To this day, many villains in London wonder why the Krays, who were so obsessed with violence, were surprised and upset that they were considered to be dangerous outsiders. Ronnie Kray did not tolerate any threat, or even competition, from other criminals. Reggie was always urging his twin brother to be more cautious, but Ronnie was permanently out for blood, and could come up with a thousand reasons to hurt anyone he deemed to be an enemy.

The Kray 'Firm' – even in those early days – remained in a permanent state of war readiness, their soldiers swiftly mobilised to clamp down on any perceived threat. New arms were regularly being purchased, with caches of guns and ammo stashed in different parts of London. Every member of the Firm was issued with his own automatic. Ronnie and Reggie purchased their own VIP Browning machineguns for £75 each. Ronnie even wanted to use limpet mines and Mills bombs, but couldn't find a suitable supplier.

The twins were not only aspiring to be the most powerful criminals in London. They didn't need any more macho gang fights to show who was boss, like Hill and Spot. Now everything had to have a purpose. Even their base at the East End billiard hall was more like a business headquarters than a club for villains. News was travelling around their manor that the young twins were genuine 'guv'nors' who looked after their own. It gave them extra status, increasing their ability to attract recruits.

The Krays installed a sense of real discipline into their firm. Ronnie's dream was to replace all the tearaways with genuine criminals. By 1956, the twins' power had spread through Bethnal Green and Mile End along to Walthamstow. Every thief and gambling club, most of the pubs and many businesses, were paying protection money to the Krays. Reggie bought himself a flashy convertible Cadillac not dissimilar from one that Jack Spot had once owned.

Criminals began referring to them as the most dangerous mob in London, the boys with the real future. But they still lacked the strength and depth to expand. Ronnie wanted to sweep into the West End, but no other gangs would form an alliance with them because of their deadly dangerous reputation.

Ronnie wanted to take them all on. He didn't help his reputation by constantly talking of 'doing' people, and of how he believed he was psychic and could read people's motives from their aura. Reggie disapproved of his brother's spiritual obsessions, but still felt he was under Ronnie's power and influence.

The Krays were here to stay.

*   *   *

On 2 May 1956, Billy Hill's archrival and enemy, Jack Spot, visited a pub called the Little Weston, off Praed Street in Paddington, on behalf of a secretive financial backer prepared to buy the property. Earlier that same week, Spot had agreed to run the place if the deal went ahead. At 10:40 that night, Spot and his wife Rita, plus a friend called Paddy Carney, were walking back from the pub to Spot's apartment at Hyde Park Mansions. As they approached the apartment block, three cars screeched to a halt thirty yards further up the street. Rita heard the sound of people running behind them. Moments later at least half a dozen men – some with handkerchiefs tied loosely around their faces – emerged from the dark and steamed right into Spot. One of those men was 'Mad' Frankie Fraser. Spot hit the deck in seconds as a cosh ripped open a gaping wound in his skull. Then he felt sharp pain tearing at him as blades sliced through his flesh.

Rita let off an ear-piercing scream before flinging herself at the attackers. She kicked and scratched them to try to get them to pull away from her husband. Spot scrambled back onto his feet and started hitting back, as a few local residents emerged from nearby homes.

Rita later testified, "I was pushed against the railings and fell to the ground. Jack got hold of me and tried to push me up the steps. We got up three steps to a platform and both fell again. I got up, but my husband was still on the ground. Men were galloping all around us. There were lots of them. They were whacking at both of us."

That was when Rita spotted the shillelagh. It was one she'd brought back from Ireland, which her husband had insisted on giving to Billy Hill as a gift. She also recognised some of Hill's boys – including Fraser, Bobby Warren and Billy Blythe – among their assailants.

Spot lay helpless on the ground as they hit him over and over again with the shillelagh, then booted him in the face. Another man they knew as Rossi then came up the steps and attacked them with what looked like a butcher's chopper. Hill's old mate Franny Daniels joined in with an iron bar. Rita shrieked at him, "I know you!" But he didn't reply. The couple's Irish friend, Paddy Carney, disappeared into the darkness, never to be seen again. Police sirens sounded in the distance. The men hastily scrambled back towards their cars before driving off.

Rita grabbed her husband's arm and dragged him up the steps. With blood streaming from his face and body and one ear flapping in the wind, Spot tried to focus on the front door of the mansion block. Then he collapsed as everything went black.

Fraser later insisted there was no intention to murder Spot: "The thing was to teach Spotty a lesson. He wasn't important enough to kill. The death penalty was about, but you couldn't care less about that because you could easy have killed him by mistake anyway. That's the chance you take. But the purpose was to let him see what a loud-mouthed chump he was."

Fraser didn't demand his usual cash-upfront fee because he believed such a high-profile target would earn him an unrivalled, almost priceless reputation in the London underworld. He then fled to Brighton, just hours after the attack. Hill had organised for Fraser to take a flight to Ireland, where Hill had specially rented a doctor's house on the outskirts of Dublin.

Semiconscious, Jack Spot was taken by ambulance to St Mary's Hospital, Paddington, where he was given emergency blood transfusions and surgery. His wife Rita's injuries were not serious and she received outpatient treatment at the same hospital. Spot refused to help police identify his attackers.

Rita, however, was far less inclined to let the attackers get away with almost murdering her husband. She said one of them was Billy Blythe. He'd hammered into her husband, she said, with that shillelagh Spot had given Billy Hill in the days when they were still friends. Nothing would shake Rita from her conviction that the men should be brought to justice. Why should she play the underworld game of never betraying another villain?

That night she provided police with sworn affidavits, which would help them to apply for arrest warrants for Fraser, Warren and Blythe. She also suggested some other names, although she admitted she wasn't a hundred per cent certain about their identities. Spot was eventually transferred to a general ward where both Rita and the Scotland Yard detectives could talk to him. But he still continued to shake his head whenever asked the names of his assailants. At the crime scene outside Spot's mansion block, police scoured the area for the weapons but all they eventually found was a man's heavy gold signet ring.

In the early hours of the following morning, police raided a well-known Soho club and interviewed numerous villains connected to Billy Hill. They were asked where they were at the time of the attack and their clothing was examined for bloodstains. Meanwhile, the police agreed to mount a twenty-four-hour guard on Jack Spot's wife and children.

Scotland Yard detective Nipper Read went to Billy Hill's flat in Bayswater and told him he was bringing him in for questioning. As Read later recalled, "He took his time getting dressed and smartened himself up. Just before we left he went to a sideboard, opened a cupboard and took out a roll of notes, which would have choked a pig."

"S'ppose I'd better bring a few quid, just in case," Hill told Read, as if he didn't have a care in the world.

Over in Clerkenwell, Hill's henchman Albert Dimes was being equally cooperative with visiting detectives. Both Hill and Dimes were taken to Paddington Green police station for interviews, but they had strong alibis and were never charged. Scotland Yard believed that neither man was directly involved in the attack. "It would have been too obvious. These men were astute criminals. Not idiots," said Read. But the Yard let it be known that Hill and Dimes had been able to provide detectives with "valuable information".

Meanwhile, the London underworld had branded Jack Spot a squealer because he couldn't stop his own wife from talking to police. Ironically, Spot himself still didn't know at this stage that Rita had agreed to talk.

*   *   *

The Kray twins had steered clear of the aftermath of the Frith Street 'fight that never was'. But on this occasion, they made a point of popping in to see Jack Spot in hospital, the day after his admission. Both Krays gleefully examined his injuries before Reg got straight to the point. "Who the hell did this to you, Spotty?" Spot didn't even glance up at the twins. He simply rolled over and looked the other way. He said nothing as the twins persisted in their questions, like blood hungry bulldogs gnawing away at a piece of meat. Eventually, Spot closed his eyes and pretended to be asleep. The Krays smiled to each other, gave their customary shrug of the shoulders and headed for the exit.

That evening, the twins held a celebration drink at their favourite boozer, the Blind Beggar in Whitechapel Road, the heart of the East End. "They were *that* happy to see Spot out of circulation," one former Krays man explained years later. Around midnight, Ronnie paid a visit to the Italian Club, in Clerkenwell, with his latest toy – a heavy Mauser automatic – and waved it menacingly at one of Billy Hill's associates. It was all done for show, to emphasise to Spot that they weren't involved in his beating and slashing, and were supposedly on his side. Back in the West End, police warned that it was highly likely the attack would spark fresh friction between London gangs. The Krays rubbed their hands with glee.

Billy Hill hoped that perhaps this time Spot would get the message loud and clear. But Spot now had more problems on his plate than just a bunch of life-threatening injuries. He may have refused to co-operate with police, but Rita had grassed on everyone.

Later that same day, Spot posed for a photograph in the *Sunday Express* with Rita at his side. His arm was encased in plaster, his nose and mouth twisted, both eyes blackened. He told the paper, "I'm the toughest man in the world. I am staying on in London. Nobody will ever drive me out."

Rita added, "Let 'em all come. We're not scared."

Hill laughed when he read Spot's comments. "That fuckin' geezer just doesn't get it, does he?" he told one associate.

A few days after the attack, Spot's latest so-called bodyguard,

Joey Cannon, requested a meeting at Hill's office in Warren Street, just off the Tottenham Court Road. Spot advised Cannon to take a .45 revolver with him just in case there was any trouble.

Cannon conveyed the message to Hill and Dimes that Spot would talk Rita out of giving evidence re the attack. The quid pro quo was that Hill should put a lid on the escalating violence between them. Hill was not pleased, told Cannon Spot was a 'wrong 'un' and that he would do no such thing. Cannon only avoided a severe beating due to Frankie Fraser, of all people, who put a good word in for him during a phone conversation with Hill from his Dublin hideout.

On 5 May, Bobby Warren – one of the tearaways recognised by Rita during the attack outside Hyde Park Mansions – was arrested. Warren had known the Whites of Kings Cross, the race gang displaced by Jack Spot, and his own brother had been beaten up by Spot in 1947. The chickens were coming home to roost.

Just over a week later, the psychotic Fraser was picked up by police after they got a tip he was flying back into Heathrow from Dublin. As Nipper Read explained, "We went in three cars to London Airport – two of which broke down on the way – and by the time we arrived the passengers had disembarked. We looked around desperately and I saw him, suitcase in hand, at the bottom of an escalator. His face was livid when it dawned on him that he was about to be nicked."

Fraser later recalled, "I'd telephoned England to get someone to meet me and the phone had been tapped. I didn't have a clue. I came off the plane and half a minute later I was surrounded."

Hill's gang had never seriously considered that they would be identified by their victims. As Fraser would opine, "Spot should either have been killed, I should have masked myself up, or no one he knew should have taken part." Everyone involved knew it was only a matter of time before other arrests were made. And the underworld blamed it all on Jack Spot – the so-called tough guy who couldn't even keep his wife *schtum*.

On 19 May, Fraser and Warren were remanded in custody at Marylebone Magistrates Court on GBH charges. Warren was described as a twenty-eight-year-old scaffolder of Chatham Avenue, Islington. Police opposed bail because of fears about intimidation of witnesses.

Hill hired his crooked legal pal, Patrick Marrinan QC, to defend his boys. By this time, Frankie Fraser and others regularly socialised with Marrinan at Hill's luxury flat in Barnes. "He was a good drinker," recalls Fraser, "he'd start with Guinness and go on to Irish whiskey. I think Marrinan was a rebel. It was the unfairness and corruptness of the legal profession he fought against. Also he got better money from fighting hard for a case. Billy Hill was intelligent enough to recognise this."

On the face of it, the evidence against Warren and Fraser was unimpressive. Even Spot's wife's identification of them had been contradicted by Spot himself. But there was a serious knock-on effect from the adverse publicity surrounding the string of underworld court cases featuring Hill, Spot and their gangs. MPs began asking questions in the House of Commons about whether "effective steps were being taken by the police to prevent the operation of criminal gangs in the London area".

Mr Anthony Greenwood (Labour, Rossendale) asked Home Secretary G. Lloyd-George, "How long have the public got to wait before the activities of these squalid, cowardly and small-time hoodlums like Comer [Spot], Dimes and Hill are going to be effectively curbed?"

Lloyd-George replied, "In the Jack Spot case within hours the assailants were apprehended," assuring the House he would do his duty to "put them out of harm's way".

But other plans were afoot.

EIGHTEEN

Billy Hill gathered up of a bunch of his boys who'd been cut by Jack Spot and had them sit in the public gallery for the Warren/Fraser trial, presided over by Mr Justice Donovan at the Old Bailey on 9 June, 1956. As 'Mad' Frankie Fraser later explained, "They were there to let Spotty know. He went white when he saw them."

Public fears about the underworld even prompted court officials to install a special buzzer warning system to alert police reinforcements to any part of the building. Fleet Street ran overkill coverage of the trial. Inside the court itself, the stench of corruption reared its ugly head after prosecutor Reggie Seaton QC put an awkward question to Fraser. Within minutes Fraser got a message to his defence barrister, Patrick Marrinan. Fraser wanted to ensure that what was said in court was carefully conveyed to his witness waiting outside the court, to ensure it backed up his evidence. Dodgy brief Marrinan stood up, bowed to the judge and claimed he had to go to the lavatory. Once outside the court Marrinan met the witness, whose evidence later exactly matched that of Fraser.

Hill – sporting sunglasses and a snap-brim hat – and his mob made their temporary headquarters at the Rex Cafe, opposite the Old Bailey, where they drank tea, smoked cigarettes and monitored proceedings. They all looked as if they'd walked off a Hollywood movie set; broad-shouldered, broken-nosed, razor-slashed characters who swaggered in front of press photographers and muttered threats for the benefit of anyone listening. They also watched the police, who were watching them in turn.

At the end of each day Hill would report back to his new best friends, the Kray twins, at their billiard hall headquarters in the East End. The Krays, for their part, assured Hill that there was no way Jack Spot would ever be allowed to make a comeback.

On the second day of the trial, Spot took the stand at the Old Bailey and insisted he hadn't seen any of the men who attacked him. Later that same day, Rita was called to give evidence and identified the shillelagh used in the attack after examining it closely.

When it was Fraser's turn to give evidence in his own defence, it was pointed out by prosecutors that he'd told police after his arrest, "Look here, you know I was in it, but you have got to prove it, and I'm not saying anything more."

Fraser claimed to the jury that what he really said was, "Look here, if you know I was in it, you can prove it, and I am not saying anything more." He insisted that, on the night of the attack, he was in Brighton working for a bookmaker. He said he often did it for £1 or £2 a night, admitting that he held neither P.A.Y.E. nor National Insurance cards.

Then Fraser did himself no favours by proudly telling the court he was a great friend of Hill and Dimes. "They said I should have said I just knew them, but I couldn't bring myself to deny they were my friends," he later explained.

Prosecutor Ronnie Seaton questioned Fraser about his visit to Ireland immediately after the attack. Fraser responded, "I asked for a week's holiday the same night Mr Comer was attacked . . . I thought I might be able to earn a living smuggling. I can't say any more as it might involve other people."

Defence counsel Marrinan described Spot as, "That vile cut-throat gangster . . . that corner boy of the lowest look . . . a man who prides himself on being King of the Underworld . . . this scum of the earth," adding, "This case has a background that is unpleasant – unpleasant and unnatural. People in it do not lead the sort of lives which ordinary respectable citizens lead. There is a background which shows that people are prepared to go to most tremendous lengths to pay off feuds."

When the jury eventually retired to consider a verdict, the chocolate-suited Billy Hill was nearby, sitting with a henchman on a *Lest We Forget* seat in the garden of remembrance at St Sepulchres Church. His flunkies sent messengers back and forward across the street to the Bailey.

Within two hours, defendants Warren and Fraser were led back into the dock. The verdicts were announced with little ceremony: "Guilty . . . Guilty . . ."

Afterwards the court heard that Fraser had fifteen convictions, two of them involving violence, and Warren also had a long criminal record. However after giving each man seven years, Mr Justice Donovan told them the sentences would have been longer if the evidence had been more cut and dried. But Billy Hill and his crew were still outraged by the verdict itself, and they began shouting and swearing in the courtroom. More than a dozen uniformed policemen had to force them to leave the room ahead of the legal teams and their witnesses, in case of trouble. Many of them swore revenge on Jack Spot. Outside, the Old Bailey was ringed with City of London police, and even Mr Justice Donovan had to be given a police escort.

A waiting Jaguar whisked Jack Spot and his wife Rita away from the court as press flashbulbs popped and a crowd of curious bystanders watched from the pavement. Spot's limo sped off in the direction of the Embankment, while his flat near the Edgware

Road was put under tight police surveillance for fear of reprisals. Fleet Street was outraged that Billy Hill could so brazenly continue to run the underworld in full view of the authorities. Columnist Cassandra in the *Daily Mirror* complained, "These hoodlums who have never done a day's work, who were brought up in borstals, who have criminal records that leave the ordinary citizens reeling with horror at their callous brutalities, turn up in vast shiny limousines outside the courts of justice to encourage 'their boys' when all too occasionally they land in the dock."

* * *

A few days later, a Scottish gangster called Victor 'Scarface Jock' Russo was out walking along Frith Street, Soho, when a large, cream-coloured Buick pulled up alongside him. An electric window slowly slid down and a finger beckoned Russo over. He recognised Billy Hill immediately. Russo had known Hill since 1940, having slashed Hill's brother, Archie, on an earlier visit to London over a pretty blonde club girl called 'Manchester Maisie'. Russo had also borrowed cash off Jack Spot on one or two occasions.

At the wheel of the Buick that afternoon in Soho was one of Hill's most trusted boys, Johnny Rice. Albert Dimes and another man were also inside the car. As Russo leaned closer, Hill turned to Dimes and said, "He'll do." Hill then told Russo, "We want someone to take a strike from Spotty and nick him, so that he gets some bird." They needed somebody who would allow himself to be slashed in order to frame Spot, meaning certain arrest and prison.

Russo accepted a ride in the Buick to nearby Warren Street, and agreed to meet Hill again at Peter Mario's restaurant, in Soho, scene of the much publicised launch party for Hill's autobiography.

At the restaurant the following Tuesday, Hill told Russo, "I'll give you a monkey, plus the expenses of a plastic operation if you'll do it."

Russo scratched his chin thoughtfully for a moment then agreed. But he said he had to go to Scotland the following Friday, so it would have to be before that.

"That's alright. We'll make it for Wednesday. It'll happen comin' out of the Astor Club on Wednesday morning. I'll get two straight witnesses," said Hill.

Two days later Russo took an early train to Scotland and called Hill to say, "Thanks but no thanks. I changed my mind and if you ever come to Glasgow we'll send your body back in a sack!"

Hill was furious. "But we've got it all lined up."

Russo replied, "Then do it yer fuckin' self."

* * *

Outside Spot's Hyde Park Mansions flat, his wife Rita and their young children noticed a man following close behind them. It was just after the Fraser/Warren trial and the man remained fifteen yards behind whenever Rita turned. She deliberately took a long loop around a nearby park to establish if she was being followed. The man stayed behind her throughout. Eventually he approached her. When she noticed he had his hand in his pocket, she grabbed the children and pulled them close to her. Then he pulled his hand out of his jacket to shake her hand, claiming he'd recognised her from the papers and wanted to congratulate her on not running away from London.

Spot later told journalists he knew the man behind it all. "He used to be a friend of mine, and I once helped him out of a difficulty." Everyone knew he was talking about Billy Hill.

The pressure was making Spot question his own sanity. He became so stressed that he secretly began consulting a Harley Street psychiatrist. In the mid-fifties such a thing was virtually unheard of, especially for a gangster. But Spot later described his shrink as "an intelligent man", and carefully absorbed his assurance that a lot of his problems were a direct result of his impoverished childhood. Spot started to believe that he was a victim of circumstance rather than a cold-blooded character who crashed into the world of crime with the greatest of relish. But if news of his treatment had got out he'd have been the laughing stock of Soho.

* * *

By this time, Jack Spot and Rita were prisoners in their own home. Neither of them dared venture out into the West End. The threatening phone calls increased. Sinister, croaky voices left messages claiming to be Spot's friends and asking where he could be found that evening. One time Rita told a caller her husband was out shopping. Within ten minutes, three carloads of men were waiting on a street corner within striking distance of Hyde Park Mansions, but out of sight of the two-man police guard parked by the apartment block.

In May 1956, Billy Hill and most of his boys disappeared from their usual haunts after hearing a rumour in the West End that Scotland Yard had 'secret agents' living and working in the London underworld, building up evidence for eventual prosecutions intended to break the rule of the mob. Now was the time to keep a low profile.

Hill's complete and utter control of the West End at this time continued to provide a useful opening for the Kray twins, who were busy exploiting the marketplace with cold efficiency. The Krays had been breathing down Hill's neck for a long time, although it was still in their interest to let him continue his reign for a while longer. "Ron and Reg wanted all the pieces of the jigsaw puzzle to be in the right place before they swooped in to take over everything," explained old-time face Jimmy McShane.

On 20 June 1956, one of Billy Hill's henchmen, Tommy Falco, an olive-skinned, part-Maltese tic-tac man, was admitted to St George's Hospital, on Hyde Park Corner, requiring forty-seven stitches. Within an hour, Falco was telling detectives Jack Spot had caused the wound. Falco had a thirteen-inch long cut along his left arm, which varied in depth from an inch to one third of an inch. It was a clean single cut and looked as though it had been caused by one continuous stroke. The doctor who treated Falco said it was unlikely to have been self-inflicted and detectives took away the left sleeve of his jacket and shirt for forensic examination.

After receiving hospital treatment, Falco and his alleged 'witness', Johnny Rice, another of Hill's most trusted boys, went to West End Central police station. Flashy Rice, broad-shouldered, six feet five inches tall, constantly fingered a heavy gold signet ring on the little finger of his right hand and was immaculately dressed in a double-breasted blue serge suit rounded off by square-lensed, half horn-rimmed spectacles. Rice described himself as a 'steel merchant' in his statement, although he was actually a getaway driver for bank robberies, as well as Hill's principal driver. Rice had even 'starred' in some pictures taken at Hill's book launch in Soho, while one newspaper reproduced snaps of him working a bookmaker's stand at Brighton races.

Rice told police how he and Falco were outside the Astor Club at 2:15am when Jack Spot had attacked Falco with a weapon. Rice claimed he caught Falco as he fell and then carried him back into the club. He didn't pursue Spot, who then ran away. But Rice insisted he did hear a car start up shortly afterwards. The open razor allegedly used in the attack was found on a nearby pavement at 5am the next morning. Falco and Rice gave full statements to the police and a warrant for Spot's arrest was issued by a local magistrate.

At 10:30am, detectives approached Spot as he was leaving St Mary's Hospital, Paddington, after receiving out-patient treatment for his own injuries. Spot was taken to West End Central where he was interviewed by Detective Chief Inspector John Mannings. Asked for an account of his movements the previous evening, Spot insisted he hadn't left his flat from 10pm on Tuesday 19 June until 8:45am the following day, when he went to hospital.

At Spot's home at Hyde Park Mansions, another team of detectives arrived seeking further evidence of the Falco attack. Detectives soon established there was no trace of blood on Spot's clothes. Rita was taken to see her husband at the police station and immediately made a statement, totally backing her husband's alibi that he'd never left the flat. However, Spot was still charged with causing grievous bodily harm to Thomas Joseph Falco and was kept overnight in a cell. Next morning, at 10am, he appeared at Marylebone Magistrates Court.

Crowds began gathering around West End Central police station as word of Spot's arrest spread. Falco and his wife had to be smuggled out of the back entrance in a police car. Rita swept out of the same nick shortly afterwards, and went immediately to the offices of the family solicitor. A couple of hours later, she arrived back at Hyde Park Mansions with three C.I.D. bodyguards. Two more officers already stood guard outside the apartment block. As Rita travelled up to the fourth floor flat, where her two children and two sisters were waiting, a police guard was placed at the foot of the stairs.

Meanwhile, 'Scarface' Jock Russo – who Hill had earlier tried to hire to set up Spot – was heading home on a train to Glasgow when he read about the Falco slashing. A few hours later, a drunken Russo called Hill and said he was planning to go to the police, but wanted to give Hill a chance to get his boys to change their statements before Spot appeared in court. In his inimitable fashion, Hill calmly told Russo to fuck off. So Russo went through with his threat, and told the police Hill had offered him money to be slashed.

Meanwhile, Falco, the 'victim', was given a twenty-four-hour guard at the home of his father off Gray's Inn Road, in Holborn. Police were aware that Tommy Falco had attended the earlier Warren/Fraser trial, when he'd been working as a henchman for Billy Hill. Now he had a wound that required forty-seven stitches, allegedly caused by Jack Spot.

At the preliminary hearing at Bow Street Magistrates Court the next morning, Falco alleged that, after the knifing, Spot had said, "This one's for Albert." (Chief witness Johnny Rice recalled the quote slightly differently: "This is one for Albert Dimes.") Falco told the court he was employed by Dimes, while in actual fact Hill was his boss. "I work for Albert Dimes when we go to the races . . . when he wins I get wages."

Spot was remanded in custody for a week. In the prison hospital, he continued to get treatment for wounds he received during the Fraser/Warren attack.

Over in Soho, Billy Hill continued to play the role of Boss of the Underworld with great aplomb. After that drunken midnight phone call from Scarface Jock Russo, Hill (accompanied by his brief, naturally) had visited his local police station and told them Russo was a cheat and a liar, and not to believe anything he told them. Hill was smart. He confronted the police and virtually challenged them to charge him in connection with the Falco slashing or forever hold their peace. After a thirty-minute interview, Hill was told he was free to go.

Two Scotland Yard investigators travelled up to Scotland to interview Scarface Jock Russo at his home. He told them how Hill had offered him £500 to "take a small stab here, one here and one here," pointing to his face, his shoulder, and the centre of his chest. Russo even told the officers that Hill's plan was for the incident to occur at the Astor Club because it was in the West End Division of the Met, where Billy Hill had a lot of 'friends'.

* * *

On that same day – 29 June 1956 – Fleet Street reported that Hill's associates Billy Blythe and Robert Rossi had also been named in connection with the attack on Jack Spot. 'Little Billy Boy' Blythe – just five feet tall – had always fancied himself as a big-time operator. In teenage fights during his East End childhood, he'd always got a thrashing. He joined the army before the war only to desert, and ended up serving a long stretch in the glasshouse. Then he got into gambling, and first encountered Jack Spot at point-to-point meetings. Little Billy then served a civilian prison sentence, this time for cutting a copper. After that, he ran a gambling den in Smithfield until the police closed it down. Then he went for broke and joined Hill's team, in pursuit of Jack Spot.

Less than twenty-four hours later, five plainclothes police officers, including one from Scotland Yard, grabbed Blythe and Rossi in a Dublin city pub at gunpoint. They'd spent three weeks in the city at the house Hill leased for them. Hill's lawyer, Patrick Marrinan, was dispatched to his native Dublin to try to prevent their extradition. The next day, a Dublin judge announced that, until he made a final decision about the detention of Blythe and Rossi, the men could not be removed from the jurisdiction of the Irish courts.

Within forty-eight hours the judge announced that the warrants had given "inadequate" reason for arrest and granted their release. But then, as the two men strolled cockily out of the court, Scotland Yard detectives swooped with new charges and thirty minutes later they were on their way to the Killeen Customs Post near Newry, on the border with Ulster. Then it was on to the

Belfast Police Office, a new building connected to Belfast Prison by a tunnel. After spending an hour in separate cells, Blythe and Rossi were then bundled into a grey police van with darkened windows, accompanied by two Scotland Yard detectives. Cuffed, and with their heads covered in raincoats, they were escorted onto the 6:15pm Belfast to London flight.

In Brighton, another suspect in the attack on Spot – car dealer Edward 'Ginger' Dennis – told detectives, "If it's a straight I.D. Spot's old woman won't pick me out." Dennis was allowed to have tea while police searched the house he was staying in. Detectives then found two letters referring to the attack on Spot and Rita. As police left the house with Dennis in handcuffs, he asked one officer, "Can't you bang those letters back to the wife? It's worth half a hundred to you." Reminded by the detective that he was still under caution, Dennis replied, "With those, I've got no chance. They'll put me out there with the other two."

Rossi, Blythe and Dennis were booked into Paddington Green police station at 9:30pm on 2 July. They were charged with maliciously wounding Jack Spot and told they would be detained overnight. At 10:45am the next morning, an identity parade of twenty-five men was arranged. After consulting their solicitors that figure was reduced to sixteen, but the three prisoners refused to take part. Then a detective said to them, "In that case you will be confronted with the witnesses." Each replied, "I don't care. I'm not standing in that parade."

At 10:55am, in a cell at Paddington Green, in the presence of a solicitor and other police officers, Rita identified all three men and said they'd been involved in the attack.

The following day, Marrinan, representing Blythe, told Marylebone Magistrates Court, "There is still such a thing as the presumption of innocence. It seems to be quite a fashionable thing for Mrs Comer to point the finger at anyone and say this is an enemy of hers or of her husband. It is quite apparent she is not a reliable witness."

Back in Soho, Scarface Jock Russo was set upon by three men and warned he'd get a much worse beating if he gave evidence. Soon he was besieged with death threats. There were too many reputations at stake.

The frame-up allegation against Jack Spot was repeated over and over again at his Old Bailey trial, which began on 16 July. But no one would identify the supposed 'Mr X' who was behind it. The police didn't want Billy Hill's name revealed in court, because they feared it could be used as a lever to get the case thrown out for legal reasons. In any case, most witnesses were too scared to utter his name.

Spot craned his head when Falco walked in through a side door to the court, looking neither left nor right. In the witness box, Falco half-turned to the judge, holding his arm awkwardly as if in pain. But when he realised the judge wasn't watching, his head turned and he stared across the court at Spot, straight into his eyes. Falco then took a deep breath before describing the so-called attack: "He came along and I saw something shining in the air and he brought it down on my arm. I gathered what was going on and brought my left arm up. I felt a pain in my arm, saw blood and grabbed hold of my wrist."

"Did Comer say anything?" asked prosecutor Ronnie Seaton. Falco replied, "Yeah. He did. He said: *'This one's for Albert.'*"

Seaton glanced at the jury for a moment, as though encouraging them to make a special note of this reply. Falco admitted his friendship with Dimes and then insisted to the court he never even wanted the police involved in the case. "I don't like putting people away. I would not do it to my worst enemy. I was afraid of what might happen afterwards if I put him away."

Then the judge interrupted. "I see how it goes on. One man

slashes another and the other man says, 'I will not put him down, my worst enemy, but I will slash him back.' There is very little sense in it is there?"

Falco – not the brightest of sparks – looked blankly at the judge before confirming to the court that he was wearing a blood-soaked jacket and shirt when the attack occurred. Falco insisted he didn't see Scarface Rossi at Peter Mario's restaurant in Gerrard Street, when Hill was allegedly planning to frame Spot. However, Spot's defence counsel, Victor Durand QC, told the court that Hill *had* been in the restaurant, and had even told his mate, *People* reporter Duncan Webb, "I want you to have a go at Spot this week." But Falco kept to his story.

Falco also denied to the court that Billy Hill was his guv'nor. "We're just friends," he claimed. He knew it was more than his life was worth to go against King Billy's wishes.

When main prosecution witness Johnny Rice took the stand, he was asked about a suggestion he and others had put their heads together to bring the charge against Spot. Rice said, "I would not risk the lives of my children, my wife and myself to do a thing like that."

* * *

The following day, 17 July, Billy Hill was a surprise witness in the Falco slashing trial. He strode, pale-faced and bespectacled, into the court, wearing a neat, double-breasted, blue serge suit. His cockney accent and casual demeanour matched the way he leaned heavily on the edge of the witness box.

Hill sneered across at Jack Spot, and then rattled off the oath like a priest in the pulpit before handing the bible back to the clerk of the court. He tugged at his coat lapels and claimed to the court he was a clerk by profession, and had been acquainted with Spot since 1937 and Russo since about 1940.

"Did you ever embark on any scheme with Russo . . ." asked prosecutor Seaton.

"Na," interrupted Hill without a flicker of emotion.

"You must wait for the question before giving answers," the judge told Hill, who barely acknowledged him.

"I've seen the newspapers," replied Hill.

Hill insisted he never asked 'Scarface' Jock Russo to 'take' a knife wound. But then he was completely thrown by a question from Spot's defender, Victor Durand QC.

"Do you know what I mean by the word 'straight'?" Durand asked. Hill leaned slightly more heavily on the witness box before replying in a low voice, "a straight line".

Then Durand demanded, "Do you mind standing up STRAIGHT in this court?"

Hill stood up straight and fiddled with the lapels of his jacket, in preparation for the next question. He admitted to the court knowing both Spot's attackers, Fraser and Warren, as well as confirming his business association with Rice.

Durand then asked him, "What title do you take for yourself, if not a kingdom or a dukedom?"

Hill puffed himself up, glanced confidently towards the judge, the jury and the public before announcing, *"I am the Boss of the Underworld."*

But Hill wasn't trying to impress the watching pack of Fleet Street reporters. He wanted Jack Spot to get the message loud and clear. Spot later admitted thinking to himself, "It's all yours, Billy. I'm not disputing the throne any longer. I'm finished now."

By making such an outrageous statement in the highest court in the land, Billy Hill was virtually challenging the authorities to come after him. Yet some would secretly admire him for having the balls to make such a statement.

Next it was Albert Dimes' turn in the witness box. He denied that he was angry with Spot and Rita, and deprecated himself as a 'nonentity'. His testimony added little else to the case. Scotland Yard's Detective Inspector Mannings then admitted to the court that his officers had not kept a continuous watch on Spot's home throughout the night of the alleged knife attack on Falco.

The following day, Scarface Jock Russo told the court how Hill had offered him £500 to be slashed outside the Astor Club. Then came Russo's prison cellmate, Bill Kennedy, known as 'the Duke'. He told the court, "He [Russo] said he was going to say the whole thing was a set-up and mentioned the names of Rice, Hill and Dimes as some of those responsible for the set-up." Either Russo was lying, or Billy Hill had managed to purchase the services of Kennedy as a key witness.

At the end of the trial, Mr Justice Streatfield advised the jury to reflect on the probability of the story. "Let us assume he [Spot] was lurking there. What does he see? Not Falco by himself, rather a little fellow, but accompanied by that giant Rice. Do you think that a man with a razor is going to lurk there and have a slash at the little one and hope to get away with it? It may be that the slashing is done quickly, but does that man slash the smaller of the two men when he can be caught by that big, burly man Rice the next second?"

Then Mr Justice Streatfield made a statement that one newspaper, the *Daily Mirror*, thought of sufficient importance to splash across both its front and back pages the following day:

"Unhappily, in London at any rate, if not in other places in this country, there has for some little time been something like gang warfare going on – and heartily sick of it all respectable people are becoming. People slash one another, by way of revenge, with razors, and everyone is getting fed up with it. These scenes that we have seen, or heard of, are a disgrace to modern life in this great city. We only wish something could happen to stamp it out – as assuredly it will be, because common sense prevails in the end and law and order will be relied on."

The judge continued: "Some people might think judges attained their positions in almost pitiful ignorance of the affairs of the world in general. However that may be, that does not go for the jury. You may think that the very existence of gang warfare as I have called it might be a factor which lends colour to the possibilities that this in truth was a frame-up."

On 18 July 1956, it took the jury of ten men and two women just twenty minutes to find Jack Spot not guilty. Many in the public gallery broke into gentle applause while a few faces glared in anger. Spot acknowledged the jury and judge with a smile and headed out of the courtroom a free man for the second time in twelve months. To avoid the gathering crowds, Spot was ushered along a corridor by uniformed police and taken out a back exit, where he hailed a taxi home to his wife Rita.

Billy Hill, still fuming over one counsel's description of him as a "miserable little character", decided to hold an unofficial press conference. He rhetorically asked reporters, "If I'm a miserable little character, then why do the police watch me night and day?" Hill continued to insist that he played no role in trying to frame Jack Spot, but it wasn't a very convincing performance.

NINETEEN

The way in which Jack Spot effectively exonerated Billy Hill by not naming him at trial made headline news. The *Daily Express* splashed the news across its front page with an exclusive interview with Hill. He said he was glad about Spot "because I don't like to see anyone in trouble. I have been inside too long – seventeen years out of forty-four – to want anyone to go through what I have been through."

Bizarrely, Hill insisted on being interviewed as he drove a green Jag with Albert Dimes sitting alongside him. "Jack Spot hates me. I do not hate Jack Spot. He has sworn that he is my enemy," said Hill, as he sailed right past the entrance to Spot's home at Hyde Park Mansions. But when he was asked if he'd make peace with his rival, he responded, "Make peace with that villain? Never. If I go to him he'll believe that's a sign of weakness."

Then, after coolly asking the *Express* reporter to "gimme a light" for his cigarette, Hill continued. "I'm staying right here. I've done no wrong, no wrong at all. Perjury? I've nothing to fear. All this talk going on that I framed Jack Spot to get even for what his wife has been saying is nonsense. I don't think the police believe this and I don't think they will charge me. What would I want to frame that oaf for? They say I offered Russo £500 to have his arm slashed and swear in court that

Spot did it. Give Russo a monkey? If I gave Russo my apple core I'd miss it.

"Gang warfare? It doesn't exist, take it from me. It's all a lot of twaddle. There are fights sure, but there's always been fights. And anyone who says I'm organising violence or plan to do anyone injury is asking for lots and lots of trouble."

But what about that twenty-four-hour police guard on Rita and Jack? "Someone says I planned to do her injury, cut her up a little for what she's said. I would never hurt a woman. I wouldn't waste my time on her."

Then Hill's passenger, Dimes, chipped in. "Get this. I'm a bookmaker. I'm an ordinary man. Ever since that fight I was involved in with Spot last year I've been called a gangster. Nonsense, lies."

A job just the previous week – a £100,000 diamond snatch in Holborn – had also been linked to Hill. "Everyone says this is a job with years of knowhow behind it so they think of me." He couldn't resist adding, "The accusing finger is always pointed at me as the brain behind every big snatch."

Later, sitting in the faded splendour of a Bloomsbury hotel, Hill ordered tea, gave away a 10s note, waved the change away and added to the *Express*, "I don't like Spot. He don't like me. I am known as the Boss of the Underworld – ex-Boss I say. I didn't frame Spot and never have. I've done time for most things – smash and grab, armed hold-ups, and that sort of thing. But never for framing."

*   *   *

Gangsters like Billy Hill began their criminal careers breaking the law in a rush, motivated by need, expediency or rage. So when they evolved into classic 'big-time' criminals, things got easier. The villain became intoxicated by his own celebrity and continued to commit crimes to maintain the euphoria. But like all addicts, he'd get so strung out on his habit that he'd inevitably make mistakes. Following the debacle of Jack Spot's trial, there were calls for Hill and his men to be prosecuted for perjury, but the police feared the case would never stand up properly in court. In the weeks following the trial, *The People* (through Duncan Webb, naturally) published yet another version of Hill's life story. But Hill would rather have been sunning himself in the Med, either in Tangier or at his recently acquired villa in Marbella. The spectre of the Kray twins was beginning to loom over every criminal enterprise in the West End and the Krays didn't like being reminded of Hill's power and influence in the underworld, seeing him purely in an 'advisory capacity'. They didn't want him treading on their toes.

Hill prided himself on his ability to avoid violence, unless it was absolutely essential. He liked to fix things before they got out of control. He didn't even like antagonising his archenemy, the police, and he certainly believed in keeping his men under control. However, up-and-coming younger hoods like the Krays weren't particularly impressed by Hill's more patient approach. Why should they care about keeping the police happy, when their overriding attitude was, "Coppers is dirt"?

Hill was fully aware of the Krays' harder attitude, and he also knew he wouldn't be boss of the underworld forever, which was why he kept the Krays onside. They'd even told Hill how they'd headed to north London in a van with guns and knives to finish off their rivals, some Islington brothers, only to find that none of the opposing gang were prepared to rise to the bait.

Hill knew the Krays would eventually try to take over the West End, so he wanted to keep them happy by recommending protection work to them, and even tipped them off about some potential robbery targets.

The twins themselves were sparking so much rumour and fear

that, when they 'went on the missing' from their Fort Vallance headquarters, some said they'd been killed in a gangland execution. Then the word was that Billy Hill had been so desperate to get them off his turf, he'd paid them to go and live in the Bahamas. Hill didn't mind that one, but he knew it was a long way off the truth.

The twins re-emerged unscathed a few days later, when they crushed a rival gang in Clerkenwell. Ronnie Kray saw their smooth victory as a portent of the future, and convinced himself that no one would be able to prevent them taking over all of London now.

* * *

Billy Hill was contacted by Jack Spot not long after the end of the trial. As Hill later explained, "He talked about owing me £500 and asked if he could call and pay it," claiming that Spot appeared in his offices with the money but was shown the door. Hill then phoned Spot and barked at him, "Keep your money and keep away from here. Try working for a living."

Spot later acknowledged the incident, and said the money was the amount Hill had wasted on trying to get him framed. He'd only wanted to make a point. Spot also insisted there was no way he would ever be friends with Hill again.

Billy Hill had more important things on his mind. He went on one of his regular PR offensives, publicly insisting he had no connections with any of the major crimes being committed in London. But when one newspaper asked him about the £100,000 Holborn diamond snatch carried out just a few days earlier, Hill couldn't resist praising the "brilliant team" involved in that robbery, and added, "It was a job well done. Someone must have studied and imitated my own methods."

The underworld had little doubt that Hill still had his finger in a lot of pies. "Planning. That's the secret. Pull off the unexpected.

That fuddles the police," said Hill, while insisting he was now a reformed character.

* * *

On 21 August 1956, one Fleet Street paper reported that a man known as 'Big Brain' was at the top of the list of six names submitted to the Director of Public Prosecutions, in connection with the plot to frame Spot. Many believed that Big Brain was Billy Hill's new codename at the Yard.

Then, in the middle of all this, there was a petty spate of libel writs between Spot, Hill and Johnny Rice. As one journalist explained at the time, "It was farcical. They were all threatening to sue each other for defamation. Yet everyone knew they were villains." Eventually, all three men dropped their actions, when they realised the only people who'd win would be the lawyers who charged vast hourly rates.

* * *

On 24 August 1956, Jack Spot's onetime sidekick, Sonny the Yank, was released from prison, still furious about being put away after doing a job for Spot and not getting anything in return. Spot hadn't even paid Sonny's family a traditional retainer while he was inside, which destroyed any loyalty that might have existed between the two men. In fact, Spot didn't have the money to keep his own family afloat, let alone Sonny's.

A taxi turned up outside Wandsworth Prison containing Sonny's wife and daughter. He hugged them warmly and went back to his home in Stepney for breakfast and a Turkish bath. That night, the Krays and Billy Hill laid on a special 'welcome home' party for Sonny, just to make sure he never returned to Jack Spot. He swore he'd never talk to Spot again

The trial of Billy Boy Blythe, Battles Rossi and Ginger Dennis – all

accused of taking part in the attack on Spot and Rita – opened at the
Old Bailey on 8 October 1956, before Mr Justice Cassels. Patrick
Marrinan was once again defending one of Hill's team, in this case
Blythe. Eight days later, Blythe, Rossi and Dennis were convicted of
unlawfully wounding Jack Spot. Blythe got five years and the other
two were sentenced to four years each. Mr Justice Cassels stressed to
the defendants, "If men like you get tough with other people you will
have to realise that the law can get tough with you."

Blythe was dragged away shouting, "It's a mockery of justice."
Rossi and Dennis looked stunned. At the back of the court,
officers mingled with members of the public in case of trouble.

Marrinan knew only too well that his paymaster, Billy Hill,
would not be very happy . . .

*   *   *

Shortly after this, the Krays suffered their first ever setback when
Ronnie was given a three-year jail sentence for his role in the
bayoneting and stabbing of a man called Terry Martin. Billy Hill
tried to persuade Ronnie that Jack Spot had played a part in
fingering him, after Spot had become increasingly suspicious
about the role the Krays played in his own downfall.

The twins acted outraged and swore that if Spot ever tried to
make a comeback they'd break his legs, "if he was lucky". But
they were shrewd enough to realise that Hill's manipulative claims
needed to be taken with a pinch of salt.

Hill knew that Spot had little more than his fat cigar to put
between himself and the Krays. Five years earlier, they both could
have seen off such tearaways with ease. Now, young as the twins
seemed, they'd openly challenged the toughest criminals in
London. Hill knew that Ronnie's jail sentence would only fuel the
climate of fear.

The twins considered Spot to be a phoney, and even Hill had

now been relegated to the level of nothing more than a useful associate. The Krays believed their powerbase would expand rapidly because, by the mid-fifties, crime had outgrown the generation that came of age with the race gangs.

*   *   *

After the Blythe/Rossi/Dennis trial, reporter Duncan Webb, encouraged by Hill, set about putting the final twist of the knife into Jack Spot. He wrote an article for *The People* to remind readers of various questionable aspects of Spot's background, and even encouraged the Home Secretary to have Spot investigated. Webb claimed that MPs wanted to know whether there was any truth in Spot's alleged boast that "the police relied on me to clean-up the West End and certain racecourses."

Hill was quoted in the Webb article: "One reason why Spot's now so unpopular in the underworld is because crooks are convinced he's a stoolpigeon for the police. They are certain he has given information which has got more than one person gaoled."

Hill knew only too well that the best way to finish off Spot was to label him a 'grass'. Spot always denied ever helping the police, and there is no evidence to suggest anything to the contrary.

Once again, Jack Spot had been well and truly stitched up by Billy Hill.

*   *   *

In late 1956, Aggie Hill gave an interview to a newspaper about what it was like to be the wife of London's first criminal godfather: "At least nobody takes any liberties with you." Aggie described Hill as "one of the gentlest, kindest fellows you could meet". She admitted they'd long been separated, but she had a nice little flat in Euston and still kept in touch with him. She revealed he'd recently bought her a bedside tea-maker and, when her poodle Chloe had died, he had immediately given her another one called Chico. She even admitted getting on well with Jack Spot's wife, Rita and how – as she didn't have kids of her own – she'd looked maternally upon their babies. Aggie added, "We just drifted apart. Certainly I would talk to her if I ran into her. But somehow I don't think we shall be meeting."

Not long after this, on 12 January 1957, Hill's temperamental girlfriend Gypsy got herself involved in a fight at the Miramar Club in Sussex Gardens, Paddington. A month later she was charged with wounding a man with intent to cause him grievous bodily harm. Naturally, Hill's number one lawyer, Marrinan, was on hand to apply for bail, but he actually failed this time around and a stunned Gypsy was remanded in custody for a week. But when she came up before a magistrate's court for a trial committal hearing, the magistrate threw the case out.

*　　　*　　　*

On 21 February 1957, Jack Spot attended the London Bankruptcy Court and insisted on using the name 'John Colmore', in the hope that Fleet Street wouldn't get a sniff of his situation. But a pack of newshounds turned up to hear Spot deny that he had twenty suits worth £40 each. He claimed he only had three suits, three pairs of shoes, two overcoats and "a few ties". The sole claimant was Duncan Webb, who wanted £1,031 18s 8d, which he said was still unpaid from the assault case dating back to 1954. Spot was declared a bankrupt.

In his hour of dire financial need, Spot turned to his old friend Vic Sims at the *Sunday Chronicle*, who agreed to run an updated version of the paper's earlier serialisation of Spot's life story. The article tried to portray him as a hero of the East End, but Spot's main priority was the £1,000 fee the paper agreed to pay, provided he put his name to the series of articles. Not even Rita's diamonds were still around to pawn now, as she'd sold them off to help his legal defence on his last court appearance.

Spot wanted to make a completely new start. He'd heard some of the rumours about what the Krays were planning once Ronnie got out of prison, so he decided to travel alone to Quebec, Canada, to check it out before sending for his wife and the kids.

Jack Spot was deported back to Britain the day he arrived in Canada. When he got back to Southampton docks, a car was waiting for him which had been sent by Reggie Kray as a 'welcome home' gesture. Spot was too exhausted from his sea journey to question his wisdom in accepting such a gift. One of the Krays' oldest associates later explained, "Reggie just wanted to remind Spot that things had changed and he and Ronnie were now calling the shots. Reggie visited Ronnie in prison a few days later and they had a right laugh about it."

Shortly after returning to London, Jack Spot bizarrely claimed to one reporter that London's underworld was by this stage in the hands of two American Mafia chiefs. He said, "One of them pretends to be a respectable citizen and claims he's left his days of thuggery behind. The other is a man everybody knows as a bookie who will stop at nothing. He is a man born of Italian parentage who was interned during the war." The two men sounded more like Billy Hill and Albert Dimes than a couple of New York dons. In reality, Spot was having one last dig at his oldest enemies, but he didn't even have the courage to identify them.

* * *

When it came to a big send-off for his boys, Billy Hill certainly did things in style. After Billy Boy Blythe died in a Liverpool jail during an operation for ulcers, it seemed only fitting to Hill that the man who scarred Jack Spot's face should be given a hero's burial. The funeral was one of the biggest ever seen in Billy

Boy's London neighbourhood, and Hill paid for it all. Three thousand people, marshalled by police and shouldered out of the way by thugs, waited outside his home at number five Myddleton Street, on the borders of Islington and the City of London, to watch Blythe's last journey. At 1:30pm on 25 February 1957, pallbearers with winged collars carried Blythe's oak coffin with silver equipages down the house's narrow staircase.

A police squad car then led the funeral cortege of twelve Rolls-Royces through the crowd. More than two hundred and twenty wreaths were packed onto the cars for the five-mile journey to the cemetery. Barrow boys doffed their caps without even knowing who they were honouring. The police saluted, not realising who had just died. Even a chief inspector stood to attention when the entourage swept into Kensal Green cemetery in the Harrow Road, northwest London.

Billy Hill marched behind the coffin and the relatives. Women in black teetered by the graveside. Hill proudly pointed out a massive wreath shaped like an open prayer book, made entirely out of white carnations. Afterwards, he paid for a boozy wake in which everyone except him got very drunk and sang the praises of the psychotic Blythe.

*   *   *

It was Patrick Marrinan's trial and dismissal from the legal profession which probably marked the beginning of the end for Billy Hill. Marrinan was accused of consorting with criminals, many of whom worked for Hill, as well as delivering messages and money to them in prison. He did win a libel action after his appeal against his dismissal was rejected, amidst allegations that his phone had been regularly and illegally tapped by the authorities for many years. But ultimately Marrinan was a bent brief. Ironically, he would eventually return to his native Ireland where he became a successful solicitor.

But for the moment, Hill continued to be involved in various businesses. He provided 'protection' for a club owner called Harry Meadows, after he'd managed to prevent the Krays twins kicking off a bloodbath following a 'mix-up' about allowing them in the club. Reggie Kray got Hill to give Meadows an assurance that trouble could be avoided. Instead of asking for a fee for his peacemaking services, Hill gave the twins £300 and told them, "Take that few quid, it would have cost me more to have arranged such a commotion to ensure my services are still necessary." Reggie later said that Hill "smiled with a twinkle in his eye". They were undoubtedly fond of him despite the fact they were already taking over his empire.

By this time, Hill was a regular at Crockford's Casino in the West End. His closest friend of the time was a fraudster called Charlie Taylor, who specialised in the so-called 'dollar premium' scam. The two men ended up fleecing a Scottish heir of his entire fortune, and then sending him packing when he dared to object. Billy Hill might have started easing his way into the backseat, but he was still capable of earning big money when he felt like it.

*   *   *

In June 1958, the Krays twins and Billy Hill were outraged when they heard Jack Spot had slipped back into the West End and opened a club – although his wife, Rita, was fronting it on his behalf. The Krays were on the verge of becoming the new club kings of the West End, and the last thing they wanted was Spot invading their space.

Hill's henchman, 'Mad' Frankie Fraser, later confirmed that Spot's club, the Highball, was a real bone of contention. As he explained, "The club had to go. Spot and his wife had broken the code of conduct time and again by going to the police. If you go to the police like Spot and his wife done, then you pay the consequences."

In August 1958, two men entered the Highball, picked up a metal bar stool and smashed a customer called Peter Edwards over the head with it. The two men then ran out to a van where a third thug handed out weapons, including crowbars. They used these to smash open the ground-floor door of the club. The men were all screaming, "Jack Spot, Jack Spot, the fucker! We're going to do him up!"

The police arrived just as the heavies were running off and a battle ensued. Three Smithfield meat porters all ended up at Bow Street magistrates court. They were accused of causing grievous bodily harm to Edwards and to PC Peter Long, with intent to resist arrest, and with assaulting another policeman. The GBH charges were eventually dropped when Edwards refused to give evidence against the three men.

A few weeks later Spot's wife, Rita, left the Highball in the charge of her doorman whilst she went to a party at a nearby flat. Three hours later – just after closing time – a mob of burly men with connections to Billy Hill entered the building through the basement. They poured paraffin over the bar stools and chairs, stacked all the tables in the middle of the dance floor and then set light to them before scrambling out through the basement door.

Minutes later the alarm was raised by a cleaning lady. She jumped in a taxi to fetch Spot and Rita, who arrived to find the premises ablaze. Later that morning, Scotland Yard issued a statement saying they feared that the blaze was an attack by a rival mob and that it might provoke fresh outbreaks of gang warfare. Spot defiantly told journalists he'd reopen the Highball and call it the Silver Slinger.

Then Spot heard on the criminal grapevine that Hill had opened a bank account with £5,000 in it to set Frankie Fraser up again, once he was released. Since being sentenced for the chiv attack on Spot and Rita, Fraser had been certified insane and transferred to Broadmoor Hospital. Spot was also told that Fraser was being primed by Hill to finish him off once and for all.

Spot finally conceded defeat. He dropped all plans to reopen the club and moved to Dublin with his family shortly after.

TWENTY

The Krays – lacking the experience and finesse of a Billy Hill – were steaming through the underworld like runaway Chieftain tanks. They wanted control of every important manor in the capital. The twins wanted everyone to know that they wouldn't tolerate disloyalty. A lot of people got cut and the word went out: don't fuck about with the Krays. They ignored the fact that Hill's power had come from his ability to avoid violence most of the time. For the Krays weren't politicians, who negotiated their way out of difficulty; they thrived on confrontation. If they needed to knock someone off to prove a point, then so be it. As Ronnie later explained, "We weren't playing kids' games any more."

Johnny Brown (a pseudonym), a retired blagger and thief now in his late sixties, and a close relative of one of the three men who escaped from the Great Train Robbery, insists Hill still had the same level of respect as the Krays during this period. As he explains, "We had a tickle, and Billy Hill heard about it. There was a list: Billy Hill and the twins were at the top of the list – you had to give a two'er down the club."

In September 1958, Hill's pet reporter, Duncan Webb, bizarrely got a papal dispensation to marry killer Donald Hume's wife Cynthia. Two weeks later, he died at the age of just forty-one – from war wounds, rather than any injuries caused by London's most notorious criminals. Just before he died, he provided police with evidence which secured the acquittal of Ian Gordon, a young airman who had been convicted of the murder of a woman he was courting.

A few months later, Hill was summoned by socialite Lady Docker to her home near Stockbridge, in Hampshire, after £150,000 worth of jewels was stolen. The two of them had 'bonded' particularly well during the launch party for Hill's autobiography four years earlier. Hill claimed he promised "not to leave a stone unturned" in his quest to track down the nicked 'tom'. It eventually emerged that the jewellery had gone missing after Lady D befriended a sailor, who ended up travelling with her and her husband Sir Bernard in their Rolls Royce. Despite claiming to have scoured the country for them, Hill came back empty-handed, claiming that the thief was an amateur opportunist and therefore he couldn't help.

In June 1959, Billy Hill started purchasing antiques with a serious view to becoming a dealer. He told associates he was providing marble pillars and fireplaces to a millionaire's home in the Bahamas.

A few months later, Hill hit the headlines for one of the last times, when he made all the arrangements for the funeral of Selwyn Cooney, the manager of his wife Aggie's New Cabinet Club in Gerrard Street, who'd been murdered in a fight. The killing was sparked by a row with a member of the Nash family, who at the time were making serious inroads into Soho. Many were horrified when a woman witness to the shooting called Barbara Ibbotson was razored as a warning not to give evidence. Old time London thief 'J.D', now in his eighties, concedes it was "a bit drastic – like the Eastern Europeans today. But it was unusual in them days," he reminisces. "Billy Hill used to cut you and put £200 in your pocket."

Many Soho observers saw the murder as some sort of turf war, demonstrating to Hill that he was no longer in charge of the West End. Then the man accused of the killing, Jimmy Nash, was acquitted, although in a second trial he was convicted of grievous bodily harm and sentenced to five years. When Hill was approached by the police to assist their inquiries against the Nashes, they were politely shown the door.

By 1959, Billy Hill had successfully managed to persuade Fleet Street that he was nothing more than a modest "ex-gangster", so when his name was linked in the newspapers to an illegal arms deal, Hill rather enjoyed being back in the limelight. Talking from one of the Krays' newly acquired clubs in Knightsbridge, just a stone's throw from Harrods, Hill told reporters, "I don't know where you get your information from but to me it seems very much exaggerated." Hill insisted that his recent "business trips" to Stockholm and Tangier had no connection to two cargoes of rifles, submachine guns and mortars. But few believed him.

By the late fifties, Hill's name had become so entrenched in the national psyche that he even got an honourable mention in a hit movie, the 1959 comedy *Carlton-Browne of the F.O.*, with Terry-Thomas and Peter Sellers. During one scene, a character is ejected from a nightclub even after a member of staff has pointed out the man is the member of a royal family.

"I don't care if he's Billy Hill," says the manager of the club.

Hill loved it, and revelled in telling his pals about how his name was used in the film.

*   *   *

In 1960, the Jockey Club was legally permitted to introduce legitimate betting shops to every high street, effectively wiping out the illegal gambling dens and street-corner bookies which had been so much a part of Billy Hill's reign. As the big credit bookmakers prepared for the legalisation of off-course betting, the smaller bookmaker and his protectors were being squeezed out of the picture.

But with these changes, new 'industries' sprang up for gangsters like the Krays. A favourite racket was the protection of the newly opened betting shops. Then there were the one-armed bandits, which began being installed in shops and clubs across the capital. A new criminal era was dawning, and Hill knew that the time was rapidly approaching when he'd have to at least give the impression of retiring gracefully. Hill and Gypsy settled down to a kind of domestic bliss at his flat in Moscow Road. Visitors were astonished by the over-the-top crystal chandeliers which hung from every ceiling, even in the toilet. There was also carpeting on the toilet seat. As one old friend explained, "Billy and Gypsy thought it was smarter than Buckingham Palace." Hill's phone number at his flat – Bayswater 7338 – was well known to many by now, especially since Hill preferred to carry out the majority of his business transactions in the apartment.

In his middle age Hill would sometimes spend weeks at a time at the flat, never actually venturing out of the front door. Associates would visit him at his home, only a short walk from Bayswater tube station. He even had a few boys earning money from unlikely sources, including one who'd pick up silver sixpences from tube stations and then have them melted down, as the silver was worth more than the actual currency.

Billy Hill may have abstained from drink throughout much of his life, but his capacity for smoking knew few boundaries. By the time he reached his fifties he almost always had a cigarette, a Capstan Full Strength, in his hand or hanging from the corner of his mouth.

*　　　*　　　*

Hill greatly enjoyed his time at his properties in Tangier and Spain. After all, he was the only one of his generation who'd actually got out of the underworld with a bagful of loot. He considered Jack Spot and many others to be part of a bygone era. Hill had gradually retreated from London to avoid any problems with the Krays, but that didn't stop him entertaining the twins at his whitewashed hacienda in Tangier, whenever they felt the need to soak up the sunshine.

Hill adored the Moroccan port the most. He used to say, "Tricky Tangier, lovely little spot." Despite his early proclamation that he enjoyed eating abroad, however, his claim turned out to be hollow when those who travelled with him later said he usually imported all his own food, including corned beef, fresh meat, tomatoes and eggs. He even became a regular at one Tangier restaurant called Nautilus because they'd always cook him up all his own private food.

In 1961, both Hill and Albert Dimes had their names mentioned in dispatches during the London trial of high-class conman Charles De Silva, who'd dared to take Billy for a ride. It turned out that De Silva had bought a load of paint from Selfridges and then simply relabelled it, before conning Hill into buying it for a 'knockdown price'.

Hill was so furious he had De Silva beaten up. Then, typically, in the spring of 1961 he financed an audacious scheme in which De Silva attempted to defraud a chinchilla breeder from Yorkshire of £100,000, by promising him a share of a chinchilla farm in Ceylon. Omar Shariff look-alike De Silva, who was sentenced to six years, had actually been a mate of Hill's for many years, and also spent some time working with the Krays. Years later he took a drug overdose rather than face yet another spell in prison.

In 1962, Hill's efforts to boost business for a new casino caused a few raised eyebrows, when he was a guest at the famous gambling club Crockford's. That same night, many of the members' cars had invitations to the new casino on their windscreens. The Crockford's chairman took it all in good spirits and described it as a good gimmick when interviewed by the *Daily Express*. Typically, Hill himself denied all knowledge of the stunt. "I wonder who put them out? I often play at this other club, though I do not own it."

At one stage Hill had a small number of card players on his books who went into another well-known casino, the Clermont Club, after being trained up as 'readers' and back-ups, to pull off a whole range of gambling scams. Hill eventually spread his team to other casinos in London and was soon at the centre of a massive gambling fraud. The scam was called the 'Big Edge', and involved crooked croupiers and cheating card players – all classic Billy Hill territory.

Although now away from the mainstream London crime scene, Hill was still raking in a fortune. Some of his contemporaries believe to this day that Hill raked in millions of pounds, all of it tax free. Hill didn't go out much by this time, but he was occasionally spotted in the Marlborough pub, in Chelsea, where the worlds of celebrity and criminality were starting to mix. Former London thief J.D. recalls how he'd see renowned society cat burglar Peter Scott "sitting at a table with Billy Hill an' that – Stanley Baker used to play cards with 'em."

*　　*　　*

Also in 1962, Billy Hill and Albert Dimes co-hosted a party for the redoubtable 'Mad' Frankie Fraser on his release from prison. It was held at the Pigalle Club on Piccadilly, and guests included singer Shirley Bassey and pianist Winifred Attwell. The Krays were nowhere to be seen.

Hill was still interested in developing his club interests outside

London, which took him to the Sussex seaside resort of Brighton. There he became partners with a man called Harvey Holford, who liked to style himself as the Errol Flynn of the south coast. When Holford murdered his young wife in a fit of jealousy, Hill even allowed him to claim in court that he was under duress because of threats from Hill and Dimes.

Holford's trial was peppered with insinuations that he'd been strongly provoked to murder his wife. There were even hints of sexual abuse when he was a child, plus continual questions about the paternity of he and his wife's child. On 29 March 1963, Holford was acquitted of murder and found guilty only of manslaughter. He received just four years in prison.

*   *   *

In the spring of 1963, Billy Hill had a meeting in an upstairs room at his latest favourite pub, the Star in Belgravia, where he proposed funding what was to become the Great Train Robbery, using the proceeds from another robbery he'd secretly financed the previous year. But the gang's leader, Bruce Reynolds, turned down the offer as Hill wanted a sixty per cent share of the proceeds.

The train robbery eventually went ahead on 8 August 1963, in Buckinghamshire, and the gang seized £2.3 million. It changed the face of British crime. Hill would no doubt have loved a piece of the action. (He later claimed he didn't even have a whiff of it – but then he would say, that wouldn't he?)

When *Daily Mirror* reporter Rex North tracked Hill down to a casino in Cannes, just after the robbery was carried out, he said, "There are veiled hints in the French newspapers, and everyone is pointing me out as a hero in the sun. This, Billy Hill does not like," adding, "I know nothing about it. Ring up Scotland Yard yourself. Now, if you like. Book plane tickets back to London, if you care to do so. I am so flicking [sic] mad about all the publicity without the money to go with it."

*   *   *

Now aged fifty-three and supposedly retired, Billy Hill undoubtedly kept a lower profile but remained London's 'chief executive', still advising and financing robberies as well as raking in vast sums from Britain's growing casino culture. Hill was even sometimes called in to throw out cheats when they caused heavy losses at West End casinos. One such incident happened at the famous Clermont Club, where an Italian-born cardsharp who'd been recruited by a member of the British aristocracy was caught playing a few tricks. Hill had his loyal minder, Bobby Warren, pay a little visit to the man, who left the country within hours.

Hill got involved with a lot of aristo types at this time, through being a regular at the Star Tavern where he was renowned for sitting at a corner table with a pot of tea and the obligatory pack of Capstans, while playing cards for large stakes with such characters as Peter Rachman, the most evil landlord in London. (Rachman's legacy was an entry in *The Concise Oxford Dictionary*, which defines 'Rachmanism' as, "Exploitation of slum tenants by unscrupulous landlords.") Regulars at the pub later recalled that Hill would openly cheat on Rachman, who didn't want to lose face by accusing Hill of such underhand tactics.

By the early 1960s, the Star had become a magnate for spivs, toffs, and even a bunch of dodgy coppers from Scotland Yard. The landlord at the Star was a larger-than-life Irish character called Paddy Kennedy, who was said to be as loud and tough as any of his customers. During this period, Hill still had a man inside the Clermont Club, monitoring all the big winners, and soon got a whiff of yet another cheat's scam which gave him a unique opportunity to earn more ready cash.

*   *   *

Soho in the mid-1960s was a much 'dirtier' place than when Billy Hill was boss of the underworld. Pornographic bookshops and cinemas, plus clip joints which specialised in fleecing customers, dominated the Square Mile of Vice. A classic scam was a smooth-talking spiv standing outside a doorway inviting punters in to see a dirty movie. Having paid up, the customers would then be directed to the second floor while the spiv, still outside, moved on to find more doorways and more victims. Well-known London criminals Jimmy Humphreys and the Mason brothers, and notorious vice barons Bernie Silver and Frank Mifsud, ruled supreme at this time. Strip bars and snide champagne clubs were controlled by more hardened gangsters like the Krays – who, just like Spot and Hill before them, had steered clear of out-and-out vice.

Over in Tangier, Hill's lover Gypsy now ran a club purchased by Hill, called the Churchill. A few days after Ronnie Kray's infamous murder of George Cornell, in March 1966, the twins were spotted being driven round Tangier in a big white limo while they visited Billy Hill at his villa. Reggie Kray was so impressed that he seriously thought about opening a club in Tangier himself – but then the local police served the twins with an immediate deportation order, and they headed back to the Smoke. Hill remained untouched though, thanks to the contacts forged all those years earlier.

Retired blagger 'Johnny Brown' was out in Morocco at the time. "I actually bumped into them in Tangier, the first time I'd been there. And I seen 'em in the Churchill club, Billy Hill's club, with my brother-in-law who was living out there at the time. And we went up there this night, and Ronnie's at the bar, he's got a little boy with him, little peasant. And he took no notice of us, as though we weren't there. And I bumped into him in the street a couple of days later, Reggie, driving an MG that belonged to Billy Hill – and I said to someone out there, another guy, 'He looked me straight in the face a couple of times, and they haven't acknowledged me.' 'No,' he said, 'they're like ostriches. They've got their head in the ground, and they pretend they haven't seen you.' Strange characters. They thought they was untouchable."

Meanwhile, Scotland Yard detective Nipper Read tracked Jack Spot down to his flat on the Gloucester Road, in Kensington, west London, to ask him about the Krays' activities in the spring of 1966. Spot was particularly furious when Read told him that Billy Hill had entertained the twins at his newly acquired villa in Tangier. Now it all made sense to Spot. "Hill and those Kray nutters conspired to kick me out of London," he later told one acquaintance.

With the truth finally dawning on Spot, he provided Read with stacks of information on the Krays' contacts and associates. Spot even linked Ronnie to the death of a bookmaker in 1957. "Spotty was out for revenge and he had little to lose," said one old lag, acquainted with Spot in the sixties. "He blamed the Krays for encouraging Billy Hill to have him done over."

Hill lived well throughout the decade of the so-called swinging sixties. The Krays even encouraged him to make guest appearances at their West End clubs. Hill's friends at the time, besides slum landlord Peter Rachman, included Lady Docker and Profumo scandal girl Mandy Rice-Davies, although he kept a low profile most of the time and even made a point of trying to steer clear of the other ruthless sixties gangsters, who'd moved into central London by this time.

In the early seventies, Hill quit his Mediterranean homes in Tangier and Marbella and moved back fulltime to the UK, settling in Surrey with the temperamental Gypsy. They ran a club together in the stockbroker belt area of Wentworth. Hill eventually grew tired of Gypsy's hysterics and, in 1976, took up with an African showgirl called Diana. She had ambitions to be a singer but had a tragic history of mental problems. Diana had a son by a thief called Johnny Dobbs, and the boy was adored by Hill, who'd never had any children of his own.

Gypsy naturally loathed Diana and was convinced she was being kept by Hill at a house belonging to his long-time pal Charlie Taylor. Gypsy frequently rang up "the tart" and threatened to come round to the house to "slice her up". One time Gypsy did indeed show up at the house, but luckily Taylor's grandmother had taken Diana out for the afternoon.

However, Billy's relationship with Diana was doomed from the beginning. In the summer of 1983, after at least half a dozen suicide attempts, she finally took her own life. Hill was racked with remorse and blamed himself, because he'd left her after a row and returned home the following day to find her body. He virtually locked himself away in his flat in Moscow Road for the remainder of his life. Gypsy took over the rearing of Diana's young son and Hill adopted him as his own.

Hill's own health had long since begun to go downhill, thanks to his heavy smoking. When he visited Frankie Fraser in prison in the late 1970s, Hill told him that doctors had warned him that unless he gave up, he had a maximum five years left. When Fraser asked him why he didn't kick the habit, he replied, "I can't, Frank. I can't."

Hill ended up being looked after at his flat in Moscow Road, Bayswater, much of the time by one of his oldest pals, Percy Horne, whom he'd first met in borstal when they were teenagers.

Billy Hill died on New Year's Day 1984, at the age of seventy-two. Former lover Gypsy Riley took over the funeral arrangements, and Hill's ex-wife Aggie travelled over from her new base in Jersey, where she ran one of the island's most successful nightclubs.

None of Hill's old underworld cronies were informed until after the service. A wooden stave marked the grave at the City of London Cemetery in Manor Park, east London, where Hill's remains were interned. Scrawled on the stave was the name 'Hill', and only a handful of close family attended the service. There were just six wreaths laid around the graveside. The Krays – long since locked up on life sentences – sent their condolences from their cells. Without Billy Hill, their reign of terror would never have got off the ground. Jack Spot bitterly described him as "the richest man in the graveyard". The stave was eventually replaced by a proper gravestone, said to have been paid for by friends and associates of the imprisoned Kray twins, despite Hill's alleged fortune.

Hill's occupation, as given on the death certificate, read 'demolition man'. He left no official will or letters of administration, but he has always been rumoured to have left a large fortune in Switzerland, which Gypsy supposedly brought back with instructions to use it to bring up Diana's twelve-year-old son.

Hill did leave a letter for 'Mad' Frankie Fraser in which he claimed he'd given Albert Dimes £50,000 to give to Frank, but Dimes, himself long since dead, had spent it all. Fraser later recalled, "Bill was a very smart man, not sharp but a classy dresser. He neither stood out or not. You could take him in any company and he wouldn't let you down."

During extensive inquiries to locate Billy Hill's adopted son, one underworld source explained that the boy was spirited away to Tangier, given a Moroccan passport, and continues to live in an apartment owned by Hill in the city to this day. "Typical Billy Hill," my source explained. "He knew the kid would be a target in London, so he made sure he was taken over there and brought up as a Moroccan so no one could get at his money. No one will ever find him now, although a few of Bill's old mates still stay in touch with him."

*   *   *

Albert Dimes and Frankie Fraser continued their careers in crime. In the early sixties, they joined the Richardson brothers, Charlie and Eddie, in south London. Dimes abandoned the racetrack for the even more lucrative business of supplying fruit machines to nightclubs. He became friendly with British film star Stanley Baker and, through him, was introduced to American director Joseph Losey. Dimes worked as an advisor on Losey's 1960 movie *The Criminal*, in which Baker played the leading character – a combination of Dimes, Hill and Jack Spot. Dimes always reckoned he never fully recovered his health following the 'fight that never was' in Soho with Spot. He died of cancer in his home in River Street, Islington, in 1972, at the age of fifty-seven.

In 1967 Fraser was convicted as one of the Richardsons' 'torture gang'. Various clashes inside prison meant he eventually served the full nineteen-year sentence. He was finally released in April 1985. In August 1991, Fraser was gunned down outside Turnmills nightclub in Clerkenwell. Naturally he refused to identify his assailant to police. In recent years, Fraser has made a living by hosting gangland tours of London's most infamous crime spots, where he proudly points out the scenes of notorious local crimes. He also occasionally pops up in Christmas pantomimes.

GLOSSARY

bang to rights	caught red-handed
bent	crooked
bird	prison sentence
blag	wages snatch, robbery etc
brass	prostitute
chiv	a taped-up razor for cutting, not stabbing
cozzer	policeman
dipper	pickpocket
drum	flat or house
face	renowned criminal
fence	criminal who buys and sells stolen goods
finger	accuse
fitted up	framed
grass	informer
guv'nor	senior policeman/gang boss
manor	territory of a villain or policeman
minder	bodyguard/troubleshooter
monkey	£500
old lag	long-term prisoner
peter	prison, police cell or safe
ponce	pimp
porridge	prison sentence

run-in	secret location for unloading and storing stolen goods
scam	deception
screw	prison officer
screwsman	burglar or safe-breaker
shillelagh	Irish stick used in fights
shooter	gun
snout	informer/tobacco
spieler	gambling club
spiv	black market trader
stretch	prison sentence
stripe	cutting someone's face with a chiv
swallow	accept a situation without protest
Sweeney Todd	the Flying Squad
team	regular gang of criminals
tearaway	small-time, but generally violent and reckless criminal
tic-tac	man at race courses who conveys bets from bookies using hand signals
tomfoolery or tom	jewellery
tooled up	equipped with weapons for a crime
turned over	premises raided by police
villain	crook of some standing
wide	aware of how the world works, of the codes of the underworld
workman	someone employed in a drinking club or spieler

BIBLIOGRAPHY

Boss of Britain's Underworld (1956) by B. Hill, Naldrett Press Ltd.

Inside the CID (1957) by P. Beveridge, Evans Brothers

Cherrill of the Yard (1953) by F. Cherrill, Harrap

London after Dark (1954) by R. Fabian, Naldrett Press

War on the Underworld (1960) by E. Greeno, John Long

Jack Spot, Man of a Thousand Cuts (1959) by H. Janson, Alexander Moring

Soho (1956) by A. Tietjen, Allan Wingate

Deadline for Crime (1955) by D. Webb, Muller

Crime Reporter (1956) by D. Webb, Fleetway

Mad Frank (1994) by F. Fraser with J. Morton, Warner

The Underworld (1953) by J. Phelan, Harrap

Cloak without Dagger (1956) by P. Sillitoe, Pan Books

Nipper (1991) by L. Read with J. Morton, Macdonald

Born Fighter (1990) by R. Kray, Arrow

Smash 'n' Grab (1993) by R. Murphy, Faber and Faber

The Profession of Violence (1972) by J. Pearson, Harper Collins

Mad Frank's Diary (2000) by F. Fraser and J. Morton, Virgin

Elephant Boys (2000) by B. McDonald, Mainstream

Tough Guys Don't Cry (1983) by J. Cannon, Magnus Books

Hit 'Em Hard (2002) by W. Clarkson, Harper Collins

Interview with 'Johnny Brown' and 'J.D.', P. Woods, October/November 2006